FOOL'S MATE

A True Story of Espionage at the

National Security Agency

Mr John W Whiteside III

ISBN: 1493597051
ISBN 13: 9781493597055

To Vasili, Patricia, all of the FBI and NSA participants, retired agents, prosecutors, MI-6 colleagues; to my wife Donna, children Jason, Brooke and Greg; to those who encouraged me to write this story; and to Grandmom Whiteside, who purchased a chess set for me at the young age of seven, I dedicate this book.

Table of Contents

Dedication   iii

Prologue   ix

Part I: *Opening Gambit*   1
   Chapter 1   3
   Chapter 2   17
   Chapter 3   29
   Chapter 4   37
   Chapter 5   41
Part II: *Middle Game*   51
   Chapter 1   53
   Chapter 2   67
   Chapter 3   77
   Chapter 4   91
   Chapter 5   105
   Chapter 6   123
   Chapter 7   139
   Chapter 8   151
   Chapter 9   163
   Chapter 10   173
   Chapter 11   179
   Chapter 12   193
   Chapter 13   205

Part III: *Endgame*   213
    Chapter 1   215
    Chapter 2   225
    Chapter 3   241
    Chapter 4   247
    Chapter 5   257
Epilogue   261
Author's Note   265
Selected Bibliography   269

Marcel & Madeleine
Sabourin
342 Wisteria Crescent
Ottawa, ON K1V 0N5

DISCLAIMER

The opinions expressed in this manuscript are those of the author and not those of the FBI.

PROLOGUE

On June, 17, 1997, FBI Special Agent John Whiteside climbed the steps to the Federal building in Philadelphia, PA. Though he was tense with anticipation, his six-foot frame let him move fast despite the heft of all the documents in his briefcase. The day was sunny and warm, but he barely noticed. Today Robert Lipka would confess.

Over the course of the past five years Whiteside had collected all the evidence, interviewed all the players, arrested Lipka, and finally brought him to court. Now, realizing that he stood no chance of walking free, Lipka was going to confess as part of a plea bargain. He would tell everything about his espionage for the KGB.

U.S. Marshals brought in Lipka, a 300-pound man in an orange jumpsuit, whom the press had nicknamed "the Great Pumpkin." Agents and officers were assembled in a drab, beige meeting room with only a rectangular table and metal chairs. U.S. Marshals unlocked Lipka's handcuffs but left his leg shackles on; Lipka was told to shuffle to a chair with his back to the room's line of windows. SA Whiteside sat at the end of the table next to Lipka and placed a recorder in front of him. Ron Kidd, Lipka's experienced criminal attorney, sat at the other end, next to Assistant U.S. Attorney Barbara Cohan. Other investigators filled in the rest of the space around the table.

SA Whiteside had to go through some preliminaries before he could start in; he reminded Robert Lipka that he was appearing voluntarily at this debriefing, then obtained Lipka's consent, and that of his attorney, to record the confession. Whiteside warned Lipka that the government wanted complete information on all his espionage activities, from the time he first thought about committing espionage until his last meet with the KGB. Ron Kidd reminded his client that his full and truthful cooperation was the key to a reduced sentence, and he implored Lipka to cooperate.

SA Whiteside turned on the recorder and started questioning.

"Bob, let's get started by talking about when it was you decided to go to the Soviet Embassy and offer NSA secrets for sale to the KGB."

"That. . . that was a really long time ago, and I. . . I simply can't remember."

"Surely you can remember contemplating the chance you were taking and risking being discovered. How is it that you can't remember that event?"

"I—I can't recall the details."

"Well, let me ask you this, how did you get from NSA to the Soviet Embassy that first time you walked in?"

Silence.

"Did you drive, take public transportation, have someone take you?" Whiteside prompted.

"I—I don't remember. See, I've had surgery on my back and neck, and my memory has been affected. There are things I simply cannot recall."

As the morning wore on Lipka kept his concentration focused directly on the recorder, rarely looking at any of the interrogators. His answers were vague. Everyone was growing frustrated, especially his own attorney. Several times Ron Kidd shouted at Lipka to tell the truth. In other moments he urged and pleaded with Lipka to cooperate during the interview.

"Bob! Stop lying to these people and tell them the truth!" Kidd shouted, his face turning red. "Start cooperating with them and help yourself. You're acting very foolish and need to answer these questions. Stop wasting everyone's time and tell the truth. And for God's sake stop making up stories."

Lipka took a deep breath and started talking again.

PART I:
OPENING GAMBIT

"A nation can survive its fools, and even the ambitious.
But it cannot survive treason from within."
Marcus Tullius Cicero

Date: September 1992
Location: Newtown Square, PA

The telephone call was directed to Special Agent John W. Whiteside at the Newtown Square Resident Agency of the Federal Bureau of Investigation in Delaware County, PA, at 11:35 AM.

"John, it's Gary," Whiteside's boss identified himself. "We have something big going on in your area, and we have some visitors arriving from FBI Headquarters today. Can you be in the conference room in Philadelphia at one this afternoon?"

"No problem," Whiteside replied in his characteristic dry manner. His Newtown Square Resident Agency was close to its parent office, the Philadelphia Division (or Field) Office—DeBuvitz's home base—and the drive would probably take about forty-five minutes.

Whiteside and DeBuvitz spoke almost daily. Whiteside was responsible for all foreign counterintelligence and espionage investigations in Chester and Lancaster counties; they were both rural areas, though Lancaster was known for its Amish farms whereas Chester was known for its wealthy villages. DeBuvitz, Whiteside's boss, supervised all foreign counterintelligence and espionage investigations in the Philadelphia Division, which corresponded to roughly the eastern half of Pennsylvania. On the org chart Whiteside was technically under Newtown Square Supervisor Sid Pruitt, but in reality he received his cases from DeBuvitz.

This morning's call from DeBuvitz was unusual, in both its urgency and its mysteriousness. DeBuvitz had called on the secure STU-III telephone used for only the most sensitive matters, and even then he hadn't said who the visitors were.

SA Whiteside immediately started the drive to Philadelphia. He was a practical man; the square-jawed, barrel-chested type who knew that questions were better asked in person. Whiteside had worked out of Newtown Square since April 1986, though he'd been working espionage and foreign counterintelligence investigations since 1975. He'd been stationed in New York City then, and had at one point risen to Supervisor in the KGB Unit at FBI Headquarters in Washington, DC. But sitting at a desk in Headquarters had made Whiteside miss the action of being out in the field; he'd yearned to get back to the excitement of daily operations against the KGB.

In 1983 Whiteside was thrilled to hear that he'd be transferred to the Philadelphia Soviet foreign counterintelligence squad. He stayed in Philadelphia three years, then moved to Newtown Square with expanded responsibilities. Since that move Whiteside routinely worked investigations involving all the menacing countries on the Attorney General's Criteria Country list, not only the Soviet Union. The types of cases varied from country to country, but privately Whiteside always preferred to work against the Soviets: they had the best intelligence service by far, and at the time posed the biggest threat to the U.S.

"Gary, what's going on?" Whiteside asked quietly as he walked into Supervisor DeBuvitz's office.

"I'm not sure, John," Gary answered cautiously in his Midwestern twang. DeBuvitz was a personable fellow who'd completed a tour of duty during the Vietnam war. Many of his colleagues knew him best by some of the many war stories he liked to tell, although some doubted that he could have been involved in all that he said he did. Nonetheless, he was a respected leader who had been Counterintelligence Supervisor for a long time. "All I know is that I had a phone call saying two FBI agents from Washington, DC are coming up for a briefing on a special case, and that senior investigators need to be present. The Espionage Supervisor from Headquarters is already here, and so is an agent from the Washington Field Office."

Just then a receptionist rang to say that visitors were being escorted to the conference room. DeBuvitz and Whiteside walked in and greeted Assistant Special Agent in Charge (ASAC) Tom Kimmel, who was also attending the meeting. Kimmel was DeBuvitz's immediate boss in Philadelphia, even though Kimmel was new to counterintelligence work and espionage cases. A tall, lanky man with prematurely white hair, whose eyeglasses dangled from a long, colorful strap around his neck, Kimmel was a graduate of the U.S. Naval Academy. He was, in fact, the grandson of Admiral Kimmel, who had been blamed for failing to anticipate the surprise attack on Pearl Harbor. ASAC Kimmel worked very hard in his spare time to try to ensure that his grandfather was exonerated by the Federal government.

Tony Buckmeier, a young, tall, soft spoken Special Agent from the Washington Field Office, was also there. He was a relatively new agent when compared with others who filled the room. Buckmeier generally kept a low profile, and mostly took care of the day-to-day needs of undercover agents; however, he'd known about a Top Secret intelligence source being debriefed by Western intelligence services from very early on.

Supervisor Michael T. Rochford from FBI Headquarters began the meeting once everyone was introduced. Rochford was an Espionage Unit Supervisor assigned to FBI Headquarters. A big man whose loud, gravelly voice filled the room, he'd worked up through the ranks from his start as a Russian translator.

"The FBI has recently received information from a source of unknown reliability," Rochford said, "which has identified an individual who was an agent for the KGB from September 1965 to August 1967. He was a volunteer walk-in to the Soviet Embassy in Washington,

DC and was known to the KGB by the code name 'Dan.' He allegedly made over fifty meets in that two-year period. He passed over 200 Top Secret documents to the KGB, and was paid $500 at each dead drop. This spy was in the U.S. Army, assigned to NSA [the National Security Agency]. Our source further said that 'Dan' left NSA in August 1967, and moved to Lancaster, PA, where he attended Millersville College. The source identified 'Dan' as Robert Stephan Lipka. The source also identified Lipka's spouse as Patricia, and said she was a nurse at St. Joseph's Hospital in Lancaster, PA."

Surprised silence fell in the conference room as the Pennsylvania contingent digested the new information; there had never been an actual espionage case prosecuted in the Federal Court's Eastern District of Pennsylvania, which roughly covers the eastern third of the Commonwealth. Whiteside was thrilled to learn that the case had a connection with Lancaster County, his specific territory. He couldn't wait to get his hands back in that work.

Before anyone spoke Rochford continued with his briefing. "The identity of the source cannot be divulged for security purposes, and I want to reiterate the fact that none of the information from this source has been verified yet. This particular espionage matter will be the first test of this source's information. If accurate, it will establish the source's credibility and pave the way for more investigations based on his information. Our colleague, Special Agent Tony Buckmeier from the Washington Field Office, is coordinating all of the information provided by this particular source, and both he and I will be the point of contact for the Philadelphia Division investigation. Should additional information be developed about Lipka from this source, SA Buckmeier will immediately provide it to Philadelphia."

Around the mahogany conference table a discussion ensued about the best way to start investigating this alleged KGB spy. They had no information that indicated whether Robert Lipka was still active with the KGB. In fact, the main question in the men's minds was whether

Robert Lipka existed. In the past the KGB had thrown out red herrings to disrupt FBI investigations of more important matters, or to protect another, more valuable KGB agent. Therefore, the first questions to answer were whether Lipka existed, whether he worked or had worked at NSA, and whether he now or in the past had access to classified information from 1965-1967. Then the team would answer secondary questions: Was the other biographic information the source gave on Lipka accurate? Where was Lipka living? How was he making ends meet?

The strategy for answering these questions was paramount: It was crucial that they conduct a criminal espionage investigation of Lipka while at the same time keeping him unaware of it. If he knew, he would probably flee before Whiteside had enough information to prosecute him.

After considerable discussion several primary starting points emerged. First, they designated Whiteside as the case agent both because he was assigned Lancaster County, and because he was one of the most experienced counterintelligence agents in the division. As case agent Whiteside would be responsible for the overall conduct of the investigation, from open to close. Second, everyone agreed that the first task would be locating Lipka's current whereabouts, which would prove his existence, and possibly verify the other biographic information.

Once the case team had these starting points, a broader "if—then" plan fell into place: If they confirmed that a Robert Lipka actually had in fact lived in Lancaster, then they would verify that he'd worked at NSA; if he did, then they'd verify that he'd had access to classified information; if they verified all of this, then the investigation would begin in earnest.

It was important that Lipka be the first person approached in the investigation to prevent possible leaks from other people they might interview; Whiteside's team had to carefully control the information Lipka would get. But to keep Lipka unaware of the investigation they would use a "false flag" approach: This maneuver involved having an undercover FBI agent falsely claim to represent another country, or flag. In this case the undercover agent would pose as a Russian intelligence officer. That disguised agent would try to talk with Lipka and get him to reveal that he'd been working with the KGB.

***

After the meeting Whiteside's mind was filled with thoughts of the investigation. He was thrilled to be back on the ground, protecting his country by taking down the spies who worked against it. The Cold War had been at its height when this alleged spying took place: 1965, the first year of Lipka's alleged spying, was also the year that the number of American combat troops in Vietnam ballooned from 16,000 to 184,000. Later that year they suffered through the bloody battles of Ia Drang and Plei Mei. In 1966 China began the Great Proletarian Cultural Revolution; then in 1967 China successfully tested its first hydrogen bomb. That same year Secretary of Defense Robert McNamara resigned over his differences with President Lyndon Johnson's insistence on ratcheting up troop levels in Vietnam. Just a few months later the Tet Offensive shocked the world by proving that the Americans hadn't stomped out the North Vietnamese communists.

There was turmoil at home during that period, too. Medgar Evers was assassinated in 1963, two short years before Martin Luther King Jr.'s historic march from Selma to Montgomery, AL. The Watts riots broke out in L.A. and New York City, and the Eastern seaboard experienced an historic blackout while multiple, massive Vietnam protests sprung up and race riots spread around the country. In 1967 the Human Be-In, and then the Summer of Love, took place in San Francisco; a Texas jury convicted Muhammad Ali of draft evasion; and *Hair* debuted in New York City.

During the entire period of Robert Lipka's alleged spying, 1965–1967, Germany continued conducting trials of World War II Nazis and concentration camp guards, India and Pakistan were fighting, and the Six Day War exploded in the Middle East. In short, if Robert Lipka had passed secrets during this turbulent period, there was a high probability that his information had costs hundreds, if not thousands, of American lives.

But Whiteside needed to concentrate on bringing this spy to justice. He was concerned with keeping the investigation low profile while his team collected evidence to prove Lipka's guilt. The following day, after a restless night, he drove directly to the Lancaster County seat without stopping at his office. The trip was about fifty miles through Pennsylvania's Amish country, a pastoral area of rolling fields and the occasional horse-drawn buggy. Some of the leaves were just beginning to change color, hinting that there might be an early autumn. Amish farm stands lined the route offering shoo-fly pies and an assortment of fresh-baked fruit pies. In Lancaster itself Whiteside's first stop was at the Duke Street library—a nice, quiet place to get information inconspicuously.

He immediately sought out the Lancaster City Directories; city directories were always a useful tool for investigators because they cross-referenced names, addresses and telephone numbers. Rochford's source had given 403 Lancaster Avenue as Lipka's residence in 1967, after Lipka had left both the Army and NSA. The first copy Whiteside picked up provided the first of many thrills that morning: The 1967 directory showed none other than Robert Lipka residing at 403 Lancaster Ave., with occupation listed as "U.S. Army." There was no mention of his wife, Patricia. But the 1968 directory identified Robert Lipka as a student, and listed Patricia Lipka as a nursing assistant at St. Joseph's Hospital, Lancaster. This was exactly what the source had said. The investigation was on.

As Whiteside leafed through the city directories year by year, the information about both Robert and Patricia appeared in the same way until 1973. In that edition, Patricia Lipka's name disappeared from the directory. The 1974 edition showed Robert Lipka at the same residence with an occupation described as "Liberty Coin Shop." Subsequent editions through 1980 held the same information. Whiteside had no idea what had happened to Patricia Lipka. Robert may have simply forgotten to list her on the annual inquiry form from the company who printed the directory, or she could have died. In any event, it was a question Whiteside wanted to answer.

The 1981 edition of the directory held another surprise: Robert Lipka was now listed as residing at 1001 Williamsburg Road, Lancaster, PA, with a new wife named Deborah. Neither Patricia nor Liberty Coin was listed. After confirming that subsequent editions contained no new information, Whiteside left the library.

On a hunch Whiteside decided to visit the Lancaster County Courthouse and look up divorce records starting about 1973. His luck continued; he quickly found Complaint in Divorce number 141, dated January 1974, naming Patricia Lipka as the complainant and Robert Lipka as the defendant. A marriage certificate was attached to the complaint which provided the date and place of their marriage. That date, September 27, 1966, betrayed the fact that Pat had been married to Lipka for almost a full year during the time he was allegedly spying for the KGB. It seemed likely that they'd dated for a while before marrying, which implied that Pat may have been with Bob for the entire two years of his espionage work, from September 1965 to August 1967.

The divorce complaint also confirmed that Pat was employed as a nursing assistant at St. Joseph's Hospital, verifying more information from the Russian source. Pat had identified Lipka as a coin dealer working out of their apartment, neatly tying together information from the city directories with information provided from the new source.

But beyond that, Pat's "Record of Testimony" provided valuable personality insights on Robert Lipka. He'd married Pat at age 21, when she was only 18. Pat gave birth to a girl, Kelly, seven and a half months after their wedding.

Pat's divorce affidavit began, "For my cause of action, I have stated that the defendant, Robert S. Lipka, has offered such indignities to me, the injured and innocent spouse, as to render my condition intolerable and my life burdensome. My husband degraded me, called me names, ran around with other women, deserted me on several occasions, for months at a time, [sic] he physically abused me and gambled us into debt. As a result I became nervous, upset and had to consult a doctor. Finally, in November of 1973, I could take no more abuse and I left my husband. Since then, my health has improved."

Pat's affidavit painted a picture of a man with no love for his partner or his child starting 1968 (two years after the wedding) and extending to 1973, the date of the divorce filing. Pat recounted that, in the beginning, "my husband started staying out at night and wouldn't come home. When I asked him where he was he said playing cards. This was at least twice a week. Some nights he didn't come home at all." Starting in 1969 Lipka would leave her and his child for months at a time, without sending money or communicating. Though he was hardly around in 1969, Lipka racked up so much gambling debt, "we had to take out a loan," Pat wrote. In 1971 he disappeared for the summer to California. And he had company. Pat wrote,

> "The night before Easter of 1971, I came home from work and put my daughter in bed and fixed her an Easter basket. The phone rang and a man asked for his daughter. I said you must have the wrong number. He said is this Robert Lipka's home? I said yes. He said well my daughter is with him. My husband told me later this girl was in California with him in June of 1971."

Other affairs, and other phone calls, followed. Then things took a darker turn:

> "He also started to slap me around. One day when I came home from work I jiggled the door trying to get my key in the lock. He opened the door and slapped me in the face. He said I was disturbing him while he was watching TV because I made too much noise opening the door."

Lipka also wasn't above berating Pat in front of her friends:

> "A couple months before I moved out, I was home with a girlfriend who he didn't like. When he saw her, he started shouting. She left. After she left he screamed at me because I had invited her to the house and he hit me along side [sic] of the face."

On top of the physical abuse, Lipka treated her with a total lack of respect: "He was always calling me stupid. Toward the end before I left, he called me a bitch and a slut. This was humiliating." Nonetheless, Pat writes, "I did everything in my power to make our marriage a success. I treated my husband as a wife should treat a husband.... I did not give the Defendant any cause to mistreat me." She also wrote that, "We last cohabitated on November 25, 1973, the date that I left." Whatever her reason—perhaps for her child's sake—Pat had stuck it out for seven years with this man before filing for divorce.

The proceedings showed that on the day of the divorce hearing Robert Lipka never showed up.

Since there was still plenty of time left in the day, SA Whiteside traveled to Millersville University, only a fifteen-minute drive from the center of Lancaster. The clerk at the Registrar's office showed him records of Lipka's attendance and verified his graduation in May 1972. The records confirmed that Lipka spent five years pursuing a bachelor's degree in education. Upon graduation, Lipka received a three-year temporary teaching certificate from the Commonwealth of Pennsylvania. However, the university had no record of whether Lipka ever got a teaching job. This was a small puzzle, but verifying Lipka's education at Millersville College further established the bonafides of the new Russian source at the same time that it confirmed Lipka's activities.

Though it had been a very successful first day of investigation, Whiteside felt real urgency to find out the most crucial thing: If Lipka had spied for the KGB was he still in contact with them, still passing classified information? In plenty of other cases even though a spy had left the arena where they'd had access to classified material, the spy continued to furnish top secret information by setting up a ring of sources. The John Walker spy ring was a perfect example: Walker, arrested by the FBI in 1985, had been out of the Navy for years. However, he'd recruited a friend, Jerry Whitworth, as well as his own son, Michael, and brother, Arthur Walker, to continue furnishing him with classified material for the KGB. Had Lipka set up a similar espionage ring?

Back at the FBI office Whiteside conducted Pennsylvania motor vehicle and driver's license checks for Robert Lipka. The results came back almost instantaneously, showing a current residence for Lipka at 1001 Williamsburg Road, Lancaster, PA, which confirmed the source's other address information. Lipka was the registered owner of a 1972 Ford Pinto and an old Ford Econoline van.

He certainly doesn't seem to be flaunting any riches from the KGB, Whiteside thought. Still, the day's evidence was convincing enough to him that he considered the Robert Lipka he'd investigated as one and the same person the new source had identified.

The following day, SA Whiteside met with the members of the Special Support Group (SSG) assigned to the Philadelphia Division of the FBI. This elite group was specifically trained in surveillance of espionage, counterintelligence, and counterterrorism targets, whether those targets were foreign nationals living in the United States, or targets like Lipka, citizens suspected of espionage activity. SA Whiteside had worked with the SSG on many occasions and was well aware of their street expertise. These support employees looked like grandmothers or teenagers just out doing their daily business, but they don't miss a thing. This skill was crucial to Whiteside in the current case because he wanted them to collect information without alerting Lipka. What set this elite group apart from others was their rigorous training in breaking off surveillance rather than risking being observed, or "made," by the target.

Whiteside had a private meeting with SSG team leader Judy Lee, a slender brunette with eager blue eyes who had worked her way up to the team leader position. "So what are the goals of the surveillance?" she asked. Lee was a master at surveillance who treated her colleagues with respect, but demanded perfection from them at the same time. As one of the FBI's best surveillance experts she also made a point of understanding the purpose of the surveillance, and often provided more than was asked for. "What's most important to determine?" she pushed.

"Everything," Whiteside half-seriously answered. He told Lee all the relevant information they had on Lipka, then asked her to get photographs to identify him. All of his routine daily activities were important, including his job, his weekend activities, and his relationships with his wife and family.

"I don't know if Lipka has an ongoing relationship with the Russian intelligence service," Whiteside concluded, "so any personal contacts Lipka has should be thoroughly investigated to determine their identities. Essentially, I want everything you can give me on Robert Lipka."

Judy chuckled aloud at Whiteside's request. "What a surprise. You want everything for a change." She knew that detail is extremely important in cases like this, and she heard this kind of request routinely. "You know we'll do our best to assist. Please keep us informed about any changes that may occur."

Suddenly there was much to do: Whiteside's investigation was truly underway. FBI Headquarters called to let him know that they'd set up a meeting with NSA in two days. Then an analyst from Headquarters called; she'd dug up a file on a Soviet "illegal" case investigated by the FBI at the same time Lipka had allegedly been operational with the KGB, involving a couple who'd lived not far from Lipka. Whiteside had asked her to review the new material from their Russian source and try to connect any archived unusual intelligence activity from the 1965-1967 time period. Combing through the old files she found that Peter and Ingeborg Fischer were Soviet operatives not registered with that country's diplomatic corps, and were therefore working "illegally" for their mother country. This husband and wife team had entered the U.S. as Canadian citizens with legal U.S. residence permits, but they'd been conducting covert operations for the KGB since 1965. The analyst promised to send Whiteside two file boxes of this material.

In addition, the analyst had found another old FBI investigation based on information from another Russian source identifying a penetration of the U.S. government by the KGB. Subsequent investigation by the FBI and NSA had determined the leak was at NSA, but no identification of the KGB agent had ever been made.

She also offered to include reports from a third source, code-named "Fedora," a KGB officer who had told the FBI during a debriefing session in 1978 that the KGB paid an agent codenamed "Dan" $150,000 for his services. This was a remarkable piece of information if "Dan" was Lipka because it meant that the Soviets paid him an additional $123,000 beyond the $27,000 the original source claimed. Equally exciting, "Fedora" mentioned that, as of 1976, the KGB was keeping track of "Dan's" father's home address, and his dossier provided that address. Both these puzzle pieces suggested a new mystery: The KGB's continued interest in Lipka well after he left NSA, and even after he'd graduated from Millersville College. What it most likely implied was that Lipka somehow continued his relationship with the Soviets. Was he, in fact, running a network of spies like John Walker? This possibility would continue to haunt the investigators as they tried to make sense of available source information.

Date: Thursday, September 24, 1992

Location: National Security Agency,

Ft. Meade, Maryland, Office of

Security

W hiteside arrived at NSA on time but had to wait at the security desk. He wasn't at the main NSA headquarters facility, but at an off-site location in a standard glass and steel office building. This was the first time he had been involved with NSA in his 25-year career with the FBI, and he wondered how he would find this Top Secret organization. It was so Top Secret, in fact, that Whiteside wasn't allowed to enter their space without an escort.

A few minutes later a young assistant opened the door for Whiteside to Bob Hallman's office, which was nondescript even though he was Chief of the Counterintelligence Division at NSA. NSA Special Agents Al Brisentine and Rodney Weidner were already waiting, and shortly thereafter, SA Dan Brennan arrived from the FBI Baltimore office. The NSA Special Agents seemed young, though Weidner looked closer in age to Whiteside than Brisentine. Bob Hallman appeared to be a grizzled veteran. Bob Schneider, an NSA analyst of many years, was also present for the meeting. The atmosphere was friendly yet reserved. Tension was clear on everyone's faces, but it seemed more out of eagerness for the briefing than anything else. No one wanted to hear the bad news about a Soviet penetration at NSA.

Brennan knew all of the NSA representatives because he was the FBI liaison with NSA. In his role, Brennan would receive requests from FBI offices around the country for contacts at NSA. Brennan was the only FBI employee to have NSA clearances.

In a few minutes more FBI Supervisor Mike Rochford, who'd been at the first meeting with Whiteside and DeBuvitz, arrived with his boss, Tim Berezney, Unit Chief of the FBI Headquarters Espionage Unit. Almost all the FBI's heavy firepower against KGB espionage was in that small, gray room.

Once they started the meeting NSA personnel were dismayed to learn that Lipka had been identified as having passed more than 200 of their own Top Secret documents to the KGB between 1965 and 1967. Everyone at the conference agreed it was imperative to determine whether Lipka was continuing his espionage through current NSA employees.

"But we can't alert Lipka, or our employees," said Hallman, "that is if in fact someone here is still operating for Lipka."

Once again investigative strategy was paramount. First, assignments were made. SA Brennan would be the contact person for all FBI investigations relating to the Lipka matter in the Maryland area (should the trail lead there), continue his role of communicating between NSA and the FBI, and would be considered a co-case agent with SA Whiteside. NSA SAs Brisentine and Weidner would coordinate all necessary investigation within NSA, and would maintain frequent contact with both Whiteside and Brennan.

"When we met in Philadelphia and Mike Rochford briefed us on the case," Whiteside began his summary, "we debated investigative plans. Because I was able to confirm most of the Russian source's information about Lipka, and established that we have a divorced spouse involved in some manner, I thought it would be nice to interview Pat Lipka first and see if she would be willing to assist us in our investigation. I know it would be a great benefit to us if she would cooperate."

"However, in so doing, we face the danger of her contacting Lipka and hurting any chances we might have in trying a successful false flag approach to him, especially if she doesn't cooperate. Therefore, after consideration, my team thought it would be better if we were to work this in two initial stages and continue with our original plan. Let's concentrate on the false flag approach and see how much evidence we're able to get from Lipka himself. Then, if the investigation does become alerting to him at a later date, at least we won't lose whatever we've already gained. While doing that, NSA can research Lipka's personnel file, identify his contacts and any current employees still working here who may have known or worked with Lipka. Let's hold off on interviews until we wrap up the work with Lipka."

Other options were discussed around the conference table, and subsequently discounted. But by lunchtime everyone seemed to be in agreement with the investigative plan Whiteside had presented. Once contact with Lipka was deemed finished for whatever reason, the interviews could begin with Pat and Lipka's coworkers at NSA.

The team walked to a local deli for sandwiches. As soon as they sat down after lunch Bob Schneider pulled out the NSA personnel file on Robert Lipka; everyone was pleasantly surprised that he could locate such an old file so fast. The material in the file confirmed that the Robert Lipka presently living in Millersville, PA was identical to the Robert Lipka who worked at NSA from January 1964 through August 1967, and that both of these Robert Lipkas matched the description supplied by the Russian source. NSA analytical employees had located a military ID card with a photograph of Robert Lipka in the file. The photo was old, of course, but the FBI would still be able to make comparisons once the Philadelphia Division SSG team got current photographs of him. Crucially, the file also confirmed that Lipka had had a Top Secret clearance along with officially authorized access to U.S. government cryptographic information.

Schneider also pulled out a "Cryptographic Authorization Briefing Certificate," signed by Lipka and dated January 22, 1964. Lipka's signature acknowledged his awareness of the provisions of Title 18 U.S. Code,

Section 794, better known as "the espionage statute." Without this find no prosecution of Lipka could take place because the FBI wouldn't be able to prove full knowledge of espionage in Federal Court.

The file showed that Lipka signed the Cryptographic Authorization Briefing Certificate on his first day at NSA Headquarters. He was assigned to a unit then-called the Collection Branch. Ten months or so after his assignment there, the unit changed its name to the Priority Materials Branch, but Lipka stayed in this unit for the duration of his posting at NSA.

"In this position, Lipka would have had access to documents of the most critical nature to the security interests of the U.S.," Schneider explained. The group around the table collectively took a deep breath as the extent of damage that Lipka may have caused sunk in. "Constant teleprinter traffic happened in Lipka's area," Schneider continued, "and he was responsible for taking the message traffic off the teleprinters and getting it to the appropriate desk manager at NSA. Originals were kept in the Special File Room for safekeeping. Essentially, Lipka probably had access at one time or another to virtually every secret at NSA."

Whiteside had seen these teleprinters on other occasions; they were like primitive fax machines. When teletypes needed to be sent, a narrow yellow paper tape was prepared with a series of holes punched throughout the tape. When the paper tape was run through the coded machines, the message would appear at the recipient's machine. The paper created a significant amount of fine dust in the small office, covering the gray teleprinter housings with a powdery layer of yellow. The teleprinters were quite noisy, and with more than one communicating at the same time it could be difficult to concentrate. Whiteside found out later that Lipka's workspace had housed about eight teleprinter machines—certainly making enough noise to distract anyone from his actions—that sent and received highly classified intelligence reports to and from NSA facilities abroad and secret locations in the field.

Schneider held up a sample of the teleprinter paper that was used during Lipka's time. There was a red watermark on each page, from the original to copies one through five. These numbers were crucial for determining who could see what. In addition, the bottom of each sheet of teleprinter paper, whether a copy or original, carried the warning that transmission to an unauthorized person is prohibited by law. Therefore, had Lipka passed any teleprinter paper to the KGB, he would have done so fully aware he was committing a crime.

Schneider explained that if there were any extra copies of a particular communication those extra copies would be placed in a "burn bag" for subsequent destruction. NSA didn't have paper shredders in the building back in Lipka's day, and no one would have known if documents meant to be destroyed slipped away instead.

Schneider also noted that Lipka's monthly salary in the Army while assigned at NSA was $200 per month. If he received $1,000 per month from the KGB, that would calculate to five times Lipka's monthly salary. That was a huge amount to be paid to a spy by the KGB. The group sat stunned by the amount.

At the end of the day-long meeting everyone realized that despite the key evidence in Lipka's personnel file it would take a lot more work to prove that Lipka had been passing information to the KGB. It would be a chillingly mammoth task: the investigative team would need to identify any current NSA employees who'd worked with Lipka, and NSA would have to review all their classified documents from 1965 through 1967 to better identify what Lipka may have passed to the KGB. The rest of the team needed to complete their background research. And all of this had to remain covert.

***

Out in Lancaster County, the SSG teams were piecing together Robert Lipka's current life. At the end of October Judy Lee met with Whiteside to review what the SSG had developed to date. "Every day we would watch his wife, Deborah, leave for work at the post office, and then see his two sons catch the bus to the local elementary school. After a bit of time passed we would watch Lipka get in his rusting Econoline van and drive to a local coffee shop. Every day he would buy a cup of coffee and a copy of the *Daily Racing Form*. Frequently he'd return home and quickly leave again for the racetrack in Harrisburg, travel south to Delaware Park racetrack, or bet on horse races at a local Turf Club. Horseracing was his passion, and he bet on the horses every chance he got. If he didn't head to the track Lipka would stop off for a Big Classic hamburger at a local Wendy's."

Judy showed Whiteside photos taken by the surveillance team. "You'll see that Lipka's quite obese, probably close to three hundred pounds. He sometimes wore large, Buddy Holly-style glasses, and has dark wavy hair. He looked like an average male his age. There was nothing fancy or unusual about his hairstyle."

"Have you seen his behavior on weekends?" Whiteside asked.

"On weekends Lipka occasionally shopped with his wife and kids, for things like clothes the boys needed. They seemed content, in that Lipka often held his wife's hand as they walked together. Sunday mornings we saw Deb Lipka taking her sons to a local church. She stayed there several hours, indicating that the boys were probably involved in Sunday school or other youth activities, while she likely went to services and participated in adult activities. Robert Lipka, on the other hand, never went to church with them, and we didn't see him."

"Our investigation determined that their boys were named James, the older boy at about 10 years old, and Tom, the younger boy, at about 8 years old. But we couldn't identify any employment for Robert Lipka. We never saw him go to work. His only activity seemed to be horse racing. He didn't seem to have contact with any local friends, only immediate family. He did his banking at the Fulton Bank, a Lancaster-area regional bank. In general, Lipka's behavior wasn't extravagant. He seemed to maintain a very low profile in the community. When not at the coffee shop, the racetrack, or Wendy's, he was at home. He was never seen working outside his house on any maintenance or lawn projects, although the house seemed to be well kept."

Whiteside thanked her for an excellent surveillance report, then he showed Lee Lipka's military identification photo from NSA. That photo, taken when Lipka was only eighteen, highlighted his massive weight gain. Looking at the old photograph next to the recent surveillance photographs pretty much indicated that the Lipka Lee had been tailing was in fact the same person who'd worked at NSA in the 1960s.

"Judy, I'd like you and your team to continue occasional surveillance on Lipka," Whiteside finally said. "Just stay current with his habits, his local haunts, his patterns of travel; I want your team ready, at any moment, in case we need more sophisticated investigation."

"We can do that. Once or twice a week," Lee said.

"Great. But I also want to challenge your team to identify any potential 'illegals' or intelligence officers who might contact Lipka."

"Any particular signs we should look for?"

"Nothing specific, though we suspect he was in touch with Russians. He goes to the racetracks a lot, so there's plenty of opportunity for him to meet shady characters there. And if anyone does contact him, we need to identify that person and find out if they're affiliated with Russian intelligence."

"We can do that," Lee said confidently. "Leave it to me."

***

At Ft. Meade, Maryland, Special Agents Brisentine and Weidner, along with Analyst Bob Schneider, were painstakingly piecing together Lipka's activities in NSA's Collections Branch. They'd put together a list of former and current employees who'd worked with Lipka, and also began to research the different classified documents that would've come in over the teleprinters, as well as other documents that Lipka would've filed in the Special File Room—from NSA and other intelligence agencies like the CIA, State Department, and Department of Defense.

One of the more bizarre finds in Lipka's personnel file was dated 1966, which would've been the height of Lipka's espionage activity. He'd entered an NSA contest that asked employees to come up with slogans for Security Week, an annual event that highlighted the ongoing need for absolute protection, including physical, computer, personnel and communications security. In any classified workplace personnel are likely to grow complacent. Security Week was designed to refocus everyone's attention. Not only had Lipka entered this slogan contest, but he'd won an honorable mention for his submission "Vigilance is the key to security."

SAs Brisentine and Weidner could only grimace at the thrill Lipka must've gotten in winning the security award while knowing how badly he was breaching it.

"What made this sick monster tick?" asked Brisentine. He'd been a polygraph expert with NSA for years, but found that Lipka's personality presented unusual questions. It seemed surreal to Brisentine that someone involved in a cowardly effort like espionage would boldly rub it in the faces of those he was hurting, despite doing so quietly.

***

At the Newtown Square FBI Office SA Whiteside received the promised two file boxes from FBI Headquarters on the investigation of Soviet illegals Peter and Ingeborg Fischer. He opened the first box and caught a whiff of musty air; this case had been investigated so long ago that SA Whiteside had been only a sophomore in college. Everything was typewritten on onionskin using carbon paper. But even after sitting in storage some twenty-six years it was possible that they'd assist in convicting Robert Lipka for espionage. Whiteside had his reading cut out for him.

But before he could start reading Whiteside believed that other matters had to be addressed. First and foremost, the fact that Robert Lipka was not employed and had no obvious income was alarming. Although he was leading a relatively spartan lifestyle, it could still mean he was receiving income from Russian intelligence. Whiteside's first priority had to be ensuring that Lipka wasn't continuing to pass NSA secrets to the Russians.

There were a number of investigative options available to the FBI which might help resolve this critical matter. The first option was to explore the possibility of requesting and obtaining authorization for a surreptitious search of Lipka's residence in Lancaster. Previously known as a "black bag job," this investigative technique was rarely used, especially when it involved a United States citizen. And although no evidence yet found showed that Lipka was still active with the Russian intelligence service, no evidence proved that he wasn't. How else would the government finally determine whether Lipka still had classified information in his possession? It was a long shot, but Whiteside considered it worth the effort to do the paperwork. If the request was denied, so be it. But there was more than enough probable cause to show that Lipka had been an agent of a foreign power.

Disappointingly, the request was denied. In fact, it was denied by FBI reviewers before it ever reached the necessary approval level.

"John, it seems like the Legal Unit at FBI Headquarters needs evidence that Lipka has been actively passing information to the Soviets within the past sixty days," Supervisor Gary DeBuvitz told Whiteside over the secure phone. "Since we can't show when he last passed classified information they've denied your request for a surreptitious search of his residence. They won't even pass it on to the Justice Department for consideration."

"Well Gary, that's disappointing as hell, but hopefully we have a second option, installing a wiretap on Lipka's home phone. I know wiretaps are generally reserved for investigations where all other possible leads have been exhausted, but there's still reason to believe that a crime is, or may be, committed via telephone. In this particular case, when national security is at risk and the subject of the investigation has no job and no visible means of support other than his wife's post office salary, getting a wiretap authorization seems possible, don't you agree?"

"Go for it John, but you know how difficult these requests are. I hope they'll agree with your line of reasoning. It works for me," DeBuvitz responded.

But when Whiteside discussed it with the FBI Legal Unit they threw cold water on his hopes. They reminded him of a legal provision requiring proof that a U.S. citizen has been in ongoing contact with a foreign power within sixty days or less of the wiretap request, a similar proviso to the one that had blocked Whiteside's request for surreptitious entry. Since the FBI only had hard evidence of contact with the Soviets in 1967 Whiteside had to find other options.

One possibility was a pen register, which FBI Headquarters had authorized in other cases. Agents could capture the numbers of all incoming and outgoing calls at Lipka's residence. Later agents could look up each number's subscriber to identify friends and associates of Robert Lipka, then compare the times of the telephone calls with surveillance logs showing when only Lipka was at home, to determine Lipka's private contacts. The frequency of incoming and outgoing calls could be monitored as well, which would identify those who knew him best—and whom the FBI could interview in the future. Additionally, the team could determine whether any of the contacts were NSA employees, or had classified clearances with other government agencies. These side investigations would be time-consuming, but they would prove, as reasonably as possible, whether Lipka was continuing to spy.

***

By the time the first days of 1993 rolled around NSA and FBI investigators had acquired a considerable amount of information about Lipka and his work at NSA. Surveillance had found that, though unemployed, he'd planned a trip with his family to Disney World that his sons were excited about. Subpoenas for his bank records at the Fulton Bank revealed that his account was normal in all respects, except for one glaring thing: A deposit of $300,000 in late 1992.

This seemed like a key to investigators, until further research revealed that Lipka had recently won a lawsuit against a sports club where he was a member. Lancaster County court documents showed that Lipka had filed a civil lawsuit against Lancaster Commercial Travelers Association. Lipka had been at the men's club on January 28, 1990, watching the Denver Broncos play the San Francisco 49ers in Superbowl XXIV. As he claimed in his lawsuit, Lipka had been given a seat with his back to the wall. A large game table of some type had been propped up against that wall to make room for more Superbowl viewers. Suddenly the table fell forward, hitting Lipka on the upper back and neck. Lipka waited two years to sue for what he claimed were two herniated discs, spinal cord damage, numbness, incontinence, and sexual dysfunction, as well as scarring and disfigurement. The suit demanded compensation for Lipka's medical bills, lost wages, and "loss of enjoyment of life and life's pleasures." In October 1992 Lipka was awarded close to $500,000 in an out-of-court settlement. The $300,000 in his account represented most of what he won after paying his attorneys.

This lawsuit also claimed that Lipka hadn't been able to work since the table fell on him. Whiteside knew that whatever injuries Lipka may have had they hadn't been serious enough to stop him from going to the racetrack nearly every day. Lipka's claim of not being able to work simply showed Whiteside more about his personality: Lipka seemed to enjoy making a living without too much work, passing American secrets and living off lawsuit money, while depending on his wife to get a steady paycheck for their family.

Investigation also unveiled another interesting episode: Lipka had entered a *USA Today* contest called the Financial News Network National Investment Challenge in 1990 which gave each participant an imaginary $50,000 in cash to invest in the stock market. The person who multiplied that money the most, after a period of one year, would win the game; the top ten winners would have their names published in the newspaper as a reward for their success. As it turned out, Lipka was able to parlay his imaginary $50,000 into $609,807. He finished 7th nationwide. While Lipka never actually received any money from this contest, investigators realized they were dealing with an intelligent man who had the skill to come out ahead in risky ventures.

3

Date: February 18, 1993
Location: FBI Newtown Square Office

O n a sunny Thursday, at 3:00 PM, SA Whiteside finally put away the last page of the last box of files on Peter and Ingeborg Fischer. He'd had to increase the magnification of his reading glasses from all of the eye strain brought on by the fuzzy carbon copies. While painstakingly pouring over the hundreds of pages, he'd found a lot of duplication because files from FBI offices in Buffalo, New York City, and Philadelphia had all been thrown together. But it had been fascinating to go back in time and read about Soviet intelligence operations going on before Whiteside had any inkling he'd ever be involved. After all, he was still in high school at the time these illegals entered the U.S. It had been exciting to read communications directly to and from FBI Director J. Edgar Hoover, as well as to see approved wiretap authorizations from Attorney General Ramsey Clark. Reading through these files was like traveling back twenty-five years into our nation's history.

But Whiteside also had the full story of Peter and Ingeborg Elsa Dora Fischer. This was the Soviet Intelligence Service at its best, better than any John LeCarré novel. Both Fischers reported a year of birth as 1929 in Germany, prior to the post–World War II division of their "homeland." While the FBI files made it clear that facts about the Fischers' birth and early years were in doubt, sometime prior to 1962 the Fischers were recruited by the KGB to work as illegals. They trained together at the KGB facility outside Moscow, in an area off-limits to all Soviet citizens. There they learned to speak both German and English so they could one day pose as German nationals residing in the U.S. They received training in radio communication with Moscow using short wave radio and simple, yet effective, encryption and decryption. They also trained in clandestine means of communication, such as dead drops and Short-Range Agent Communication devices, better known as SRAC. Further, they practiced various methods of photography and secret writing in order to communicate covertly using a one-time code and cipher pad, which would be destroyed after each use by placing the paper sheet into a container of water or flushing it down the toilet.

The Fischers learned defensive measures as well: They learned about conducting surveillance detection routes, or SDRs, in an effort to identify hostile surveillance coverage from counterintelligence services. They practiced different methods of eluding surveillance, as well as making brush contacts (short meetings meant to look as if they were coincidences in passing), and filling and clearing drops (special sites where spies would stash secret documents for intelligence officers to pick up), even when surveillance was detected. They also learned methods of conducting sabotage operations, including using explosives, so that in the future they could destroy military or civilian targets, such as bridges, communications systems, railroads, radio and microwave transmission towers, or fuel storage sites.

The training was intense and specific, and included firearms practice and defensive tactics. Most important, of course, was that they could never divulge the fact that they were in the employ of the KGB. This is why they were "illegal": all employees of diplomatic agencies are required to register with the State Department in Washington, DC, and some are required to stay within a twenty-five-mile range of their country's embassy. But "illegals" stay hidden from the State Department and the FBI, and can roam at will within the host country. In the event of war or a break in diplomatic relations, when all other diplomatic personnel are sent home, illegals remain in-country, in a position to forward valuable intelligence to their home nation and continue espionage activity, clandestine communications, and potential sabotage as ordered.

The last illegal known to be in the U.S., before the FBI found out about the Fischers in 1965, had been Rudolph Abel. Abel was arrested in 1959, then in 1962 he was exchanged for U.S. pilot Francis Gary Powers, who had been shot down over Soviet airspace in 1960 while flying a U-2 reconnaissance plane. Abel's services had been that important to the USSR.

The Fischers had also been poised to do important work for the USSR. When they completed their training they were sent to Germany via an underground intelligence network, and placed in the East Germany sector controlled by the Soviets. KGB experts forged birth certificates, passports, and other documents for them. An altered marriage certificate showed that the couple was married in 1961 in West Germany. Sometime in 1962, the Fischers immigrated to Canada from West Germany. At that point it was up to the Fischers to blend into Canadian society posing as German expatriates.

On February 28, 1965, the Fischers lawfully entered the United States from Canada into Buffalo, NY. During their stay, the FBI, along with the assistance of other intelligence agencies, determined that Peter and Ingeborg Fischer were in fact Soviet illegals. The FBI launched a concentrated investigation against them, careful not to let them know they were being watched. This secrecy was absolutely necessary: should the investigation be identified, the Fischers would simply flee. But the FBI also didn't want to arrest the Fischers. With the risk of nuclear destruction at its peak, it was far more important to observe the Fischers' activities and trace what was important to Brezhnev's government, rather than prosecute the Fischers. Following their clandestine activities would both reveal the KGB's plans and lead the FBI to the higher-ups giving orders. As long as the FBI had the Fischers under surveillance, there would always be time for an arrest.

Or so the FBI thought. They tailed the Fischers when they moved to New York City in late 1965, and then to Upper Darby, PA on May 15, 1966. At the Fischers's Upper Darby apartment the FBI installed a phone tap and searched the apartment twice. But ultimately, in July of 1968, Peter and Ingeborg took a "vacation to Europe" and never came back. The mail carrier who had delivered the Fischers' mail had also been passing the FBI information on the Fischers' movements, and alerted agents when the Fischers started selling off the contents of their apartment. Ironically, the FBI agents bought almost everything, and the postman sent their money to the Fischers in Berlin.

In all the material Whiteside had sifted through about the Fischers what stood out was a list of twenty-five sites in Pennsylvania and New Jersey from a notebook the illegals had once left in their apartment. His interest was also piqued by the transcript of a conversation the bugs had picked up. On Wednesday April 17, 1968, Ingeborg Fischer, speaking in German in their home, asked Peter, "Where is the letter, where you wrote it down?"

He replied, "I have written everything down here."

"Okay, okay. In Lancaster, isn't that right?"

"Yes, sure, where we put it earlier."

"Yes, yes, there are Germans living there."

"I have studied it. Not far from the college, about four miles."

After this conversation, the room became silent and the activities of the Fischers were temporarily unknown. Several hours later, the Fischers came back to the topic. Ingeborg said, "My goodness, I must destroy this."

"Show me the name," Peter replied.

"What name?"

"I wrote it down."

A few minutes later Peter said, "There are only two names in all of Philadelphia, that means it is not very widely spread." (Subsequent research by Whiteside's team established that there were only two listings for "Lipka" in the Philadelphia phone book at that time).

About eight minutes later, after a period of quiet over the mics, Ingeborg asked, "Saturday or Sunday?"

"I don't know when we'll go," Peter said.

FBI Supervisor Norris Harzenstein and Special Agent Charlie Silverthorn had been the primary FBI Special Agents on this case, and Whiteside saw notes showing that they believed this conversation indicated the Fischers would be taking a trip that weekend. The file further showed that the following Sunday morning, April 21, 1968, at about 10 AM, the Fischers did leave in the direction of Lancaster. The FBI team tried to tail them but unfortunately too few surveillance vehicles were ready because the Fischers hadn't previously been active on Sundays. With few cars, the agents couldn't keep the Fischers in view without becoming obvious. Grudgingly, the team leader had called off the surveillance.

Five hours later the microphones in the Fischers' house had crackled with German conversation: "It is over with," Peter had said.

"We must be careful," Ingeborg had added.

"It is okay, okay, okay," Peter had assured her.

Whiteside pondered this intercepted conversation, and the trip toward Lancaster, PA. *Did these involve Lipka, someone else, or just another sabotage site?* He knew, of course, that Lipka had been living at 403 Lancaster Avenue at that time, but Harzenstein and Silverthorn hadn't known anything about Lipka. Further, Lipka's address wasn't on the list of twenty-five sites the FBI had found in the Fischers' notebook. Only the neighboring fuel depots were, which seemed consistent with the other types of sabotage sites in the notebook.

However, another thing in the notebook had caught Whiteside's eye: A notation about the fuel storage site near Long's Park in Lancaster with the word "ROECK" scribbled nearby. The Fischers had written notes next to all the locations in the notebook, and they were obviously personal references to help them find the locations. But there was no clue, contextual or otherwise, about "ROECK."

Whiteside couldn't guess the significance, but had an intuition it might be important. A fluent German-speaking colleague said that "roeck" wasn't a German word, though. Whiteside puzzled over it himself for many days, but couldn't come up with anything. He contacted Mike Rochford, their Russian speaker, at Headquarters over the secure STU III telephone line and asked if the word meant anything in Russian. "Mike, I've tried my best to determine its origin, or a possible German derivative, with no success. Do you know if it's a Russian word?"

"John, I've never heard the word before, but I'll check my Russian dictionary and talk to some other Russian speakers at headquarters to see if anyone is familiar with the word. Do you think it's significant?"

"I simply can't tell Mike, but it certainly meant something to the Fischers or it wouldn't be written down."

A return call from Mike Rochford several weeks later determined the word was not Russian, and that no one at Headquarters had any idea what it meant. Not what Whiteside wanted to hear.

Sitting next to the two boxes of files that sunny Thursday afternoon, he thought glumly that there were no leads to follow from the Fischers' massive file. The only thing to do was request that the twenty-five sabotage sites be revisited by FBI agents. Though they'd been checked by Harzenstein's men twenty-five years ago it couldn't hurt to look again. This way Whiteside could at least determine whether the sites still existed, and whether there was evidence of intelligence activity. The rural sites particularly interested him because the telephone and electric poles might display easy to spot signals, like chalk marks, tape, or thumbtacks. Plus, it was possible that these sites were still in use for Russian intelligence; it's poor espionage tradecraft to reuse a site, but the Russians had been known to do so.

Supervisor DeBuvitz was happy to let Whiteside check the Long's Park location himself, though he assigned the other sites to his veteran agents. Whiteside took Long's Park because he not only drove by the area frequently, but because in the Fischer files he'd found an intriguing map of Lancaster he wanted to explore. It had been prepared by Harzenstein's agents in 1968, and they'd thickly penciled in a square that included Long's Park and the two fuel storage facilities, Esso and Sico.

Long's Park proved to be a lovely, eighty-acre wooded recreation area which would have made an ideal place for a KGB operation. There were literally hundreds of locations that could have been drop sites. At the moment it was deserted for the winter, except for a few hardy joggers and a woman pushing a baby stroller. A five-minute drive later Whiteside was at the location of the two fuel storage facilities at the intersection of Harrisburg Pike and Route 30. The site looked almost identical to the 1968 FBI photo. A traffic light or two had been added to an overhead cable, and a Toys 'R Us Store had been built nearby, but both fuel storage stations themselves were unchanged.

After taking photographs SA Whiteside drove past Lipka's former apartment at 403 Lancaster Avenue. He was surprised to note that Lipka's former residence was just five short blocks from the park, and inside the penciled-in square drawn by the now-retired FBI agents. The coincidence of a site from the Fischer's notebook located so close to Lipka's old apartment was certainly interesting.

4

Date: March 1993
Location: Washington, DC

By the following month it seemed clear to Whiteside that his team had collected all of the background information they could without talking to anyone. Lee's SSG team had provided a large volume of helpful information, but continued surveillance would simply be risking exposure for little gain. Whiteside asked her to take her team off the job for the immediate future. Only he himself would keep reviewing the pen register of Lipka's calls.

NSA continued to report that, to date, none of Lipka's identified contacts were affiliated with NSA. In the same vein, NSA had been unable to identify any problems with who was left of Lipka's former colleagues from the Priority Materials Branch. The Washington Field Office of the FBI, while continuing to support the investigation, wasn't able to pass on any additional information about Lipka from their new, Top Secret Russian source. However, there was some hope: In Maryland, SA Dan Brennan had located Lipka's former wife, Pat, and her telephone number never showed up on Lipka's pen register. The FBI had generally found angry ex-spouses to be very helpful sources.

Whiteside wanted to move the investigation to the next phase. Still, he was cautious enough to want assurance that, if his team made a case against Lipka, then the Department of Justice and the United States Attorney's Office would prosecute a case this old. It made no sense to continue the intense investigation, with potentially hundreds of interviews remaining, if the case would never be considered.

This was an unusual move. The FBI usually completes an investigation before it ever seeks a prosecutive opinion from the local U.S. Attorney's office. But this case was unusual. First, this was the first espionage case being investigated based on information from the new Russian source; if successful, it would establish his credibility and empower investigators to investigate other important espionage cases suggested by his information. Second, there had never been an espionage case worked out of the FBI's Philadelphia Division office and the Eastern District of Pennsylvania's U.S. Attorney's Office. Therefore, in order to avoid letting the case fail on a legal technicality, or improper investigative technique, Whiteside felt it was important to get a prosecutive team together for legal advice.

Whiteside had worked with Justice Department attorney John Dion from 1980–83, when Whiteside had been a supervisor at FBI Headquarters. Dion was a slender gentleman, dark complected and soft-spoken with a resonating, deep voice. Tall and impeccably dressed, he always appeared to be full of self-confidence and ready to confront any issues at hand. They'd both learned to trust each other in delicate situations handling KGB matters. When Whiteside called Supervisor Rochford to request a meeting with the Department of Justice, Internal Security Section, Espionage Unit, he asked for Dion to be part of the team. Fortunately Rochford was able to make that happen. A newer attorney on the staff, Michael C. Liebman, also joined the team. Dan Brennan, Mike Rochford and Tony Buckmeier completed the group in the meeting at FBI Headquarters.

Whiteside started off explaining the Lipka case to John Dion, trying to communicate its seriousness. "John, I'm not sure if you know, but a recent Russian recruitment-in-place has given the FBI the name of Robert Lipka. Lipka allegedly committed espionage against the United States while working at NSA from 1965 to 1967. According to our source, he passed over 200 Top Secret documents and received $27,000 for his efforts, being paid $500 at each of some fifty dead drops. We have fully identified Lipka through background investigation and surveillance, and have confirmed his military assignment at NSA, where he had access to almost every classified document."

SA Buckmeier chimed in, "Our source's existence is not known to either the Russians or the U.S. intelligence community for reasons of his safety. He's provided other information regarding persons of interest who may be cooperating, or have cooperated, with the KGB in the past. This is the first actual espionage case opened on information from the source. I am not at liberty to divulge his name or background, or where he's living currently."

Supervisor Rochford supported the information from Whiteside and Buckmeier. "John, John Whiteside and his team have drawn up plans for a false flag approach against Lipka using an undercover FBI Special Agent. We at FBI Headquarters are in full agreement with his plan and are looking forward to its implementation."

Dion finally spoke to the group. "Is there any additional investigation that's been conducted in this matter?"

SA Brennan answered. "John, I think you'd be pleased to know that we are working closely with NSA and their security group. They have confirmed Lipka's work there and determined he had access to many of their classified programs in his role in the teleprinter room. His access to documents was vast. We are also in the process of identifying current employees who may have worked with Lipka, and past employees who worked with him. We have some concern that he could still be running an espionage ring, like John Walker."

Dion smiled a bit, as he was one of the lead government attorneys who helped prosecute the Walker spy ring.

Finally Whiteside directed the big question to Dion: "I realize that you will not, and cannot, authorize an espionage prosecution of Robert Lipka at this time. We have not finished the investigation by a long shot and proven his guilt. In fact, we are only at the beginning of a long investigation. However, if we are able to build a successful case against Robert Lipka, will you consider prosecuting it, despite the fact that almost twenty-eight years have passed since he first walked into the Soviet Embassy? Or will the age of the case, which probably gives it less jury appeal, cause the case to be declined? I don't want to waste the efforts of so many professional counterintelligence officers in building a prosecutable case, only to see it be declined over a technicality. We have the opportunity to prosecute someone for espionage and proclaim to other potential spies out there that time won't erase your betrayal. There's no statute of limitations for espionage."

John Dion sat quietly for a moment. Whiteside began to wonder if he'd made any headway. But he finally spoke, firmly and slowly: "The age of this case will have no bearing on any prosecutive decision I will make in the future. If a solid case is made against Lipka, prosecution would certainly be considered."

Whiteside, Brennan, Rochford, and Buckmeier grinned at each other and let out deep breaths they hadn't realized they'd been holding. John Dion's statement was about the best they could hope for at this early stage of the investigation.

"Michael, I'm assigning you to this case for my office," Dion continued, "but John, you also need to contact the Philadelphia U.S. Attorney's office and get an attorney appointed there to work on the case. You'll also want to contact John Martin, the head of the Internal Security Unit. He's met with your Russian source and he's closely following all cases that come from his information."

Martin was well known in the intelligence community for all his prosecutions of espionage subjects, and his interest meant big things for the FBI team. Whiteside walked out of the meeting with a smile on his face. He had confidence that John Dion would be true to his word. If his team could make a good case against Lipka, Lipka would pay for his treason.

5

Date: April 1993

Location: Newtown Square, PA

With the U.S. Justice Department supporting them, it was time for Whiteside's team to plan the false flag operation. False flags were often used by intelligence services to get unsuspecting agents to provide information of value. While a potential agent might refuse a recruitment pitch to provide information to the Russians, that same agent might agree to provide information to what he believed to be a representative of India, for example. These false flag approaches are often successful ways to reinitiate contact with former agents because the agent quickly realizes that the contact knows about his or her past; ignoring this type of contact would leave the agent wondering just who it was that knows about his or her past efforts, and what the consequences might be.

Keeping those thoughts in mind, SAs Brennan, Whiteside, Weidner, Brisentine, and Rochford planned the false flag approach to Lipka. Rochford began, "Unless you fellows know of a better candidate, I would suggest using undercover FBI Special Agent Dimitry Droujinsky for our false flag operation. I've worked with him in the past. He's a charismatic man who's proven himself in several other cases, and he has a Russian look. Droujinsky speaks several foreign languages fluently, including Russian. And although he would deny it, he even has a Russian accent when he speaks English. Droujinsky is also a black belt in Tae Kwan Do and a former U.S. Marine who can take care of himself in a tussle."

Whiteside added "Well Mike, none of the rest of us have used this technique before, so I guess we'll go with your choice, Droujinsky." SA Brennan and the NSA SAs concurred.

"We need to select a position for him to represent," said Whiteside. "I think it best not to be affiliated with the SVR [the new name for the old KGB]. We don't know whether Lipka's still affiliated in some way with the SVR, and I think it best to distance ourselves from that. What if we say Droujinsky's from the GRU? My thought being that if he is from the GRU, he can make some mistakes during conversations with Lipka and perhaps save face, if needed."

After much discussion the team decided that Droujinsky would represent the Russian Military Intelligence Service, or GRU. This agency hadn't changed its name since the fall of the Soviet Union, so it would be more realistic than claiming Droujinsky was from the KGB, which no longer existed.

"I agree with John's idea," Brennan replied. "All we need to do now is to come up with a cover story for Droujinsky. Why would the GRU be reaching out to Lipka after all these years?"

"They wouldn't be," piped in Brisentine, "but he doesn't know that." Everyone laughed; they knew it was unusual for any intelligence service to attempt recontact after all those years.

"Why don't we have Droujinsky tell Lipka that the GRU had recently learned from old KGB files that he'd been a very effective agent for the KGB," Whiteside offered. "After the fall of the Soviet Union in 1991 the GRU was taking over some of the KGB's former agents. He can then try to encourage Lipka to renew his relationship with the GRU."

Rochford replied, "The approach is a risk, in that if Lipka is still active with a Russian intelligence service, he would be suspicious about encountering a GRU officer who knew nothing of that fact. Nonetheless, I think this scenario still seems to be the best option we have."

Discussion turned next to the desired outcome of Lipka and Droujinsky's meeting. Rod Weidner asked, "What are we hoping to have Lipka tell Droujinsky?"

Whiteside answered, a bit tongue in cheek, "Ideally, a fully cooperative Robert Lipka will talk proudly about all of his intelligence work with the KGB from 1965 to 1967 and perhaps beyond, and would detail every Top Secret document he'd ever passed. He will identify his handlers, drop sites, emergency instructions, and contact telephone numbers. He will talk about his motivation to spy and why he stopped, if in fact he ever did. He will discuss his pay, and what he did with his money. In short, he will give Droujinsky everything."

"Fat chance of all that happening," someone piped up.

SA Brennan replied, "Anything he gives up is more than we have already, and it comes straight from his mouth. It will be difficult to explain to a jury, coupled with the information we have from our Russian source."

But the team knew it would be difficult to approach Robert Lipka; there were numerous things that could never be predicted or controlled. In this case, they knew little about how Lipka had gone about his espionage and what motivations he'd had. They had no idea what the quality of his relationship with the KGB had been, either. It would take all Droujinsky's conversational charm, and the entire team's preparation, to make this false flag operation a success.

The meeting lasted all day, but the group made concrete decisions. These operations don't take weeks of soul-searching; FBI agents are trained to strategize, and they do it well and quickly.

"We need to select a date for the operation," Rochford said, moving everyone along.

Whiteside answered him: "Based upon the results of our surveillance, Tuesday is out, as that seems to be the day his wife is off from her job at the post office. If we start with a Wednesday, that will still give us Thursday and Friday, if needed, before the weekend arrives and his sons and wife are home."

Brennan, looking at a pocket calendar said, "How about May 12, 1993, a Wednesday? A Wednesday would leave enough time for the necessary manpower to arrive in Lancaster early in the week; there would be a lot of surveillance to prepare. A middle-of-the-week operation would also allow for additional days, should they be needed."

"Sounds good to me," Whiteside replied, "and of course we'll be prepared to remain in Lancaster as long as the operation lasts." All agreed to meet at the Comfort Inn on Monday, May 10, 1993, to begin the setup.

***

SA Whiteside and Assistant Special Agent in Charge (ASAC) Tom Kimmel of the FBI Philadelphia Field Office went to the U.S. Attorney's Office in Philadelphia together to meet with the U.S. Attorney, Michael Rotko. Anytime an FBI Special Agent was to meet with the actual U.S. Attorney, protocol required an FBI manager to be present at the meeting. On the walk over ASAC Kimmel said that he didn't care who was assigned by Rotko to prosecute the Lipka matter, but he didn't want Assistant United States Attorney (AUSA) Barbara Cohan to be the one.

"Why?" Whiteside asked. He had never met Barbara Cohan.

"There was a case—probably about two years ago—that I worked on with her, and sensitive information got out."

"Two years ago. What kind of case was that?"

"It was a drug case. Seems some information got out to one of the subjects in the case and created some problems for us. I'm not sure who was responsible for the leak but it certainly didn't help us."

"So what happened?"

"It was a delicate case. We can't afford having this Russian's cooperation leaked to the press. I don't want her to be part of this investigation."

"Sorry to hear that."

"Yeah, it really messed up the case."

"Mmm. Well, I've never dealt with the U. S. Attorney's Office here in Philadelphia—you know us counterintelligence guys, we're out in the field in trench coats and dark glasses—so I don't really care who we get. All I want is someone competent and aggressive."

"Which might be asking too much anyway, in government!" Kimmel guffawed.

But Whiteside didn't take the warning lightly. He knew that the FBI was concerned about the sensitivity of the Lipka case; they were very strictly limiting knowledge of both the Russian source and Robert Lipka's espionage activities. Any leak of these matters would torpedo the false flag approach, and therefore any hope of successful prosecution.

He and Kimmel took the elevator to the twelfth floor of the office and were ushered into Mike Rotko's conference room. Rotko entered, made introductions, and then Whiteside briefed Rotko on the case. "I spoke with John Dion at the Department of Justice," Whiteside finished, "and he suggested that a local Assistant United States Attorney be assigned to work with their departmental attorney, Michael Liebman. Who's your best?"

Rotko looked over his list of attorneys for a few minutes, flipping back and forth between pages. "I only have one attorney who has responsibility for security cases. She'll be excellent. Her name is Barbara Cohan."

Tom Kimmel was ready to explode, but he never said a word in argument or disagreement. Rotko called Cohan to the conference room. She walked in with an energetic smile and her blonde hair pulled tight in a ponytail; her confident aura and square jaw made her presence fill the room. She was a young attorney who had graduated from Temple University School of Law. Prior to working for the U.S. Attorney's Office, she'd been employed as a prosecutor for the City of Philadelphia, where she'd been born and raised.

Cohan listened intently to the background of the case to date, and the plans for the false flag approach. "I'm really thrilled to be involved," she said matter-of-factly to the entire room, not seeming to notice that Kimmel looked away. "I'll contact Dion and Leibman for their slants. This is exciting—it's the first possible espionage prosecution in the history of the Eastern District of Pennsylvania. And my first. I'll have to read up on spy cases!"

After the meeting, Whiteside accompanied Kimmel back to the Philadelphia FBI office. Despite his disappointment at Barbara Cohan being selected to represent this case, Kimmel said little about it.

"I'm just concerned about her loose talk," he said. "I'm not saying she's not competent. But this is a sensitive matter, and any slip can create a problem."

"I understand, Tom," Whiteside replied, "But remember, there are a few controls here. No one knows our Russian source's true identity, so there's no threat to that Top Secret matter. There are also very few people who know about Lipka. As long as she understands the way counterintelligence and espionage investigations work, it should work out."

In subsequent meetings leading up to the false flag operation, Whiteside met with AUSA Cohan numerous times. She seemed to grasp what was at stake and was quick on her feet, both qualities that Whiteside appreciated. He needed to have counsel available for quick inquiries in the middle of the false flag operation. It seemed reasonable to take a chance on inviting her into the team. "Do you want to be in Lancaster for the operation?" he asked her on the secure phone one day.

"Thanks, John, I'd love to, but I think I'd better stay in Philadelphia," Barb answered in her booming, confident voice. "If any legal problems come up I can answer them better from my office, next to my books, than a hotel room. Still, I wish I could be there. I've never seen anything like this false flag work!"

***

The SSG team leader Judy Lee leased ten rooms at the Comfort Inn on Centerville Road, in Lancaster, PA using fictitious identification to hide the government operation. Judy was known for her uncanny ability to operate unobtrusively under dangerous and difficult situations. Her team only worked counterintelligence and counterterrorism cases but she was the best at what she did, and those who needed to know knew it. Whiteside knew it, and entrusted to her the delicate job of setting up several adjoining rooms as a command post, plus a technical room next to the room where they hoped Lipka would meet with the undercover agent and confess his espionage activities.

By Monday afternoon, May 10, 1993, Lee's entire SSG surveillance team was in place, along with members of the FBI technical squad. The investigative team, including SAs Whiteside and Brennan from the FBI, SA Droujinsky, and NSA SAs Brisentine and Weidner, had arrived. NSA brought mobile secure communications with them so that any necessary communications from Lancaster wouldn't be intercepted. Departmental attorney Michael Liebman arrived later that evening from Washington to assist as needed.

After dinner and a few beers, Whiteside gathered his group and reviewed plans. They'd decided at the planning meeting in April, where the details of the false flag operation had been hammered out, that a morning telephone call to Lipka, once his wife and children left the house, would be the best way for Droujinsky to initiate contact. Droujinsky would be posing as GRU intelligence officer "Sergey Nikitin," who would say he was posted at the Russian Embassy in Washington, DC. But the challenge wasn't how to contact Lipka, it was what to do if he refused contact. That might spell the end of both the operation and investigation.

Brisentine finally raised the question they'd all been fearing that night: "What do we do if he answers, listens to Droujinsky, then hangs up and refuses to meet? We need some plan for that eventuality."

Whiteside said, "I know the Russian intelligence service would never go to an agent's home. That would be the absolute worst tradecraft ever. But I don't see any other option left, if Lipka refuses to meet with Droujinsky. The only option, now that we've invested so much time and energy in this case, is to go and knock on his door. Sure, it's terrible tradecraft, but we have no choice. And after all, it's simply a social call inviting Lipka to become involved again."

"What if he doesn't accept Droujinsky at his home and slams the door in his face?" asked Weidner.

"Well, unless anyone has any options left or better ideas, we'll just have to rely on the shock of the call to work in our favor. I suppose we could have the SSG tail him to a racetrack one day, and approach him at that location. The problem there is having Droujinsky nearby to effect a contact," Whiteside replied. "If this entire false flag idea fails Wednesday, we'll push on with the investigation and consider interrogating the former Mrs. Patricia Lipka. I don't know what else we can do. It won't be the first time or the last that we'll need to adapt to a changing scenario."

Whiteside didn't realize how prophetic those words would be. His team members met the thought with silence. But by the time they'd divvied up specific assignments everyone was fired up. The technical agents got to work that night installing equipment to capture Droujinsky's anticipated conversations with Lipka. The surveillance team planned shifts to keep Lipka under twenty-four hour surveillance in case he decided to drive to the Russian Embassy in Washington, DC after the meet. SA Whiteside called Tony Buckmeier to ask for FBI Special Agents from the Washington Field Office to be ready to detain, but not arrest Lipka, should the Department of Justice approve the order. Detention would hold him until a decision could be made for an arrest. An arrest at this point was the last thing anyone wanted because a prosecutable case had not yet been made against Lipka; a judge would let him go quickly based on the scant evidence verified to date in this investigation. However, the thought of Lipka escaping via the Russian Embassy was even worse.

On Tuesday, as the technical squad completed the wiring preparations for the command post, SAs Brennan, Whiteside, Brisentine, and Weidner spent the better part of the day meeting with SA Droujinsky, preparing him for his meeting with Robert Lipka.

PART II:
MIDDLE GAME

"The mistakes are there, waiting to be made."
Savielly Tartakower, Chess Grandmaster

1

Date: Wednesday, May 12, 1993
Location: Lancaster, PA

The moment of contact arrived. Surveillance reported that Lipka's wife had left for work and both sons had boarded their yellow school buses. Lipka was at home by himself. It was time to make the phone call. Whiteside suddenly broke into a cold sweat: *What if Lipka didn't answer, or answered then hung up, essentially ignoring "Nikitin's" request?* he thought. They had their plan, but realistically this was their only shot. Whiteside knew, though, that whatever happened, "Nikitin" would make contact with Lipka that day. Period. Even if Droujinsky a.k.a. "Nikitin" had to drive to Lipka's house and knock on the door, or corner him at the racetrack, or Wendy's. Too much effort had already been put into the case to let Lipka ignore them.

At 9:25 AM, SA Droujinsky, posing as "Sergey Nikitin," dialed Robert Lipka's home telephone number. "Hello," said a rather soft voice from the other end of the line.

"Mr. Robert Lipka?" said Droujinsky, using a thick Russian accent.

"Yes."

"My name is Sergey Nikitin, and I am from the Russian Embassy in Washington, DC."

"Yes?" Lipka replied, more softly this time.

"My superiors in Moscow have instructed me to meet with you and discuss with you something very important about your safety and security. You understand?"

Lipka did not reply. Silence weighed on the line. It's difficult to imagine Lipka's thoughts: Close to twenty years had passed with no contact from the Russians; now, suddenly, a phone call and a request for a face-to-face meeting.

"Nikitin" continued, breaking the awkward silence, "I am here today in the Lancaster area and I'd like you to come and meet me. Can you come to the Comfort Inn on 500 Centerville Road in Lancaster? Do you know where it is? It would be just for a short meeting, and I will explain everything to your satisfaction, but it is very important. Is eleven good for you? Or is twelve better?"

"No," Lipka said softly, "I have a doctor's appointment at one."

"Okay."

"Yeah, so I could only meet with you in the morning, and I have no idea what this is about."

"Well, this is what I want to explain."

"Well okay, you don't have to say anything more."

"Yes, well I'm glad you understand."

"Where, where are you?" "Nikitin" told him the name of the hotel and address for the second time. "Okay, the Comfort Inn," Lipka repeated.

"I'll meet you at the front door. I'm wearing a gray suit with a red tie, and I'm about six feets [sic] tall, and I'll hold a magazine in my hand. When you come we can go inside and discuss things."

"Ah no, no," Lipka stammered. "I'll meet you outside."

"Yes, we meet outside, okay."

But suddenly Lipka's cautious, quiet demeanor changed radically to a bold, outspoken, confident one. "I can be there in fifteen minutes," he volunteered. "I'm driving a bluish green van and it says 'Jayco' on the back of it. And I'll pull into the parking lot and wait for you. Just come up to my van and I'll meet you there. Your name again?"

"Sergey Nikitin, and of course, as usual, please do not call my embassy. You know why."

"Okay, yes, no problem. Is this related to Ollie North?" "Nikitin" responded that it was related to some embassy business, though the FBI agents were intrigued to hear Lipka bring up the Marine Corps colonel who had testified before Congress in 1987 about illegally selling weapons to Iran to finance the El Salvador 'Contras.'

Lipka said, "Okay, well you don't have to explain any further." "Nikitin" told him he wasn't going to explain, and appreciated Lipka being careful. Lipka said, "Correct, I'll be there shortly," and the call ended.

The investigative team was thrilled that Lipka was at least curious enough to meet with "Sergey Nikitin." High fives were passed around as the FBI technical squad immediately started to wire Droujinsky with a recording device. They also did a final check of the hotel room that "Nikitin" would take Lipka to, should he agree to come inside and talk.

The SSG radioed the command post that Lipka had departed from his residence in a new conversion van with the description he'd given the undercover agent. At some recent point, Lipka must have gotten rid of the old Ford Econoline van. He arrived in the parking lot of the Comfort Inn before the undercover agent was ready, and Droujinsky a.k.a. "Nikitin" had to scramble to get downstairs while Lipka drove slowly through the parking lot. The team was shocked that Lipka actually arrived, and further, arrived early.

Lipka pulled up in front of the door, and "Nikitin" approached his van. "Hello," "Nikitin" said. "Why don't you come inside? I've rented a room in a different name and we can talk easily there."

"No," Lipka said firmly. "Get in and we'll go for a drive." Droujinsky tried his best to encourage Lipka to come into the hotel room to no avail, even mentioning that he had a colleague who would be arriving at the hotel soon who would grow worried if "Nikitin" wasn't there. But Lipka insisted they go for a short ride around the area, so Droujinsky eventually got in. The SSG team kept up surveillance as Lipka drove to the area of a small park.

In the hotel command post, the SSG reported Droujinsky entering Lipka's van and moving away from the area. However, the investigative team couldn't hear Droujinsky's conversation with Lipka, so they had no idea why he'd entered the van. Whiteside's immediate supervisor, Sid Pruitt, began to panic about the safety of the undercover agent. Sid Pruitt had come to Newtown Square at about the same time as Whiteside, but from different experiences: He'd worked on a bank robbery squad in Los Angeles and was subsequently assigned as a firearms instructor at the FBI training facility in Quantico, VA. His southern drawl was proof of his Texas upbringing, and his large size hid the fact that he really had a soft heart. Pruitt wanted to grab ASAC Kimmel and follow Lipka so that they could arrest him before Droujinsky got hurt.

"Come on Tom, let's go after them," Pruitt shouted as Lipka drove off with Droujinsky. Kimmel was eager to join Pruitt in the chase. It was all Whiteside could do to almost physically stop them from leaving the command post.

"You can't follow Lipka," Whiteside said, looking straight into Pruitt's eyes, trying to calm him. "He's been trained to look for surveillance. First of all, the undercover agent holds a black belt in karate and is a former Marine. I think he would be able to physically subdue this obese, 300-pound man with no problem. Lipka is obviously in poor physical condition. Secondly, the SSG is trained in this kind of surveillance much better than two FBI managers are, and they need to be left alone to do the job they're trained for. This isn't a kidnapping case yet."

Fortunately, Kimmel and Pruitt gave in and returned to the command post. When they re-entered, the SSG reported that the van was sitting in the small park, and both Lipka and the undercover agent were chatting amicably.

In the van, Lipka and "Nikitin" were making small talk until "Nikitin" mentioned that he was from the GRU, and that they were very interested in learning more about the National Security Agency. Lipka told him that "he had no contacts with NSA at all any more, but did maintain contacts with the National Security Council, Oliver North and the good doctor." Droujinsky recognized this second reference to Oliver North, who'd laundered money for the Contras, but "the good doctor" was a reference that meant nothing to Droujinsky.

Lipka continued on, saying that money laundering was the only thing he'd been involved with in the last 20 to 30 years, and that North and the good doctor were two of his customers. He admitted using a mail order business named Liberty Coin as a front for a long time, and told "Nikitin" that the name is "very American, and not without some irony."

After more small talk Lipka said he didn't know what "Nikitin" had in mind for him to do. "Nikitin" replied, "The GRU wants to know how you started, and how things went, so they can learn, and maybe get new people in NSA." Lipka responded that he didn't think he could help in that way, so "Nikitin" changed course and said he would be interested to learn how Lipka "used to bring the stuff out, how you can go in, and how people can do it safely and securely."

Again, Lipka replied that that was something he had no knowledge of. Instead, he started rambling on about a friend of his who was a brilliant man, but whom Lipka always beat in chess. "Nikitin" replied, "You are a good chess player, yes?"

Lipka looked directly at "Nikitin" and said, "You didn't know that?"

"Well, like I told you earlier, we don't know much as we are just taking over from our brothers in the KGB, and so that's why I'm talking to you, to find out how things were done and why."

Lipka didn't seem to accept the answer. "Just for purposes of identification, I want you to write—right on this magazine—I want you to write a code word. You know what it is."

"Nikitin" truthfully replied, "No, I'm afraid I don't. You see, the files are in Moscow and I am in Washington."

"You don't have a code word for me?"

"No, I don't," said "Nikitin." "And I'll be truthful with you; we are taking over because we are interested in the organization where you used to be before. You understand me?"

Lipka took the magazine "Nikitin" had brought from the hotel, and with a red pen printed:

R_ _

"The next time we meet, if you can't write the code word, write the finish to that, I won't talk to you again," Lipka said. "Nikitin" answered that he was sorry to hear that and protested again that the code word was in Moscow. "Well," said Lipka, "by the next time you'll be able to get it." "Nikitin" promised to try his best, but Lipka said, "If you can't write that out for me the next time, I don't think I want to continue."

Droujinsky, making an effort to see if there was still contact with the Russians asked, "But this is old code word from, from when, from before or the current one?"

Lipka told him, "Let's just say that you must find the correct solution to the problem that I've presented to you. That's for my safety. Always, always was."

"I understand your caution. But again, you understand my position that I'm with the GRU, and the KGB was dealing with you before. And that is why we are sort of, how do you say it, taking over."

Lipka replied, "You're saying KGB, I can't say anything beyond that. I worked strictly for money."

Bingo—Lipka made his first strong statement about his motivation for his espionage activities.

"I understand that," "Nikitin" responded, "and this is what it is going to be, you know, also for money. Because we are always looking for people who can be reliable and trusted friends."

"I'm surprised at this."

"Well, you have to understand with our change over there, and things are in flux now, but this code word is there. I don't have it. It doesn't mean we don't have it, you know. That's all."

"Well, I expect you will have it the next time you talk to me. Ah, and if not, well, I guess you know, that'll be that."

"Well, I understand your concern and I appreciate it very much, and then I appreciated you being very careful on the telephone also. But I'll be truthful with you, we have it but I don't have it because it is in Moscow. It is not here. And with people such as yourself it is very highly guarded. We don't pass that around to many people. Very few people know about it, so. . . ."

"Well, I can understand that," Lipka said, but then changed the subject to babble on about his back injury and the surgery to correct it. Then he drifted into a discussion of his work for Ollie North and "the good doctor," the coin business he used to cover those activities, and his fondness for horse racing. Droujinsky let Lipka ramble, and eventually Lipka mentioned the fact that he'd been divorced.

"Ah, never call me on a Tuesday, never. The hours to call are, ah, Monday, seven to three PM, preferably mornings."

"Oh," said "Nikitin," "I'm glad I didn't come yesterday."

"Yeah, extremely so, extremely so. That's my wife's day off and she knows nothing about this. I'm divorced since last time."

"Now, did the other wife know about our connection?"

Lipka replied, "Yes, but I explained it away that I worked for this man who is an NSA employee, who dropped over dead. I mean, how convenient that I noticed his death notice in the newspaper. I just told her that I was working for him, Milt Robey, and doing whatever as a project for them. I noticed his obituary in the paper and told her what I did was his project. If he's dead as a stone he can't deny anything," Lipka bragged.

"Nikitin" asked Lipka, "Do you think that she is. . . was it an angry divorce? Do you think she will try to do something bad to you by revealing something that you did for us or even did for him?"

"This would be my cover if that ever did happen. I'd just say, everything I did I did for this guy on his instructions. I thought it was an NSA project. That's what I've determined as a good cover story and I'm sticking with that. I've burned it into my mind. Dead people can't defend themselves. Regarding my ex-wife, I've had no contact with her in many, many years and there's nothing to create animosity. I have no idea where she even lives anymore."

Lipka continued, "I read the *Washington Post* as one of my newspapers every day, and rarely read the obituaries. That one just happened to pop out of the paper at me. I cut it out and memorized everything about it, and the more I thought about it, I thought, y'know, if anything ever came up I would just say I thought this was a legitimate project."

"Yes, and I'm sure you came to your wife with a very sad face and said, 'Oh my poor friend. My boss is gone'," "Nikitin" laughed.

"Yeah, but I'm happily married now. But that first experience, I ah, made the decision with the wrong organ."

"Yes, of course you were young at the time..."

Lipka interrupted and said "You didn't get that joke?"

"Oh, I'm sorry I missed it. What?"

"I said the first marriage I made the decision with the wrong organ."

"Oh, okay, I see. Yes, yes I understand!" said "Nikitin," laughing.

Lipka pointed to his brain and said, "Then the second time you use this organ."

"Yes, the upper one. You should have used it all along."

"I've had no contact with her in many, many years and there's nothing to create animosity. I have no idea where she even lives anymore. And not for five or even ten years have I known. Nor do I care, so. . . ."

"Well, as long as she will not make any problem for you."

"No, but this man is dead and just by the virtue of his position that he held within the unit that I was attached to, this becomes a very convenient and plausible alibi."

Nikitin followed up: "Now by position, you mean in the military service or in NSA?"

Lipka replied, "NSA"

It was incredible that Lipka had provided his alibi to Droujinsky in the event he was ever caught, even though "Nikitin" had yet to provide a satisfactory code word. This was yet another wonderful admission from Lipka. His mention of the fact that his ex-wife knew of his connection to the KGB was just as incredible an admission.

Finally, Lipka asked "Nikitin" what he had in mind for him to do. Droujinsky tried to steer him back around to his espionage experience so GRU could recruit new people, but this only set Lipka rambling again, this time about the NSA hiring "intelligent unsophisticates" because they were easy security clears. He was essentially slandering NSA staff from the surrounding Maryland countryside, implying they were hicks who were good in a naive sort of way; since they weren't exposed to the temptations of city life, they had squeaky clean records and would easily clear NSA background checks.

Droujinsky tried again, asking Lipka why people do this kind of thing, referring to espionage without saying it. Lipka replied, "People do this kind of work for different motivations, and the biggest motivation is of course money. Pure green greed, that's all that counts. People do things for money, strictly. And so that's the only ideology that counts. Some do it for sex—that's silly. Because if you do it for money, sex isn't a problem. Some do it out of a weird sense of idealism—those are the most unreliable. When you pay a person a dollar for doing something, his loyalty is to that dollar. Nothing interchanges in between and he doesn't feel guilty because he set a price and has been paid the price."

"Nikitin" jumped in: "And he's waiting for another payment, hopefully."

"Precisely, and yet he does, just does what he's required to do to get that particular amount and, ah, you know, ideology is a funny thing. From one country to the next the only ideology I see that's common is greed. Pure green greed. No matter where you go that's all that counts. People do things for money. Strictly. So that's the only ideology that counts."

"Nikitin" replied, "A small percentage make it for adventure, also."

"Well, that's foolish. The person who does anything for adventure belongs with Evel Knievel in the circus."

"Yeah, they want to be like James Bond!" laughed "Nikitin."

"James Bond was a very conspicuous character, and would have been found out in a minute."

The SSG suddenly reported that the van had started moving in the direction of the Comfort Inn. The command post hadn't been able to hear the conversation between Droujinsky and Lipka, but there was relief that the undercover agent was okay, and that the length of time they'd spent together was certain to yield good things. Everyone was anxious to hear Droujinsky's full debriefing.

While returning to the hotel, Lipka said, "As spy thrillers go, the spy business is pretty damn boring when you get right down to it. And when it isn't boring, you're in trouble."

"Nikitin" added, "It takes time and a lot of stress as well."

"I don't think so. If you have a steel-sharp, even mentality, it can be done without compunction, without any fear of error."

As Lipka pulled into the hotel, Droujinsky asked him, "When you started with us, you started on your own, or were you recruited by our people?"

"I'm not saying until you come up with that," and pointed to the back of the magazine, with the notation 'R_ _'. "I won't say anything until you come up with this. That only goes without saying. I won't say how that was accomplished."

Just before getting out "Nikitin" asked Lipka if he would be available for a meeting in the morning, and they agreed to meet at the same place at 9:15 AM. Rather unexpectedly, Lipka told "Nikitin" that he wanted to show him something, and drove back out of the parking lot for a short drive to a company named Ferranti International. On the way Lipka talked about the coin business, and the value of gold. The only information Droujinsky thought interesting and relevant was the fact that Lipka denied having a passport, but did admit taking one trip to Canada. When "Nikitin" asked him if that trip was for his Soviet contacts, Lipka said he wouldn't comment on that, but if need be he would be willing to travel overseas in order to transact "business." No passport was necessary to enter Canada back then, but this exchange as a whole suggested that Lipka was willing to travel clandestinely—when he felt he needed to. Certainly that need might arise if he figured out the FBI was investigating him.

Just after those remarks Lipka and "Nikitin" returned to the hotel parking lot and firmed up the meeting for the next morning. Lipka dropped "Nikitin" off away from the front door and drove away.

Minutes later, the undercover agent arrived at the third floor command post. He passed his recording device to a member of the technical squad who immediately began to make copies of the tape for review by the investigative team. While the tapes were being made, the investigative team broke for lunch. ASAC Kimmel and Supervisor Pruitt returned to their respective FBI offices, but the rest of the team ate an Amish-style lunch at a local Mennonite restaurant.

Two hours later, with full stomachs, the investigative team got Droujinsky's full debriefing and listened to the recording. Droujinsky told the group that he felt Lipka had provided some key details relating to his past espionage. He also pointed out Lipka's lengthy digressions as possible evidence of his fear of providing incriminating information to someone who appeared out of nowhere. But when Droujinsky reported that Lipka wanted a code word or he wouldn't meet again, Whiteside's heart sank.

Droujinsky showed the investigative team the magazine Lipka had written on, and Whiteside knew the code word would be a major problem. There was simply no way that a recognition word or phrase could be identified that would satisfy Lipka. If their Russian source had provided it, they'd still be in business. But prospects for future contact were looking dim. Whiteside kept his feelings to himself, but suspected everyone recognized the same problem. They were all counterintelligence professionals and knew that a development like this was the kiss of death. The room grew very quiet, and people's faces creased in concern.

The way Lipka wrote the clue could mean one of several things: It could represent a three-letter word starting with the letter *r*. Or it could represent a three-word code, with the first word starting with an *r*. Perhaps it could represent any word length starting with *r*, or simply an entire sentence that Lipka would respond to with a sentence of his own. But Droujinsky would have to meet with Lipka again, code word or not, in an effort to keep Lipka talking. More of the unnamed Russian source's information had to be verified before anyone could dream of taking Lipka to court.

The fact that Lipka still talked to Droujinsky for forty-five minutes after Droujinsky failed to provide the code signaled that Lipka was curious enough about the relationship to keep talking. After all, despite the fact Droujinsky couldn't prove he was from the Russian Embassy, thanks to his lack of the code word, Lipka still admitted that he worked for money, that greed was his motivation, and he even offered his alibi should he ever be caught. Lipka also explained that his ex-wife knew about his contacts. The fact that he had been given a code word by his handlers was hard evidence as well. Droujinsky had collected fantastic information, almost the best it could be under the circumstances. Everyone was hopeful that even without the code word Lipka would continue to drop bits of significant information confirming his espionage work for the KGB. It was a relationship that needed to be continued, for as far along as it might go.

As afternoon turned into evening Brisentine, Weidner, Whiteside, Brennan, Droujinsky, and Liebman all sat in the command post and listened through headphones to the recorded remarks of Robert Lipka. They played the tape over and over again. Despite the fact that they were sure they couldn't come up with a code word by the following morning the assembled team's spirits were high. It was possible Lipka would talk regardless, and Droujinsky could buy time by saying a cable had been sent to Moscow for the information but the response hadn't arrived. It was a long shot, but it was a shot.

The team sent out for pizza and kept listening to every word. They sifted through the contexts of all Lipka's remarks looking for subtexts and clues. There is a saying that it's better to be lucky than good, and luck would enter into this case time and time again. However, sometimes it's possible to make your own luck, especially when preparation and hard work are involved. So at 9:00 PM, after hours of listening repeatedly to the ninety-minute tape, particularly the section where Lipka asked for a code word, Whiteside suddenly had an idea.

"I think I know the code word, and here's why!" he shouted, throwing off his headphones. "It's 'rook!' "

The other agents took off their headphones and looked at him skeptically.

"Look," Whiteside continued, "for starters, there was no mention of the code word by Lipka until Droujinsky told him he didn't know Lipka was a chess player. Then, at that very moment, Lipka seemed very surprised, and asked him to write down his code word on the magazine. When Droujinsky couldn't do it, Lipka wrote the 'R_ _' as a clue. And there's more. The two Soviet illegals, Peter and Ingeborg Fischer, had cased out sabotage targets near Lipka's old apartment. They were posing as Germans, but they even admitted themselves that they spoke lousy German. Anyway, they'd written 'ROECK' next to the address of the targets. Until now, I've never been able to make sense of that word. That may be how they spelled 'rook,' phonetically."

Whiteside had never really forgotten about the scribbled "ROECK" since he'd seen it; in fact, the day before he'd headed to Lancaster for the false flag he'd asked the office typist, Anne, to try to figure out if the word "Roeck" meant something else. Anne liked doing the crosswords and Jumbles in the daily paper, and this word, written by the illegals, had remained a puzzle. She was unable to come up with a logical answer. Whiteside had been pondering the word since, especially in light of the German and Russian speakers who'd said it wasn't a word in either language.

Brennen looked incredulously at Whiteside as the thought of identifying the code word sunk in. Liebman was wide-eyed with curiosity.

Rod Weidner was first to speak: "John, by God, I think you may be right. It's amazing how the Soviet illegals fit into the picture now. It certainly would be no surprise, based on the access Lipka had at NSA, to involve illegals in some way."

Dan Brennan added, "Good job, John. Now let's go have some beers."

Absent any other suggestions, the group decided to take a chance on the code word being "rook." Whiteside was thrilled, but deep down he was concerned that if he was wrong, Droujinsky would be left to his own wiles. They only had one shot, and it had to be right.

Date: Thursday, May 13, 1993
Location: Lancaster, PA

It was a clear, beautiful spring day in Lancaster County but tense anticipation reigned as the investigative group got ready for the second meeting with Robert Lipka. Droujinsky stood in the center of a buzzing group. The technical squad was taping recording devices to his torso, while Whiteside and Brennan tried to remind him of the points they wanted him to cover with Lipka. NSA agents Brisentine and Weidner chimed in to remind Droujinsky about the kind of documents they suspected Lipka might have passed, and went over their own list of questions for Lipka.

"Lipka is leaving his house and driving the green Jayco van," the SSG radio suddenly blurted to the room. His departure was about fifteen minutes earlier than expected; panic ensued as everyone hurried to get the undercover agent ready. In ten minutes, the SSG team reported that Lipka had arrived in the parking lot of the Comfort Inn and was driving slowly up and down each parking lot lane, looking at the vehicles parked in the lot. He drove around to the rear of the hotel and checked the cars that were parked in that location. Fortunately, the FBI cars resembled normal vehicles and wouldn't give them away. The SSG teams were staying at a different hotel in the area so their cars were offsite.

But promptly at 9:15 AM, SA Droujinsky, again posing as a Russian GRU military intelligence officer named Sergey Nikitin, walked calmly downstairs and out to the front parking lot. When he saw Lipka's parked van, he walked over and greeted Lipka, "Good morning, I looked for you inside but didn't see you. Why don't you come inside please?"

Lipka said, "No." "Nikitin" asked why and informed Lipka it was safe to go inside. Lipka replied, "No, no! Come on, sit in here. I want two questions answered first." After Droujinsky entered the passenger side of the van and closed the door, Lipka said, "Circle the name on there, correctly," and handed Droujinsky a piece of paper containing three Russian names written on it.

"In connection with what?" "Nikitin" asked.

"None of those names means anything to you?"

Droujinsky quietly panicked, but tried to cover up the fact that he had no idea who the names represented. He said, "Well, they're familiar in some way but I don't know in what connection."

"Do you have a packet for me?"

Droujinsky had no idea what Lipka was referring to; he took Lipka's request as a sign that he hadn't answered either of Lipka's two questions satisfactorily, so he felt it was time to try the code word. He prayed that it would work. "Do I have a packet?" "Nikitin" said. "Ahhh, does 'rook' have any meaning to you?"

"Yes!" Lipka replied with a grin.

"Very good!" Droujinsky said and laughed from genuine relief. The code word "rook" had worked like a charm! Lipka took his right hand and brought it to his chest, in obvious relief. At just that moment he looked out of his window directly into the SSG's hidden camera lens; it was a priceless photo. He shook hands with "Nikitin" and immediately raised the window so no one could listen to their conversation.

Droujinsky saw the cue, though, and told Lipka that they needed to sit down so he could show some things to Lipka, and discuss his past.

"This whole area makes me very nervous," Lipka said. "It's very close to my home."

"Well, you know, I mean you live here. You have been out of the service for a long time and there is no suspicion to you. I mean, you can come and go. People around here don't know me."

Lipka balked and talked about caution, but "Nikitin" soothed him and gave Lipka directions to the room he'd "rented" on the third floor of the hotel. He had to go over the directions several times before Lipka seemed to understand. "Okay, so I see you in like five minutes?"

"Okay, let me run this by you. I go into the lobby, over to the left, take the elevator to the third floor."

"Right, see you soon."

At the command center the SSG reported that "Nikitin" was exiting Lipka's van, and the van was driving away. People started panicking—surely this was a sign that Lipka didn't buy off on the code word. There was much disappointment until suddenly the SSG reported that Lipka had parked his van in the rear parking lot and was walking toward the hotel. Hope surged again. And, a few minutes later, when the SSG confirmed that "Nikitin" had let Robert Lipka into his hotel room, the team silently celebrated. This was exactly what they'd wanted! Everyone was eager to hear Droujinsky's debriefing to find out if he could pull more information from Lipka about his past espionage activities. If so, this false flag operation would surely lead to a successful prosecution.

Meanwhile, "Nikitin" was welcoming Lipka: "Please have a seat. I bought some coffee and doughnuts if you would like any." Lipka refused, but smiled as "Nikitin" continued, "I brought you a writing pad as I know how you like to write."

After sitting down at the small table in the room, Lipka said, "Will you please turn on the TV?"

"The radio isn't enough?"

"No!" Lipka said. "Turn the TV on please."

Droujinsky stood up and moved toward the television set but mimed confusion about how to turn it on. Lipka got up from his seat and turned on the television with the volume very loud. As he turned away to sit back down, Droujinsky quickly touched the volume control and turned it down a little bit.

The jousting for information began. Droujinsky asked questions of Lipka, and Lipka hesitated to provide answers. "You're not doing things right," Lipka said at one point.

Droujinsky showed Lipka photographs of Soviet KGB officers who'd been at the Soviet Embassy during the time Lipka was spying, but Lipka wouldn't admit to knowing any of them. Finally Droujinsky said, "If we are going to work together, we have to trust each other, y'know? And, if you recognize this photograph because it is the person who let you in and the first one who met with you..."

"That's a lie," Lipka broke in.

"I mean it's a fact. Okay?" retorted "Nikitin."

"Okay, and those are your facts, right? Then, listen very carefully to me. I'm not saying. One way or the other."

"Okay. That is okay. I just want to establish some things with us so that we can trust each other. Now, in the car, we recognize something and now we have another thing. Okay, now, so the date is 1965."

"What month," asked Lipka.

"Well, I don't have all the details with me now, but I just want to establish a basis together. I don't have your file here with me. The exact day and time and all is not very important."

"Well, it is to me."

"I understand that in 1967 you terminated our relationship. And then we had some people looking for you to reestablish contact from instructions from Moscow."

"Well, that would have been rather easy."

"Well, for some reason they could not."

"Did they leave a postcard?" Lipka asked.

"I don't know. Now our name for them was Fischers, Fischer's couple. I wanted to know why you broke contact with us."

"Well, I had no choice, since my situation changed."

As the verbal jousting continued, Droujinsky finally told Lipka that he wanted to give him a new code word to use just between them; he suggested the chess term "en passant," or simply "E.P." Droujinsky gave Lipka an accommodation mailing address in Washington, DC, and said he'd use a simple code if he wanted to meet. Since Lipka was a coin dealer, "Nikitin" would use numismatic terms, like gold coins, and sign his messages "C. M." for "Checkmate." Amusingly Lipka didn't pick up on the reference to his being "checkmated" by the FBI; he agreed, telling "Nikitin" to sign his letters "Carl Max," to correspond to the initials "C. M." "Nikitin" told Lipka he could think up a name to use for "E. P.," as long as he didn't forget that the new code word was "En Passant." Lipka chose "Enrico Passante" for "E. P."

Lipka also insisted on obtaining a post office box for written communications with "Nikitin." "I don't want anything coming to my home address," Lipka said. "I did mail some things to you in the past, but I know they never got there."

"We did not receive them?"

"No."

"Okay, see, some of these things are what I want to discuss with you."

"Well, I was very careful how I did it. I did it exactly according to procedure and there was a response to be made, and that response was not made."

"Do you remember what it was and when it was?"

"Approximately two years later."

"And nobody tried to make contact with you or anything?"

"Subsequent to what the Fischers were to do." Lipka eventually told "Nikitin" that the Fischers had left a postcard for him, and that he'd responded in the way he was supposed to. But Lipka would go no further, and said he needed a glass of water from the bathroom. More than likely he was making sure there was nothing in there that didn't belong.

When Lipka sat down again Droujinsky asked him if he had any material still at home. Lipka said no, but implied he had things hidden somewhere else. Droujinsky asked him to mail these things to him, and Lipka responded that he saw "no net worth in it for me." The discussion then turned to missed drops, where Lipka alleged he didn't receive a payment as expected, or didn't get the amount he hoped to get.

"How many times did that happen?" asked "Nikitin."

"Twice, twice the payoff money."

"Really, and did you bring it up with our people? Either by contact or by message? And what was their response?"

"No response. I found the place but couldn't find the money."

"Okay, do you remember where you used to go?"

"Yes." Lipka began writing on his pad of paper some of the drop sites he had used.

"I was wondering if you and I could go have a look at them some day," asked Droujinsky.

"I was told never to do that and I would never go back there."

Eventually Lipka gave "Nikitin" the specific information that on three occasions he got no money at the drops, and on eight other occasions, he only received one-half of what he expected to get. He discussed drop sites by writing them down on his pad of paper. He identified the Triadelphia Reservoir, the U.S. National Arboretum, the Chesapeake and Ohio Canal National Historical Park, Rock Creek Park, and the Franciscan Monastery of the Holy Land in America, all in the general area of metropolitan Washington, DC. He thought several of the former drop site locations might have become overgrown after all these years.

"Needless to say, that's why I was upset," Lipka remarked. "And that was a tremendous risk. Well, you can only die once, though."

They discussed mail correspondence again, and "Nikitin" reminded Lipka to use the address he'd just provided, along with a name for him to use on the envelope. Droujinsky also tried to probe Lipka about how much his ex-wife knew about his past activity. Lipka admitted taking her on drops but said she really didn't have any interest in what he was doing. When Droujinsky told him the records showed he made about fifty drops, Lipka answered that sounded about right. He admitted that he made them monthly, and sometimes every two weeks. Then he claimed to have made a brush contact—a very brief meeting in person.

"How many times did you meet my people face-to-face?" asked "Nikitin."

"Three or four," Lipka responded. I can tell you one time was very stupid: A busy street, and he wanted me to pass some stuff in the middle of a busy street while he was going the other way. It was in the middle of Washington. They wanted me to throw it into his car from my car."

"Did you do it?"

"No."

But then Lipka commandeered the talk to blather about playing chess and poker for money. When Droujinsky asked him what his chess rating was, Lipka said he was never rated—but saw fit to advise Droujinsky that when playing poker, never play with anyone who is as good as you or better. Then he asked again for a packet, saying, "They always had a packet."

When "Nikitin" demurred Lipka boasted again about the extent of access to Top Secret information he'd had at NSA, and hinted that he'd had difficulty making the KGB understand just what he'd had access to in the files.

"Once the game's over you can't play it over again," Lipka remarked. Droujinsky took the opportunity to ask him if he had any current connections at NSA, but Lipka only shook his head no.

When Lipka tried to go on a tangent about horse racing and a "brilliant" friend of his, Droujinsky pried him off of the topic by showing him more photographs of KGB officers who were stationed at the embassy in the mid-1960s. Lipka was very hesitant to identify any of the photographs, saying, "You make me nervous." Then he blurted, "I'll expect a money order sometime soon."

"For what?" "Nikitin" asked.

"Well, for what I think I'm owed. And I want two money orders. If I only get one it means there's trouble and we're done. One means done. Remember to send them in these amounts," and he wrote figures down on the paper in the amount of $2,500.

A few minutes later "Nikitin" asked if Lipka had any technical equipment the KGB had given him, and Lipka replied, "Yes." Droujinsky tried to tempt him to send it, implying that Lipka could get more money for that item. Lipka refused to describe what it was, but he did sketch a box -shaped item on the paper pad, and indicated that it was a communications device. When asked if he had any emergency instructions from the KGB, Lipka said he was told never to discuss that, but would listen to any instructions that superseded the previous instructions. With that, the meeting ended and Lipka left the hotel room. About ninety minutes had transpired between them and significant admissions had been made.

SA Droujinsky returned to the command post and a few minutes later SSG teams reported that Lipka had returned to his residence. In his debriefing, Droujinsky highlighted how Lipka had asked him questions about a list of names, then how he'd visibly relaxed when Droujinsky had asked him if "rook" meant anything to him.

The team was ecstatic that they'd gotten the code word right. Without it, everything they'd worked for in the case would most likely have been lost. Now "Nikitin" could maintain contact with Lipka and collect more evidence.

One thing Droujinsky took pains to point out to the team was that Lipka wanted money he believed he was owed. This insistence on alleged back pay made SA Whiteside suspect that Lipka was conning them, and had probably tried to con the KGB out of money in the past as well, based upon previous source reporting.

"Remember," Whiteside reminded the group, "we have additional source reporting from 'Fedora' that a KGB agent code named 'Dan' was paid $150,000. How can we explain the additional income when Lipka was going to college until May 1973, then operating a coin shop? Does anyone think it possible that he might be leading the KGB on, telling them that he was willing to go back to NSA if they could help him with some finances? Surely the KGB would pay dearly if they thought they could position an agent like Lipka back into NSA."

SA Brennen piped up: "Of course, Lipka may be telling the truth that he was cheated by the KGB on some of his payments. We know they've done that to agents in the past. Who is the agent going to complain to, the FBI?" Chuckles filled the room.

After a brief lunch the investigative team returned to the command post to listen to the conversation. By turning on the television volume high Lipka had made it very difficult to hear the audio. However, it wasn't impossible, and the team listened as Lipka talked about missed drops, drop site locations, money owed, and other snippets of information indicating his participation in espionage at NSA. Droujinsky tried all afternoon to remember the three names Lipka had written and asked him to circle, but still came up with nothing.

Nonetheless the team had to find ways to continue drawing out Lipka. That evening they decided Droujinsky would mail two money orders to Lipka in the amount of $2,500 each. Lipka had requested them, and they hoped it would get him to mail them a piece of KGB communications gear, along with possible classified documents from NSA.

NSA, for their part, wanted to investigate a two-story rolling file cabinet which Lipka claimed—in his last conversation with "Nikitin"—held vast secrets that the Soviets hadn't seem particularly interested in getting from him. They also wanted to research more deeply what

Lipka's duties had been, and whether he would've had access to such a thing, if it existed. NSA also decided to direct their research toward identifying members of the NSA chess club at the time; this might yield names of Lipka's NSA associates.

After the technical squad dismantled the command post at the Comfort Inn, the investigative team had dinner and drinks together at a local sports bar near Long's Park, which they thought had an ironic appropriateness. And they were safe to do so: Lipka was under surveillance, he hadn't shown up here before, and he would've recognized only Droujinsky. After a few Coronas the team toasted "The Order of the Rook" to celebrate the incredible success they'd shared so far. They were certain they had the right man; it was simply a matter of obtaining sufficient evidence to convict Lipka for betraying his government and perhaps the troops in Vietnam.

The video tape of Lipka reacting to the code word "Rook" was clear proof that "Nikitin" had passed the test. But "Nikitin" had also failed a crucial one, a huge one, one that would take a long time for the investigators to discover.

Date: June, 1993

Location: Baltimore, MD

As they'd previously decided, Droujinsky sent a letter to Lipka's post office box enclosing two money orders in the amount of $2,500 each. The money orders would be made out to Lipka's true name. A brief letter from "Carl Max" explained that the money was for "coins" received, as they'd discussed at their May thirteenth meeting—a reference to the back pay Lipka thought he was owed. But at the last minute the team had also decided to sweeten the deal by offering an additional $5,000 upon receipt of the "coins" promised by Lipka, staying intentionally vague; Lipka had made his greed clear, so the team hoped that $5,000 would induce him to send some kind of incriminating document or intelligence-related item. SA Buckmeier would make arrangements with the bank who issued the money orders to recover them for evidentiary value once Lipka cashed them, though the money would stay in Lipka's account. This way Lipka would never be able to deny receiving them. Technical experts would photograph them as evidence, then send them to the FBI Identification Division for fingerprint detection. Lipka's fingerprints were already on file from his military service. The team agreed that if nothing else, Lipka would have a difficult time explaining his receipt and cashing of the money orders in a court of law, especially in connection with testimony from Droujinsky.

On July 13, 1993, SA Tony Buckmeier found a letter from Robert Lipka at the accommodation address monitored by the Washington Field Office. The original was preserved for fingerprints and photographed, but Buckmeier forwarded copies of the letter to all of Whiteside's team. The letter read as follows:

> "Attn: Carl Max
> By now you should have received the coins that I sent to you. Please excuse the condition they were in, but they were probably buried in the ground for a long time as in the case with most valuable treasure. I will expect payment of the balance shortly and have found one other coin that you might wish to add to your collection. If you are interested, I will send that to you after I get the balance on our previous order. Please note my new address is Liberty Coin, P.O. Box 444, Mountville, PA 17554-0444. Please use this for all future 'orders.' I suggest that you get a subscription to the publication (form enclosed) and take note of the schedule of coin shows held around the nation and some of the foreign coin shows also. The ANA coin convention will be in Baltimore this year at the Inner Harbor convention center. I plan on attending this show for a day or two. Perhaps the last Friday in July. Perhaps I will see you there and if I can get a few minutes away from my friends we could have a glass of soda together. Our mutual friend Enrico Passante says Hello."

New excitement shot through the team with this letter. Clearly, Lipka hadn't given up on the undercover operation and was hinting at another meeting in Baltimore. This was great news; however, it was tempered by the tone of the letter. First of all, no package of "coins" had been received from Lipka. Secondly, the enclosure Lipka mentioned with this letter, a form for a subscription, had not been received. And lastly, the "balance of payment" remark implied that Lipka wanted the additional $5,000 for missed past payments from the KGB. Saying that he was also holding back on another "coin" until he received full payment could have been a threat, or a bluff to get the money.

The letter confirmed to SA Whiteside that Lipka was simply trying to con them out of money in return for nothing. However, some members of the investigative team believed that Lipka had sent the items and they'd just been delayed in the mail. SA Droujinsky, in particular, was convinced of this based on the relationship he'd developed with Lipka. SA Whiteside didn't accept the possibility, but he agreed to wait a few more weeks. The important thing was to maintain contact with Lipka and to try to record more incriminating statements of his espionage. To that end, they needed to attend the meeting Lipka had proposed at the coin show in Baltimore.

Privately, though, Whiteside continued to think that Lipka was playing games, and in fact may have done the same thing with the KGB after he broke contact with them in 1967, then responded to their later efforts to rekindle the relationship.

Still, it should be noted that it was quite possible Lipka hadn't received every packet of money, or at least the full amount of cash due him by the KGB. During the 1960s the KGB was known to shortchange many of their agents by claiming they could only get half of the promised funds, while handlers actually pocketed the money for themselves. They might be less likely to do this to an agent as valuable as Robert Lipka, but it was a common practice. An agent might complain to a handler about missing payments, but because the activities were illegal anyway the agent had no one else to turn to.

Nonetheless, there were pieces of evidence Whiteside felt were concrete. He accepted the information from Mitrokhin as accurate, especially since Whiteside himself had verified much of it. The tapes of Lipka and "Nikitin" were also painting a fuller picture of Lipka's duplicitous personality. He'd essentially admitted his guilt during those conversations.

Lipka had also made himself out to be someone important enough to be involved in White House press conferences, and with Oliver North, a U.S. Marine and a former National Security Council member. Nothing in Whiteside's investigation remotely hinted that these comments were true. His team had made a general check of the FBI indices to see if Robert Lipka appeared in any other investigations, with negative results. Had Lipka been involved in the Ollie North case in the late '80s that information would have come up. But if Lipka had done legitimate work with Ollie North or the Security Council, it was unrelated to his espionage. Priorities demanded that Whiteside focus his investigation directly at Lipka's relationship with the KGB. This Ollie North issue was a minor, insignificant matter when compared to espionage.

Whiteside was realizing that Lipka was a complicated person, and it would be important to move slowly and analyze every move Lipka made. However, Lipka's claims that everything he did was for the dollar, for "pure green greed," seemed a good indication of what made Lipka tick. The extra $5,000 was a tease to see if he would actually try to earn the money by furnishing classified documents to "Nikitin."

The following day the believers were partially vindicated: A separate envelope arrived from Lipka. It contained only the subscription form to a numismatic magazine that he'd obviously forgotten to enclose with his last letter. There was no message and no communications equipment.

It was an amazing coincidence, Whiteside thought, that items Lipka wanted to be received were, in fact, received, but the important items—relics from the KGB espionage operation—never appeared. The fact that Lipka's wife worked at the local post office only added to Whiteside's unease; surely she would have made sure that packages from her husband of important "coins" were safely sent. This behavior only strengthened Whiteside's impression that Lipka was trying to be the one in control of his contacts with the undercover agent.

Despite some disappointment, the investigative team gathered once again in Baltimore at the offices of the NSA security staff to plan a response to Lipka's letter. On July 21, 1993, a letter written by "Carl Max" was posted to Robert Lipka. "Carl Max" wrote that the "coins" he'd ordered were not yet received, but he agreed to meet Lipka at the Inner Harbor convention center at noon on Friday, July 30, 1993, at the main entrance.

***

Friday was a beautiful sunshine-filled July day in Baltimore, and not nearly as hot and humid as most midsummer Baltimore days. As the Baltimore FBI technical squad team placed appropriate recording equipment on Droujinsky, other members of the team finished final preparations in a hotel room; they hoped Droujinsky could lure Lipka in again the way he had in Lancaster the previous May. The SSG teams and Baltimore FBI Special Agents who'd worked on the surveillance squad had posted themselves in positions both inside and outside the convention center. They were prepared to take videotape of the meeting between Lipka and "Nikitin." While not direct evidence of espionage, it was one more thing Lipka would have a difficult time explaining in court.

This meeting would be crucial for the success of potential prosecution. First and most importantly, Lipka indicated he had an additional item, possibly from the KGB; they needed to recover and examine it. Second, Lipka would have to discuss the fact that the package he allegedly mailed to the accommodation address had not been received, and he would be pressed to identify it. Last, Droujinsky was planning to tell Lipka something alarming.

Whiteside's team had invented the story that one of the KGB officers Lipka had worked with in the past had gone missing, and there was some concern that the missing KGB officer defected to the West, thereby placing Lipka's past espionage activity in jeopardy of being compromised. Alerting Lipka to this uncomfortable situation might make him more responsive to the undercover agent. "Nikitin" would assure Lipka that by learning more about what Lipka had done, "Nikitin" could figure a way to protect Lipka. The investigative team knew this was a tall order for Droujinsky, but it was a good opportunity. Lipka seemed to enjoy taking control of their previous interviews, so the team hoped that pointing out his personal danger would throw him off. Only time would tell.

As the time approached 12:00 noon, all participants moved to their respective places. SA Droujinsky, again posing as GRU officer Sergey Nikitin, walked from the hotel to the main entrance of the Inner Harbor convention center, alone, in case there was any counter surveillance of any kind. The SSG teams reported seeing Lipka's van arrive and park at a nearby parking meter. Contrary to what he'd written about meeting friends at the conference, it seemed that he'd arrived from home.

Lipka walked to the main entrance of the coin convention and shook "Sergey Nikitin's" hand. "Nikitin" invited Lipka up to his hotel room, but Lipka refused despite his pleadings that it was safe place to have a quiet chat. Instead Lipka wanted to take a short walk, and actually led the undercover agent back to his parked van while they chatted about the weather. Lipka asked Droujinsky to sit in the van, and Droujinsky entered the passenger side, as he had in Lancaster. After some chat Lipka asked if Droujinsky had received the package, and Droujinsky replied, "No, ah, until this morning it still has not arrived. A person spoke to the postal authorities twice and they said if a package does not arrive, then the person who sent it must start a tracing."

"I'm not tracing that. That would be a disaster."

"I received two letters from you."

"But now here's the thing," Lipka said, "We're safe. I have no fingerprints on it. I used my head when I went to mail it. I carried it in a plastic bag and dumped it on the counter. And had the lady address it at the counter."

"Did she write the correct address on it?"

"I double checked it. Sure. It's in a mailing bag in her handwriting. I mean, if it ends up in a dead letter office there's no way it can be traced back to me. There's no return address."

"Well, that is good. Now what exactly do you have in the envelope?"

"The item that was given to me."

"You mean the radio?"

"The item that was given to me. I won't comment further than that. I still have some [*laughs*] strange doubts here because you didn't give me the correct code word the last time and I'm still rather nervous about that."

"You have doubts about me? I thought we were already beyond this. I thought we already trust each other and are working together."

"Well, that's, that's, that's something that we'll have to work out from this point on. I'm, I really, ah . . . [*laughs again*]. The item that was sent to you is worthless to either one of us. Correct?"

"Nikitin" replied, "Well, if it is what I think it is, it is not worthless to us because we need to retrieve it."

"For what reason?"

"Like I mentioned, well because we don't want it to wind up in somebody else's hands because then they can figure out our methods and technology and things like that you know? So it is very important."

"Nikitin" went on to tell Lipka that he should consider the $5,000 already paid as a down payment for the documents he still had, ignoring the situation with the alleged piece of communications equipment. Lipka would receive the other $5,000 once he sent the documents to "Nikitin" at the accommodation address. Lipka responded that the NSA documents he retained were buried at two different locations.

He wouldn't identify those locations to Droujinsky, but said he also had one document the Soviets had given him. Lipka seemed disappointed that "Nikitin" didn't have any money for him at the meeting; he said he'd hoped to use some of it at the coin show. Droujinsky said his superiors at the Embassy won't pay for something they haven't received, but he hoped to get the money for Lipka once the documents arrive.

Lipka demurred, and turned the subject to a friend. "You know, if your Russian friends would invite this brilliant doctor friend of mine to Russia, and also allow the good doctor to invite a friend, I would be the person he would bring. A good cover story would be to ask the good doctor to deliver a lecture in Moscow. That would allow me some free time to go over whatever you wanted to go over. I would feel more comfortable meeting in Russia."

"Do you have a passport?"

"No, but I will apply for one. I've never been out of the country with the exception of one trip to Canada."

"Was that in connection with business for us?"

"I will not answer that question. This invitation to the good doctor must be written on official Russian Embassy letterhead, and written in such a way that the doctor would invite me to accompany him. Here is what I believe to be the proper wording for such a letter." Lipka thrust several sheets of paper at Droujinsky and told him to pull the center sheet out, so it wouldn't have his fingerprints on it.

"Nikitin" took the paper but tried to steer Lipka back to talking about evidence. "I think it would be good to meet face-to-face in September, in Lancaster, to make an exchange of the buried documents for money. My supervisors at the embassy would not want to take any more chances with sending important materials through the mail."

"Well, you're the one who breached security by placing your return address on the envelope containing the bank checks."

"That address is safe from detection, and it's the only way to ensure that the money was delivered to you and not lost in the mail. It would be foolish to send that much money without a return address."

"Well, it still connects to my address, and I don't want any connection like that."

The conversation continued going back and forth. Lipka would get off of the subject of the missing item, while Droujinsky tried his best to return to it, and to let Lipka know that there simply would be no more money unless it showed up. Droujinsky also pointed out that passing any future classified information would have to be in person to avoid missing mail deliveries. It was very important to the investigation to recover any old NSA documents Lipka may be holding as concrete evidence of espionage, but also so that investigators could know what information had been of interest to the KGB.

Eventually Droujinsky was able to broach another delicate topic: "Now one thing that, ah, I don't know if I explained myself clearly the first two times we met, is, ah, by the way, do you have any kind of access through any people who worked with you, friends or anybody. I mean, can we count on more things coming now, or is this finished?"

"You mean down there, at NSA?"

"Yes."

"Totally finished... totally finished."

This seemed like a dead end, so Droujinsky decided it was time for the warning. "One of the things is, ah, and I'll be truthful with you, like I mentioned to you when I called you on the telephone the first time, there is a security problem, or possible security problem. One of our officers has disappeared and we are not sure where he is right now. And we want to protect everybody involved. Okay?"

"Which, which person?"

"Well, when I meet you in September I bring some documents to show you that Moscow is sending me and I bring you picture. But now, I just want to explain to you in principle what it is all about."

"So, in other words, he could, he could, ah, have told people about me?" Lipka asked.

"Well, we don't know yet. Now don't get nervous because we don't know yet, ourselves. But we are working on it. As soon as we know we will let you know and take the proper precautions."

"Ah, I had—I had been worried about that when the whole thing ended. I had worried from that point on what might—might occur."

"We and the other Eastern European countries always protect our sources, even with a change in governments. So don't worry about that. But we want to make sure everything is correct. So now, the next time we meet I'm going to bring some documents that we think you passed to us, because we want to see if there are any missing things. Because if he is missing we want to be sure he did not take some with him that can identify you or someone else."

"Okay," Lipka replied.

"So this is what we need to know. And you are probably wondering last time when I asked you about some details. We need to know what kind you passed, if there were any gaps in information you provided. See, you understand? We are doing such an investigation to make sure everything is there and everybody is protected."

But Lipka refused—again—to look at any documents of this type in the United States: "I'll tell you what. Don't bring those kinds of documents in September. I would rather sit down when you break me away from the professor; I'd rather do it that way."

"Well, but what if we don't break you away."

"You will, you will. This is something you can do."

"Well, like I said, I'll tell my superiors."

"All right. Well let's leave the discussion at that because I don't want to discuss any specific documents and certainly not here in the U.S."

"Yes, I'll bring the photograph. So you don't want me to bring documents?"

"No," Lipka said, "I would only go over these documents in a foreign country, such as during the proposed trip to Moscow. Bring a photograph of the missing KGB officer to the meeting in September."

"Because I have diplomatic immunity, you know."

"But I don't."

"No, but I have, I have it with me. They cannot take it from me. Nobody can touch me."

"I understand that, but I'm not going to discuss ah, any—any documents on American soil."

"Well, how about Canada?"

"No, to me that's American soil."

"Because we have embassy there also and can go there."

"I understand, but you go back to them and take that letter to them and see what they say. Invite the professor with the wording of that letter, done exactly as it is written there, and we'll go from there. It makes sense to me. I mean, there is no profit in this for me. You understand that I have been careful all along and I want to remain careful. I don't want to do anything that, ah, is not safe."

They discussed possible dates for a meeting in September, during the second or third week; Thursday was usually a good day, Lipka said. But he was beginning to get anxious, and told "Nikitin" they needed to end the contact; while they'd been sitting in Lipka's van, they'd been approached several times by Baltimore Oriole fans asking for extra tickets to the game. Both men exited the van, and Lipka put another coin in the parking meter. Then he handed Droujinsky three coins that appeared to have come from the coin show, or from Lipka's own collection, telling Droujinsky to "put 'em in your pocket." They walked together to the gate of the Orioles' new ballpark and said their goodbyes. The meeting had ended in under an hour.

✳✳✳

Returning to the hotel, the Baltimore technical squad agents took the recording of the meeting from SA Droujinsky and made copies for review by the investigative team. The SSG and Baltimore surveillance agents reported that Lipka went into the numismatic convention briefly, and left without talking to any of the friends he allegedly had there. In less than half an hour he departed and headed back in the direction of Lancaster, PA.

The investigative team had lunch with SA Droujinsky prior to heading to the command post to listen to the tapes. During lunch, Droujinsky, who'd faced many espionage subjects in the past, declared that without any doubt Lipka was the most difficult spy he'd come up against. "I'm not sure what it is about Lipka, but he still seems much more cautious than others I've met under similar circumstances," Droujinsky said. "By this time, in other cases, the spies would be opening up and talking about their activities. As soon as we get into some of the substance of his espionage, he deflects the conversation to an area which isn't threatening to him. I tried many times to bring him back to talk about the package he mailed, but he simply avoided the topic. He still acts like I am not doing something right."

***

Several days later SA Buckmeier found a ranting letter from Lipka at the accommodation address. In pencil, scribbled on the back of a blank U.S. Postal Service form, they found a hastily written message to "Carl Max." from Robert Lipka. The brief message said that Lipka would not meet with "Max" in September, or any other time, unless Lipka got paid for the package he'd sent back in June. The note was in a hand-addressed business envelope, and mailed from an unknown post office.

Buckmeier contacted SAs Droujinsky and Whiteside to pass along the news. Since there was a significant change in Lipka's attitude toward further meetings they decided to gather the investigative team again to brainstorm their next action. The following week, when they were all at NSA's offices, the team discussed the fact that Lipka still had doubts about "Nikitin's" bonafides. That had been expected to some degree, but no one was familiar with Lipka's true personality at this point in the investigation, so no one knew what to expect from him. The recent letter seemed to be Lipka's greed rising to the surface: He wanted another $5,000 and didn't want to wait for a meeting.

After about six hours the investigative team decided on two courses of action. First, SA Whiteside would send a report to the FBI Behavioral Science group at Quantico, VA for their psychological evaluation of Robert Lipka. Whiteside would include everything from the background investigation, surveillances, and undercover contacts in his report. The team hoped that psychological analysis might suggest a better method of making contact with Lipka, as well as a way to put him more at ease with the undercover agent.

The team's second decision was to style the next contact with Lipka after a dead drop. People thought Lipka might feel better in an operational mode similar to what he'd done in the past, rather than more face-to-face meetings with "Nikitin." Whiteside's team also decided to place the $5,000 in the dead drop, despite the fact that no additional documents or equipment had arrived. In this instance it was more important to keep contact with Lipka than to press for items that he may or may not have.

The drop was planned for October 13, 1993, in Long's Park, Lancaster, PA. October thirteenth was a Thursday; a day Lipka was usually available. The site in Long's Park was on the list Whiteside had found in Soviet illegals Peter and Ingeborg Fischer's 1967 notebook, and near Lipka's old residence. Droujinsky would send a letter to Lipka directing him to a concealed site at a telephone booth in Long's Park. A letter would be waiting there directing Lipka to proceed to a second site in the park to retrieve his money. While none of the members of the investigative team knew whether Lipka would respond to this dead drop technique, they guessed that any of his fears would evaporate at the thought of receiving another payment.

4

Date: August 17, 1993

Location: FBI Headquarters,

Washington, DC

The next major crisis of the case hit on a hot Tuesday afternoon, with a telephone call picked up by Supervisor Mike Rochford. The caller was well-known author Ronald Kessler, who had earlier been given access to FBI personnel and case files for a new book entitled *The FBI: Inside the World's Most Powerful Law Enforcement Agency.* Kessler asked Rochford to confirm that the FBI had initiated major investigations into allegations of espionage by hundreds of Americans, and that the information was provided by a former KGB employee who had access to KGB files. Rochford said, "No comment," and hung up. But the next day the *Washington Post* laid out Kessler's story for all to see. A note said it was an excerpt from his forthcoming book. Somehow Kessler had found out about the FBI's secret meeting at Quantico, VA to plot investigations into a large number of cases based on the new Russian source's evidence, a meeting that SA Whiteside had attended.

Rochford telephoned SA Whiteside and delivered the upsetting news. The major concern with this leak was the possible threat to the identity of their Russian source. Just because the source wasn't identified in the article didn't mean the information hadn't leaked out.

Not even people inside the FBI knew the source's identity. In reality, though, this source was a man named Vasili Mitrokhin who'd been a KGB intelligence officer. Vasili Nikitich Mitrokhin was born unceremoniously on March 3, 1922, in the small town of Yurasovo, located in a very rural province in Soviet Russia called Rayazan. Hidden away from the turbulent social unrest present in Bolshevist Russia some four years after the revolution, Yurasovo was a bucolic collection of squat houses, dusty streets, and wandering livestock several hundred kilometers south of Moscow. His family, while as poor as most Soviet households at the time, farmed the land, managing to scratch out a meager existence. He ate kasha every morning for breakfast and never once complained, knowing how fortunate he was to go to school with a stomach full of food, unlike so many other Russians throughout his country. The revolution did nothing to help feed those starving in the new Soviet Union. Yet it was an early time in the birth of the new country, and he knew it would take time to see the socialist system work out. He enjoyed hunting and fishing with his father, as well as working the soil in the garden, which helped keep them alive. He was fond of hunting for wild mushrooms that grew in abundance throughout the countryside.

He'd excelled in history and law, and after World War II ended Mitrokhin had entered the Higher Diplomatic Academy in Moscow. But World War II's devastation, including huge losses of his countrymen, affected him greatly and pushed him to serve his country. He studied law and history for three years, and in 1948 was recruited into the Committee for Information, which was a fledgling external security service; it was subsequently absorbed by the KGB in 1954. In Mitrokhin's new position as a KGB officer, working under Joseph Stalin's rule, he and his colleagues kept close watch on the activities of any Soviets who posed a threat, real or perceived, to Stalin and his rule. He also served in several postings outside of the Soviet Union for the KGB. A KGB intelligence officer was the most prestigious assignment Mitrokhin could have ever wished for, and he was extremely proud to serve his country.

While he felt that his work was excellent, and that he was a devoted patriot to the Socialist cause, his superiors thought otherwise. Mitrokhin was accused of botching an assignment and was ordered back to a post in Moscow. All intelligence officers in the KGB knew that a posting back to Moscow, without reason for a promotion, was the end of a dashing career. Mitrokhin was no different in this regard. Upon his return to Moscow he was sent to work in the KGB archives, located in a large vault at headquarters: No. 2 Dzerzhinsky Street, near the famed Red Square. Mitrokhin was angry with the new assignment. He still hoped, however, in a naive sort of way, that if he worked hard in this new but disappointing position, his career might get back on track. He'd loved being a KGB intelligence officer. He also desperately wanted to serve in a Western embassy one day.

However, as he read in the archives about innocent civilians being mistreated, even slaughtered, he began to turn against his own country. He knew nothing of this while growing up, or even while serving in the KGB. By 1972 his rage was boiling over. At that time the KGB was preparing to move to a new building and Mitrokhin was charged with organizing the archives for the move. Under the cover of sealing each document, Mitrokhin secretly began reading as much as he could, and taking notes. He planned to use the information to expose the murderous Soviet regime for what it really was.

In 1984 he retired from the KGB, and in 1991 the USSR fell. At last, Mitrokhin saw his chance to volunteer information. He risked crossing the border into Latvia, and found an audience with British intelligence. He'd gone to the American embassy three times, but had been turned away every time. MI-6 eventually shared Mitrokhin's information with the FBI because there was so much on Americans who had been spying for the KGB.

However, neither Whiteside nor any of his team members knew Mitrokhin's identity until long after the Lipka case ended. If the writer Kessler had exposed Mitrokhin's name and information in 1993 it could have destroyed the possibility of bringing hundreds of people to justice. His identity was classified at the highest level.

The other potential complication brought on by the *Washington Post*'s disclosure was the fact that Robert Lipka could read it. If the article hit the wires it would appear in almost all the newspapers. If Lipka read it, would he realize that the person he was meeting was indeed a plant, and not a Russian GRU officer? Would these disclosures bring down the entire Lipka investigation? Obviously, Whiteside had no answers. The investigation would simply have to continue as planned, although everyone would have to be aware of this damaging disclosure.

On September 29, 1993, the undercover agent addressed a letter to "Dear Friend" and enclosed with the letter a sealed package of instructions that were to be given to "Mr. Passante." In that sealed packet were instructions to go to two different drop sites in Long's Park, in Lancaster, PA on October 13, 1993. Lipka was given a time period of anytime between 10:00AM and 12:00 noon to make the drops. The letter was signed "C. M."

***

At this point in the investigation, the bulk of the work fell on the Philadelphia FBI technical squad; the SSG's specialty is limited to line-of-sight, or physical surveillance. However, the technical squad Special Agents possessed the expertise to install microphone and telephone taps, clandestinely record court-quality conversations, and perform other complex technical tasks as required in sensitive investigations. In this case, the team worked hard to install remote-controlled video and audio cameras in the areas of both drop sites where Droujinsky's letter directed Lipka. State of the art concealment devices and other systems made it impossible for anyone to locate the cameras or other recording devices. All that was needed was for Robert Lipka to enter the park, follow the dead drop instructions, and find his cash. Again, while this wouldn't be direct evidence of espionage on his behalf, Lipka would have a difficult time explaining his actions to a Federal jury if he did visit the drop sites and pick up money.

SSG surveillance reported that Lipka was at home the night before the drop was scheduled. There was no apparent reason for him to miss the drop, unless he was too wary of the circumstances. In order to lend more credibility to the effort, SA Droujinsky would be the one to place the drop under the ledge inside a telephone booth in Long's Park at 9:00 AM. Should Lipka have a confederate in the park observing the telephone booth, the investigative team wanted "Nikitin" to be seen. Once he placed the first drop, Droujinsky would proceed to the second site, where he would leave the $5,000 payment along with instructions for a December meeting.

The following morning SA Droujinsky's tasks went smoothly. He placed the first drop under the telephone booth ledge with some duct tape, and placed the money and additional instructions at the second site, located in a defined section of ground plantings easily identified with directions. The site was a bit removed from the more common area of the park and its relative seclusion afforded some measure of natural security for Lipka if he approached the area. When he finished, Droujinsky returned to the hotel command post. The investigative team watched from a secure area near the park where they were able to video monitor both of the selected drop sites. At 8:30 AM the SSG team radioed that Lipka's wife and children had all departed from the house, and that Lipka was there alone. Now the team had up to a four-hour wait to see if Lipka would take the bait.

Time seemed to pass slowly. SAs Whiteside, Brennan, and Brisentine were in one car, along with DOJ prosecutor Michael Liebman. Their remote location, far from the park, eliminated any chance that Lipka would observe them. Besides, Lipka had never seen any of them and therefore wouldn't recognize them. They spent the time planning what to do in the future on this case, depending on the way the day's events played out. Ten AM arrived and passed with no report of Lipka leaving his residence. Then it was 11:00 AM and 11:30 AM, with still no action from the Lipka residence. The group was beginning to get concerned that Lipka wouldn't show up. He only had until 12:00 noon to make the drop.

Suddenly the SSG radioed that Lipka was leaving his residence and entering his green van. It was 11:50 AM. Mike Liebman began giving high fives to the others in the car. He seemed to be the most excited of all. The SSG reported that Lipka was heading in the direction of Route 30, the most direct route from his residence to the park. Then, just as quickly as the elation began, disappointment set in: The SSG radioed that Lipka had passed the intersection where he should have exited for the park, and had continued on, possibly en route to Harrisburg.

The teams stayed in place in case Lipka was driving around to elude a tail. However, thirty minutes later, the SSG reported that he'd arrived at Penn National Race Course and was seen walking to the betting windows. While it was possible that Lipka had forgotten the date of the dead drop, it was just as likely that he was beginning to suspect something was up. Perhaps he'd read the *Washington Post* article.

After recovering the drop site items and money, the investigative team returned to the command post and began a review of all of the correspondence and conversations between Lipka and "Nikitin" to date. When taken together it seemed that Lipka was slowly growing more suspicious of the contacts, and somewhat less forthcoming with the undercover agent. Still, the team decided to try one more personal meeting. If Lipka continued to balk and didn't open up about his espionage activity, that would be the last meeting. There was too much investigation yet to be accomplished. As it was, the FBI already had a lot of incriminating conversation on tape relating to Lipka's espionage at NSA. If Lipka became aware of the FBI interest in him it would be tolerable at this time; the undercover phase was about to end.

***

British intelligence was also concerned with the recent *Washington Post* article. When Vasili Mitrokhin met with them in 1991 he'd made it clear that his goal was to eventually publish all of his notes and show the world the horrors that the former Soviet Union had perpetrated. MI-6 agreed to assist him in publishing his treatise—once all necessary investigation was finished, including debriefings with various trusted intelligence services. Mitrokhin was well on his way of reaching that goal, thanks to his careful notes and the attentive assistance of MI-6.

When he'd been preparing the KGB archives for their move, Mitrokhin had developed a system. Each envelope had to be categorized so it could be correctly placed in the new archive wing. As he packed each document into a protective folder for the move, Mitrokhin couldn't spend too much time reading each file; there was simply too much information. Often, however, there were abstracts attached to the front pages of the file describing the contents and significant information. He tried to copy all of the abstracts as closely as possible, and then, if the contents seemed truly sensational, he took the time to copy large sections. He also had to make sure he accomplished what appeared to be a full day's work so no one would suspect his other activities. Occasionally he would hear footsteps echoing in the hallway, coming towards his file room, but he could quickly get back to legitimate work. Fortunately, very few individuals had access to the archives.

After writing down a day's worth of abstracts and sensitive file information on small bits of paper, Mitrokhin would conceal these papers on his person. He knew the KGB guards would check his briefcase and any carryout items as he left the compound, but he wouldn't be body searched.

Mitrokhin routinely left for home at different times so he could occasionally work longer hours like a dedicated KGB officer. Once home, after he greeted his wife, Nina, and their son, he'd go upstairs to change; Mitrokhin stored his notes from the archive under some floor-boards he'd loosened there. Later, when his wife and son were in bed, he would retrieve his fresh notes and translate them into a code that he invented. This would keep anyone who searched his place from identi-fying exactly what he had stashed. Once he was finished rewriting the material with his code, he would burn his original notes in the fireplace, carefully stirring the remaining ashes to destroy any paper revealing his treachery. His wife and son knew nothing about his project.

On weekends his family loved spending time at their *dacha* in the Soviet countryside. He'd built the house himself of aromatic cedar. Turning the rich soil in his garden gave Mitrokhin much-needed release from the stress he felt at work, which had mounted considerably since he'd started copying classified information. He and his wife, a doctor, were also concerned about their son's health. Despite the fact that KGB officers were able to get the best medical care in the Soviet Union, the doctors were unable to diagnose and treat Mitrokhin's son. Since he was a baby, their only child seemed to be suffering from some neuro-muscular disorder that was progressively, though slowly, getting worse. His fine motor skills were most affected. The good news was that they were sure he didn't have muscular dystrophy or multiple sclerosis. But sadly, the doctors weren't sure what he did have. Mitrokhin and his wife could only hope the disease was something that could eventually be stopped, and maybe even reversed.

But weekends at the *dacha* brought great joy to all of them. The country air was sweet, and Mitrokhin and his son would fish together from the banks of a nearby lake. Hunting for wild mushrooms in sea-son was another joy Mitrokhin cherished, and his wife made delicious stews and salads with them. Trips to the *dacha* had another benefit for Mitrokhin: While his family slept, he crawled under the house and hid his coded copies of notes from the KGB archives in old milk cans stored there. Mitrokhin was sure that no matter what happened, Soviet authorities would never find his notes here, and even if they did, his code would prevent anyone from knowing what they meant. Perhaps Mitrokhin didn't realize that the KGB would certainly be suspicious of coded notes in milk cans. He may also not have realized that it wouldn't take long for KGB cryptanalysts to break his homemade code. Nonetheless, Mitrokhin had continued copying these precious documents from KGB Center, translating them into code, and hiding them in milk cans.

MI-6's work with Mitrokhin was going well. They'd successfully exfiltrated Vasili Mitrokhin and his wife and son from Moscow, and recovered all of his voluminous notes from the milk cans buried under his *dacha*. MI-6 intelligence officers were amazed at the content of Mitrokhin's work. In concert with FBI counterintelligence officials and DOJ Internal Security Section Chief John Martin, the Brits began sharing the portion of Mitrokhin's work that contained information directly relating to the United States. The British Secret Intelligence Service and the FBI had a highly trusting relationship with each other and cooperated in any way possible, especially in working against a common threat: the KGB.

Based on the nature of information furnished in each case, FBI Headquarters made the decision to start checking Mitrokhin's bonafides with the Lipka investigation first, unbeknownst to Mitrokhin. There were hundreds of American names furnished by Mitrokhin concerning targets identified by the KGB; some were individuals recruited who provided information of value, and others were people in various stages of recruitment by the KGB. From the outset of the review of this material, everyone involved believed that Mitrokhin's work would easily be the most damaging information to the Soviet Union ever obtained by Western intelligence services.

Information identifying Robert Stephan Lipka as an agent who worked for the National Security Agency was promptly furnished to the FBI. The specificity of detail provided on Lipka and his wife seemed to make this particular matter a good test case. MI-6 and the FBI knew that a successful espionage prosecution of Lipka would lend considerable weight to Mitrokhin's documents, as well as to his future credibility.

While the Brits were extremely pleased that the espionage information provided by Mitrokhin was totally accurate as it pertained to Robert Lipka, they were not at all pleased to learn that facts about a former KGB employee who was providing hundreds of names to the FBI was being plastered all over U.S. newspapers. Fortunately, Mitrokhin had not been named; the Brits had done a fine job in limiting his true identity to all but a small circle of trusted colleagues. However, Mitrokhin's very existence and the material he was providing were classified Top Secret. He was considered to be a recruitment-in-place by the intelligence and counterintelligence community. Simple knowledge of his existence was a major concern.

Mitrokhin himself, with his family, had been moved to a location carefully guarded by MI-6. He was met frequently by MI-6 case officers at different safe houses to assist in going over his work, and to debrief him for additional information where available. Mitrokhin had his material carefully indexed; when MI-6 asked him, he could provide additional clues and evidence to augment what was in his manuscripts. His son was receiving better medical attention than he had received from the Russians and was improving, although his neuromuscular condition was not expected to improve over the long term. It was a gradually debilitating problem that would affect him his entire life. Mitrokhin's wife was also by necessity forced into retirement to look after their son while Mitrokhin worked closely with his MI-6 contacts and wrote his manuscript.

***

Two days after the failed dead drop attempt with Lipka, SA Whiteside received a call from SA Buckmeier. Buckmeier reported that a letter had arrived at the accommodation address from Robert Lipka, postmarked October 13, 1993, the day of the scheduled dead drop operation.

Buckmeier faxed a copy of the letter from Lipka to SA Whiteside via the secure fax system. The letter read as follows:

> "A meeting is quite impossible at this time, due to medical problems for your friend. Also, no such coins remain in inventory at this location and the short notice plus the failure to pay the full amount for coins sent previously makes any further contact ridiculous at this time. Nothing further until full payment is made for coins previously sent. You seemed satisfied with the replacement coins given at show as a proper time for return is 30 days for refund. Failure to act on letters transferred to you plus other inconsistencies makes you suspect. You have less than three weeks left to extend the proper invitation. Continued failure to do so indicates to me that you are <u>not</u> who you say you are."

The letter was ended with the notation, "E. P. Double is a good horse to bet on at the races."

The letter was typed on a computer using a very small font. When Lipka's cryptic phrases were broken down, it essentially implied the following: First, Lipka had no classified material in his possession (or any that he planned to provide "Nikitin"). Second, he wasn't about to do anything more with "Nikitin" until he received the additional $5,000. Third, "Nikitin" had not yet provided an invitation to Lipka's "good doctor" friend on Russian Embassy letterhead, inviting him and a guest to Moscow, as they'd discussed in Baltimore. Lastly, Lipka was still uncertain about "Nikitin's" actual identity. The letter was signed in a way Lipka approved when they first met in the hotel room in Lancaster: He used his identification letters "E. P." for "en passant" and threw in the word "double" to indicate that Droujinsky should send two checks, not one, as "one means done."

SA Buckmeier was forwarding the letter to the FBI Identification Division for the possibility of lifting fingerprints from it or the envelope. Whiteside alerted the members of the investigative team, including AUSA Cohan and DOJ attorney Liebman, to the contents of the new letter. It was time to gather again and plan the next move. It should be noted that by this time in the case, each new move was being planned around the most recent contact from Lipka himself. The team realized it was still important to keep the contact between Lipka and Droujinsky viable, to get even more incriminating evidence from Lipka. He might just open up to "Nikitin" to get his greedy hands on another five grand.

At the meeting all eventually agreed that it was time to play hardball with Lipka. He would definitely be chastised for not clearing the drop and leaving $5,000 in the park for anyone to find. The investigative team also decided to turn the *Washington Post* article to their advantage. They would take the tack that this leak was what "Nikitin" had alluded to in the July meeting, when he told Lipka that a KGB officer had disappeared. This news article would be "Nikitin's" proof. He would warn Lipka that he faced exposure, arrest, or worse, then offer to help. This would put the FBI in a good position; most people in Lipka's position panic and do just about anything to save their skins.

The team also wanted the undercover agent to take two money orders in the amount of $2,500 each, and give them to Lipka only if he provided evidence of value to the prosecution.

"Wouldn't it be better to take cash this time?" asked SA Brennan. "My thought is that when Lipka sees the cash in Droujinsky's briefcase, it may get him to act a bit more helpful."

The team quickly agreed with Brennan's observation and decided to use cash this time, rather than money orders. To that end, NSA case officer Brisentine offered to prepare a number of documents from the time Lipka worked there that he might have had access to, and may have passed to the KGB. Handwritten notations would be put on the documents in Cyrillic script, as if they'd been looked at by the KGB.

SA Whiteside would contact the FBI Laboratory about preparing the letter Lipka had asked Droujinsky for offering a trip to Russia, to be given to his friend, "the good doctor." Through a little research Whiteside had discovered that "the good doctor" turned out to be Dr. Gerald Weinberger, a former professor at Millersville State Teachers College whom Lipka had met as a student there. They took to each other, perhaps because of similar personalities. How close they were at the present wasn't something Whiteside knew, and he didn't feel it was a priority in the investigation. But he did conduct some record checks to further identify Weinberger, with no significant results. NSA also checked their records and found nothing regarding this associate of Lipka's. There was nothing pertinent to the espionage case that merited any further investigation of Weinberger at the time, and no need to pursue this matter. Besides, there was never any intention to have Lipka and Weinberger travel to Russia for meetings.

For the next meeting Droujinsky would also have a photograph of an unknown white male that he'd present to Lipka as the person who was missing from the KGB. And there would be a copy of the newspaper article mentioning the KGB officer for Lipka to take with him. The team felt that with all of these props, it would be possible to scare Lipka into needing to trust "Nikitin." The investigative team also agreed that if the meeting didn't go well this would be the final contact between Lipka and Droujinsky.

To initiate contact with Lipka, the team decided to send another carefully worded letter. Dated November 5, 1993, "Carl Max" explained that since Lipka had failed to follow instructions and clear the dead drop, he hadn't received his payment. The invitation to "the good doctor" could not be extended at that specific time due to political problems at "Carl Max's" home. Lastly, Lipka was advised that if he met with "Carl Max" on December 8, 1993, at 10:00 AM, in Lancaster, at their usual location, he would be paid the balance of the money he was owed.

***

Before Robert Lipka responded, the FBI Behavioral Science Unit at Quantico answered SA Whiteside's request for psychoanalysis of Lipka, and offered suggestions for getting him to fully accept the undercover agent in his role as Sergey Nikitin. In short, Quantico suspected Lipka was a sociopath. Without more professional evaluation and observation, they were unable to break down his personality definitively, but this diagnosis was the best they could do with the evidence.

Sociopaths are difficult to deal with, but they're not all the murderers Hollywood makes them out to be. The American Psychiatric Association defines a sociopath as someone with an anti-social personality disorder; common traits include a lack of remorse or empathy, persistent lying or stealing, a tendency to physically or verbally abuse peers or family, and a history of childhood conduct disorder. Superficial charm, shallow emotions, and a distorted sense of self can also appear in the affected person. These symptoms seemed to fit Lipka to a tee.

Still, the team thought the undercover operation had gone exceptionally well and they couldn't figure out why Lipka remained so leery of the undercover agent. The analogy provided by the psychologists was that the operation had placed the fish hook in Lipka's mouth, and only needed to set it for a success. Unfortunately, the Behavioral Science Unit couldn't provide any tips on exactly how to set that hook. It would be up to Droujinsky to truly hook Lipka.

5

Date: November 1993
Location: Newtown Square, PA

Shortly before the Thanksgiving holiday SA Tony Buckmeier telephoned SA Whiteside to say that a letter for "Carl Max," not postmarked, had been received at the accommodation address. Buckmeier faxed the letter by secure fax to SA Whiteside and forwarded the original to the Identification Division for processing and examination. The letter read as follows:

"Carl M.

I will meet you on the date indicated. Please be prepared to take a short drive with me for a light lunch. Dress casually in a golf type shirt. The last location chosen by you is a known daytime hangout for homosexuals and is carefully watched and video monitored by certain individuals. I have no interest in being anywhere that these individuals gather as that is not my style. And I certainly do not wish to have myself photographed near them, even by accident.

I will assume that you will have full cash payment for past coin transaction which I carried out to the letter.

I will set that aside for use as traveling expenses for future assignments or coin transactions. Absolutely no discussion of past transactions will be permitted. I regard them as closed issue. Olympic jobs offer wonderful opportunities for worldwide travel I am told??? I envy those with Olympic jobs for that reason??? E. P."

SA Whiteside was thrilled to learn that Lipka seemed to take the bait one more time and was willing to meet with the undercover FBI Agent. Whiteside contacted the other members of the investigative team as well as the Philadelphia FBI technical squad. It was important to the success of the investigation to be prepared for any contingencies, and one of the necessary items was a hotel room—which they hoped Lipka could be persuaded to come back to. Whiteside remembered that the hotel room in May had made Lipka very nervous, and Whiteside doubted that Lipka would enter one again, especially after refusing to do so in Baltimore. However, the technical squad would have one ready in case SA Droujinsky could convince Lipka to join him in the room.

Whiteside alerted the legal team of Cohan and Liebman about the new letter and the date of the next meeting. He also contacted NSA, whose agents started preparing a set of actual documents for the encounter. They were all from the time Lipka was an active KGB agent, and of the type that NSA suspected he may have passed, based on information from Mitrokhin and Lipka's own comments. The FBI Laboratory prepared a letter for Lipka's friend, "the good doctor," on Russian Embassy stationery and forwarded it to Philadelphia. The SSG team agreed to keep track of Lipka several days prior to the anticipated meeting to ensure he was still in the area as preparations were made for the meeting. Whiteside reviewed the pen register information and didn't see any change in the pattern of Lipka's incoming and outgoing calls. There hadn't been any extremely questionable calls to date, although there were people in frequent contact with Lipka who would need to be identified and interviewed at some point. For now, everyone was focused on the upcoming December meeting with Robert Lipka.

A few days later, the investigative team gathered at NSA to review the letter from Lipka and to discuss operational goals for the meet. The letter from Lipka did pose several immediate concerns. The most important dealt with his comment that "absolutely no discussion of past transactions will be permitted. I regard them as closed issue." Lipka was showing his usual effort to control the meeting and set the parameters. If he wasn't willing to talk about documents he'd passed to the KGB, there wasn't much to gain from the meeting.

SA Droujinsky would have to hold out on giving him the additional $5,000 for "...past coin transaction which I carried out to the letter." In fact, neither the communications device Lipka claimed to have sent nor old NSA documents he'd claimed to have mailed ever reached the accommodation address, although every other piece of correspondence since had arrived. It was bold of Lipka to demand money for something he hadn't done, especially from a man who could just as easily turn his name over to the authorities. The team felt that Lipka had convinced himself he was safe from prosecution, and was simply trying to take advantage of a confused Russian GRU officer.

SA Droujinsky was briefed by SA Whiteside on what props he would have at the meeting. Whiteside told him to only use the props he needed, and that he didn't have to show everything. For example, if Lipka wasn't going to ask for the embassy letter to "the good doctor," Droujinsky didn't need to show it to him. Lipka may have thought Dr. Weinberger could travel to Russia, so he brought up the name—but it could be a bluff. Lipka didn't even have a passport (or at least a legal one in his true name), so it seemed his offer had little substance to it. Certainly, the FBI wasn't going to Russia to continue this operation. Unless Lipka decided to pour out his guilt to "Nikitin," this would be the final meeting.

Regarding the money, Droujinsky was instructed not to pay Lipka the $5,000 unless Lipka specifically identified documents that he'd passed to his KGB contacts. It was important to make him work for the money and not just hand it over. Lastly, Droujinsky was tasked with making sure that Lipka knew about the former KGB employee in the news for spilling information, and imply that Droujinsky's own warning at their last face-to-face meeting in Baltimore referred to this. It was imperative that Droujinsky put pressure on so Lipka would feel that his only choice was to rely on Droujinsky for protection.

***

It was a cold, damp day as the investigators from various places arrived at the Comfort Inn. The technical squad had finished their installations in the hotel room and SSG surveillance had been following Lipka the past several days. They reported that Lipka had been at home, and they hadn't observed anything unusual. The investigative team met with SA Droujinsky and furnished him with all of the props, including the cash totaling $5,000, to place in his briefcase. Together, they reviewed the interview plan and goals of the meeting in great detail. Everyone knew that Droujinsky faced a difficult task, but they trusted his experience. Still, it was important to keep him mindful of the primary goals for this meeting. When the briefing was finished, the group went out to the Grandstand restaurant for dinner and necessary liquid refreshment before the big day.

When it dawned, the team was already up and preparing. The only instructions SA Whiteside had for SA Droujinsky was a simple—yet stern—reminder to use his props judiciously, and not pay Lipka unless he delivered concrete information on his espionage. Whiteside stressed that this might be their last chance to deal with Lipka, so they had to draw as much from him as possible. But if they could maintain a trusting relationship between "Nikitin" and Lipka, Droujinsky needed to drive home the issue of the missing KGB employee.

Essentially, there were two ways this meeting could go. One possibility was that Lipka might balk at all Droujinsky had to say, thus bringing an end to the undercover phase of the investigation. If that occurred the rest of the investigation would proceed down other paths; it wouldn't matter if Lipka learned about it since there would be nothing he could do to stop it or interfere.

But the possibility also existed—however unlikely—that Lipka would identify documents, become fearful of the missing KGB officer, and thus rely strongly on "Nikitin" to assist him. In that case additional meetings might be planned to collect more evidence from Lipka. Whiteside's team had to be prepared for both scenarios. Undercover operations like these take on a life of their own, and despite the planning, experience, and skill involved, investigators must adapt to ever-changing circumstances. While everyone hoped Lipka would panic, confess, and plead for "Nikitin's" assistance, most of the team expected this would be the last meeting.

Following breakfast the investigative team returned to the command post and the technical team attached a recording device to SA Droujinsky. The team wasn't entirely sure Lipka would make the meeting, but all bets were that he would show up for the $5,000.

At 9:45 AM the SSG team watching his residence radioed that Lipka had entered his van and was driving a route that would bring him to the Comfort Inn. When Lipka finally arrived in the parking lot, and as he had done in the past, he drove around slowly looking for any suspicious cars or people. Finding none, he parked in front of the main doors and awaited the arrival of "Sergey Nikitin." Droujinsky headed downstairs, exited the hotel doors, and walked over to the driver's side window to greet Lipka. "Good morning. Won't you come upstairs? We have something very serious to talk about and it would be safer in the room to talk together."

"No," replied Lipka. "Why don't you get inside and we can take a short ride to a place that is safer than here. I'm known to too many people in this area."

Droujinsky entered the passenger side of the van and sat down. When he asked why Lipka hadn't made the drop in Long's Park in October, Lipka claimed that the local police had the park under sur-veillance as the result of homosexual activity there and that he didn't want to be photographed for any reason. Droujinsky responded that his people had chosen the park because "...the couple who made contact with you in the past used that park."

Lipka said, "Well yes, things change." It was an implicit admission that he'd been contacted by Soviet illegals Peter and Ingeborg Fischer.

"Did you meet them there by any chance? Did they leave anything for you there in the park? I know they used it and thought it would be a good place."

"Once, once again, tell me who you represent, precisely."

"Okay, like I mentioned to you before, I'm with the GRU. You know what is the GRU, yes?"

"Yeah. You can drive by the way, right?"

"Yes."

"I want you to mentally follow this route here because it is a very simple route and a very simple place to go. And—and. . . ah. . . an okay place for drops."

"Yes, yes, okay," replied Droujinsky.

Lipka chatted about the park he was currently driving to, Amos Herr Park in Landisville, PA, saying it was out in the open and a better place to meet, away from crowds. At one point he pointed out a picnic bench in the park and said, "It would have been a better place to tape something under." Lipka may have been referring to his past clandes-tine activities in Rock Creek Park in Washington, DC where he made previous drops for the KGB. The park had numbered picnic areas with picnic tables located in each secluded area that he may have used.

Lipka asked Droujinsky again what was so important to dis-cuss. Droujinsky opened his briefcase and brought out a copy of the *Washington Post* article mentioning Ronald Kessler's book, which held that a KGB officer was providing information to the FBI about former espionage cases. Lipka told Droujinsky that he'd read the book; he even said he'd watched Kessler be interviewed by Larry King.

"If the KGB officer has proof, then they can arrest you," "Nikitin" warned. "And y'know the consequences. You can go to prison. And that will ruin your life, and your children's life, and your wife's life, and everybody."

Lipka replied, "The statute of limitations has run out."

"No, I understand in American law that the statute of limitations never runs out. And you can check on this, but my legal person in the embassy told me that on espionage, American law statute of limitations never runs out."

"My—my understanding, well, that's been changed subsequent to my being discharged from the service. At that time it was twenty years. So, that would fall under an ex post facto situation within the law." It was clear to Droujinsky that Lipka didn't know anything about the espionage statute laws. Lipka continued, "First of all, I would never admit to anything."

Droujinsky tried to brush Lipka's bravado aside and stress that he was the only person who could help, and that the situation was just between the two of them. Lipka responded, "Do you have equipment that I can use to sanction the guy?"

"You mean kill him?" asked Droujinsky incredulously.

"Yeah," Lipka said, "Bandera style." Here Lipka was referring to a KGB assassin who murdered Stefan Bandera, an exiled Ukrainian leader. The assassin took an antidote just before firing a capsule of gaseous prussic acid into the face of the victim. Bandera breathed in the gas and was poisoned, which caused a fatal heart attack. The assassin was close enough that he, too, breathed some of the gas, but he survived because he'd taken the antidote.

"Well. . . ah. . . we have everything. We have stuff like that. And, like I said, we will help you."

Droujinsky then took a photograph from his briefcase and showed it to Lipka. It was a photograph of a former Soviet KGB officer, Yuri Linkov, whom FBI Headquarters and the analytical unit suspected had likely been Lipka's handler. "Do you recognize him?"

"No."

"You don't recognize him?"

"No."

"Remember the last time when I showed you pictures in the hotel. You said his hair was different at that time, remember? This is how he looked then when you worked for us."

"No." Lipka either would not or could not identify Linkov as his former handler. Lipka then asked, "Explain to me why you didn't know who Pavel Grachev was."

"Pavel Grachev?"

"Yeah, one of the first times we met I gave you a list of three names."

"Yes."

"And you didn't know Pavel Grachev's name. Explain to me why?"

Droujinsky immediately grew concerned about the situation. "Well, who's Pavel Grachev?"

Lipka said laughing. "Well, that would be your boss."

"My boss?"

"And he's the head of the GRU! You're telling me that you—you're GRU."

Droujinsky, trying to recover from a most difficult situation said, "And. . . uh. . . but at that time??"

"No," replied Lipka "I'm talking now."

"Oh. . . no, I thought you are referring to people you were dealing with them at that time. That those names were from that time. You see what I mean. In other words, twenty-eight years ago, that when you were dealing..."

Lipka laughed. "Well, I'm—I'm—I'm at the point where I'm confused now whether. . . see, I'm not a hundred percent sure I can even trust you. You're telling me you want me to go into—to a hotel room, that's standard entrapment procedure to. . . ah. . film somebody. I'm very reluctant to do something like that."

At this point Droujinsky tried to move the conversation along by providing Lipka with a packet containing new emergency instructions, again noting the potential danger Lipka faced should this unknown KGB defector identify him to the FBI. Lipka ignored the comment and said he'd memorize the new emergency instructions then destroy the written information. "Nikitin" handed Lipka the original *Washington Post* article and asked Lipka if he had a passport. Lipka replied in the negative, then asked, "By the way, that package never showed?"

"No, it never did."

"I'm not worried about it," Lipka said, then launched into another diatribe on all the alleged precautions he took when preparing and mailing the package. "Understand that I have nothing at my house. They can search through it, top to bottom, inch by inch. I have nothing at my house that even remotely. . . ah. . . would be suspicious."

From there discussion turned to getting Lipka to travel to Russia as a possible member of the Olympic Committee for the 1996 Games. "Nikitin" showed Lipka a copy of the letter he'd prepared inviting Lipka's friend, Gerald Weinberger, and a personal guest, to travel to Russia. Lipka approved of the letter but said that his friend's residence had changed and that he would have to get the new address for "Nikitin."

During a conversational lull Droujinsky asked about the classified NSA and KGB documents Lipka had alluded to during their meeting in Baltimore. First Lipka told a story about a bank building being built over one place where he'd buried documents. But then he said that as a result of the Kessler book he didn't want to have any incriminating evidence at his residence, so he'd discarded the old, unclassified NSA documents, interesting newspaper clippings, and military records he kept at home.

After a few more digressions Droujinsky brought conversation back to how it was that Lipka had become involved with the Soviets. However, Lipka refused to discuss the details, only saying that his recollection was that it had involved a girl.

Droujinsky's next tack was to draw Lipka into a discussion of missed drops and problems with payments for meets. "One thing I need you to talk about," "Nikitin" said, "remember you told me before that eight times you were underpaid? And three times you were not paid at all? Right? Is this correct? Or you did not find money in a drop, or something like that?"

"I would say that eight times I was vastly underpaid."

"Underpaid, yes. And I thought you said three times not paid at all."

Lipka lifted up one finger.

"One time? Okay. So one time you were not paid. But we need to know on those times when you did not get what you were supposed to get; do you remember what material you gave?"

"I have no recollection of that," Lipka said. He claimed that his back surgery had caused some memory problems and made it difficult to recall details. Droujinsky pushed but Lipka continued to say that he couldn't remember any details from that long ago; even when Droujinsky reminded him he'd discussed some of these issues in May.

For the next twenty minutes conversation ebbed and flowed as Droujinsky tried to get information and Lipka stonewalled. Lipka denied his former wife's involvement in accompanying him on dead drops. He wouldn't say what he brought out, but did say that the KGB couldn't ask him for specific information from NSA because there was no way for him to search for, and thereafter retrieve, documents from the building. When Droujinsky asked how he took documents out of the building at NSA, Lipka simply used his finger to print "H A T" on the dashboard. While he'd not had access to copying facilities at NSA, Lipka said, he'd had access to literally all NSA's material, based upon the enormous quantity of documents that passed through his work station. Then he chuckled at the irony of the fact that his training at the Army's intelligence school, Fort Holabird (which no longer exists—intelligence training is now conducted at Fort Huachuca, Arizona), had assisted him in avoiding detection while removing documents from NSA.

Droujinsky let that comment go and pumped Lipka for information about the Fischers again. Lipka finally admitted that they'd left a postcard in his mailbox, without a postmark, as if it had been placed there by hand.

He got excited talking about one occasion when he received $500 in the mail and was told to report for a meeting at a park in the Bronx, NY. Lipka had been instructed to bring a copy of *Life* magazine to identify himself to the agent, someone who had been assigned to the UN. Droujinsky pushed to get a name for the agent, but all Lipka would say was that the agent "played chess very well." And although Lipka said they'd played chess, he wouldn't divulge what they discussed. He was also vague on the date, saying the meeting might have occurred in 1974, but he wasn't sure.

Lipka was surprised that "Nikitin" didn't know about this meeting. Droujinsky protested, and repeated his story that Lipka's file was torn apart in Moscow, passionately presenting his argument that contacting Lipka was to alert him to the danger he may be facing, and to help him out where possible.

Droujinsky then took five NSA documents from his briefcase and showed them to Lipka, one at a time. "Just look at these and see if you can remember," he urged.

"I've never had access to that one, throw that out." He also claimed not to recognize a second one.

"Nikitin" showed Lipka a third document. "Something like that I might have seen," Lipka admitted.

"Yeah? So you, you gave things like this here?"

"No, no. I'm saying I might have seen some. But see, I can eliminate based on stuff that I know I never had."

"So this is a possibility, yes?"

"That's a possibility, yes."

Another document was shown to Lipka. "No, I wasn't cleared for that," he said.

"Okay, how about this, shall I open it?" It was the last document.

"Open that one up. I would have had access to that."

"Okay, so you probably passed something like this?"

"I don't know. Look, I had one hundred percent access to everything except counterintelligence files." When asked how he took the documents out of the building Lipka replied, "I'm not going into that with you. I don't think that's necessary."

Droujinsky continued to press Lipka about the method he used to get documents out of the building, and how he packaged the material for drops. Droujinsky also asked about Lipka's wife's involvement in various dead drop activity.

Finally Lipka said, "You're telling me that there is no statute of limitations on—on—on this particular thing and. . . ah. . . for me to say how I. . . what procedure I actually used in something like that would be the key that could put me in ...I hope you understand that."

"I understand your concern, yes. But of course, we are both taking chances."

"Well, that's one chance I—I don't even want you to even ask me to take. Enough about it." Lipka looked at all the NSA documents Droujinsky held and said, "I would have had access to all of these. I don't remember bringing out anything like this."

Lipka said he needed to use the restroom and left "Nikitin" in the car. Upon his return, he said the bathroom was closed and he needed to leave the area.

On the way back to the Comfort Inn they chatted about Lipka's surgery again. But finally Lipka asked that they "complete the transaction." He'd seen the money in "Nikitin's" briefcase, and was getting impatient.

Droujinsky had a decision to make: Had he received enough incriminating information from Lipka to pay him? If he didn't pay, would the relationship end? There was no way to meet with the investigative team and discuss options. Droujinsky needed to make the call on his own. "Right, okay yes now, one thing Bob, what I need from you . . . because I have cash."

"Okay."

"So, I'm going to give you cash. And I need the receipt because you—you know how you say..."

"Yes, yes, I understand."

"So you can write it any way you want, as long as my superior knows that the money was delivered to you. Do you have a pen?"

"Yep. How much do you have there?"

"Okay, I'm going to give you five thousand dollars. Okay? And that will take care of everything. And please, if you remember any more things. . . because that will help us. And you can sign your code name if you want."

"How's that? Is that good enough? Or I can put 'E. P.' right below that?"

"Yes, maybe better, and from me. . . put my code name also. That'll be better."

After receiving his money, Lipka rumbled on about possible travel overseas to international shows. But Droujinsky brought him back to matters at hand. "Bob, remember last time, when we met in Baltimore? You told me you had something my people had given to you and you were going to bring it with you. Did you bring it by any chance?"

"No, no, I—I..."

"Can you give it to me tomorrow?"

"No, there's. . . ah. . . the bank building is sitting on it."

"So there is nothing left?"

"Believe me, there is nothing left."

Droujinsky started prodding again, and Lipka eventually said that he'd attended the intelligence analyst course at NSA. "So that was your job, intelligence analyst?"

"Yes, therefore, there is a complete computerized record on everybody and what they had access to."

"Ah, the course at Fort Holabird, did that help you in doing what you were doing? In other words, not to get detected and everything?"

"Yes." laughed Lipka. "Yeah, by its own bizarre circumstances, I'll—I can never forget. . . when I came there, I replaced Jack Dunlap." Droujinsky knew that Lipka was referring to Jack E. Dunlap, an Army Sergeant in the National Security Agency and decorated Korean War veteran, who died on July 23, 1963. Dunlap's body was found slumped over the steering wheel of his yellow Cadillac with a bottle of whiskey on the front seat and a hose running from the car's exhaust system into a front window sealed with masking tape. The local medical examiner ruled the death a suicide. FBI and NSA investigation ultimately determined that Dunlap, who had been with the Army and the NSA eleven years, had been delivering copies of Top Secret documents to the KGB. However, debate raged for years afterward about how much information Dunlap had passed, and how many American lives it had cost.

"Really?"

"Yes, and this old Colonel said to me, 'You turn out to be like Jack, I'll shoot you myself.' There's a certain irony in everything, isn't there?"

"Now Bob, you made an interesting comment before. You said that there was a woman involved that got you into it. Helped you get in this situation. Start working with us. What—what happened?"

"No, no I'd rather not get into that. But your recollection of how this all started is a little different than—than mine."

"Well, why don't you tell me what happened then?"

"This is. . . this is another one of those areas that is better left unplumbed at this point. I must go... I—I. . . ah. . . I'm going to drop you off in that supermarket parking lot. Um. . . as I told you, my reluctance, my reluctance to go into a hotel room is twofold. What I explained to you before about Abscam, although I'm quite aware of other procedures to record... ah... meetings. Including bugging this vehicle."

Despite his unease, though, Lipka drove back to the hotel instead of the supermarket. He made "Nikitin" tell him how to return to the park, to prove that "Nikitin" had in fact memorized the route. As they parted company from the Comfort Inn, Droujinsky reminded Lipka to contact him using the emergency instructions should any problems develop with his safety and security. As Lipka drove away, Droujinsky walked back to the Comfort Inn for one more debriefing session.

This meeting between Droujinsky and Robert Lipka was by far their longest one. During the debriefing session with the investigative team Droujinsky vented that of all the other false flag approaches he'd made in his FBI career, Lipka proved to be the most difficult.

The group was at least relieved to find out why Lipka had been so doubtful of "Sergey Nikitin:" "Nikitin" had failed the simple test of identifying Pavel Grachev as the head of the GRU (actually the Soviet Defense Minister). It was tantamount to asking an FBI agent the name of the Director of the FBI and not knowing the answer. Droujinsky had tried to cover up the mistake, but the rest of the conversation seemed to show that Lipka would never fully trust him. SA Whiteside took the blame for the error, since he'd assumed—without checking—that whatever role the undercover agent was playing would have been carefully rehearsed. Lipka was certainly no brain surgeon, but he knew enough to try a few simple tests that led him to feel either comfortable or alerted in the meetings.

One other useful conclusion the team drew was that Lipka didn't have current access to NSA classified information, or if he did, didn't plan to pass it to "Nikitin." The team thought that if he'd had a continuing pipeline of information at NSA he would have worked a deal with the undercover agent to continue passing information for money.

But in the professional opinion of the investigators, Lipka was simply a con artist. Whenever questioning became focused on his espionage activities, Lipka would play the memory loss card. There were times when he clearly couldn't remember some of the incriminating details of earlier conversations with Droujinsky, and others when Lipka couldn't remember his own lies. It was also noted that Lipka would start stammering when answering questions about his direct involvement with the KGB, an indication of guilt via body language.

Lastly, it was evident that any further contact with Lipka would be fruitless. It would be better to begin the next phase of investigation and try to build a solid case against Lipka using other strategies. The contacts between "Nikitin" and Lipka had more than confirmed Mitrokhin's information; all the team needed now were a few good witnesses.

***

On February 7, 1994, SA Buckmeier found a surprise inside the accommodation address mailbox: A letter postmarked January 24, 1994, from Lancaster, PA. Buckmeier eventually opened the envelope and found a short typewritten note along with a copied article from the February 1994 issue of *Worth* magazine. The article mentioned that authorities believed the Iranian and Syrian governments were printing counterfeit U.S. currency in the form of $100 bills. The typewritten note read:

> "An interesting story. My curiosity as a coin collector is such that I would love to personally see about three or four huge boxes of this stuff. Imagine the damage that converting this stuff to gold coins and silver coins would do???? 60-/40???"

The note was simply closed with the initials "E.P."

Lipka's purpose for the letter wasn't clear to Whiteside. It's possible Lipka was simply testing the new accommodation address; he might also have been sending the message to "Nikitin" that he was still open to making a deal; or he might have thought his Russian contact was such a soft touch that he'd pay for even this useless information. It's also possible that he genuinely wanted to start a money laundering scheme—but because Whiteside's team hadn't found anything remotely related to other charges against Lipka, he decided not to sidetrack the espionage case to look into this. Overall the note seemed like Lipka's attempt to dodge espionage questions and cajole more money out of a hapless GRU officer. And in typical Lipka fashion, it fell short of giving away anything valuable.

After discussion the investigative team decided to ignore the letter and see what Lipka would—or not—do. Since the undercover work with Lipka was finished there was no reason to respond to another of his strange letters. Instead, the team was anticipating opening up the Lipka investigation to include all of his former family and work associates. His ex-wife Pat was of primary interest, and NSA employees who'd been Lipka's colleagues were a close second. More meetings between the investigative team members determined that the former Patricia Lipka would be the first interview target.

The team had gleaned all the intelligence they could from Robert Lipka himself, and if he learned about the investigation against him there was nothing he could do about it. He did have the emergency telephone number and mailing address for "Sergey Nikitin" in case he saw fit to use it. This might even benefit the investigation, since Lipka might feel forced to confide in the undercover agent.

Whiteside's team wasn't too worried about interviews with NSA on duty personnel because they were still subject to occasional polygraph testing as a component of their classified clearances. Any previous espionage activity on their behalf would have already been ferreted out by the polygraph. The pen register was still working on Lipka's telephone, so any call from a former NSA colleague would be identified. Most importantly, the team was reasonably sure, based on experience, training, and past cases, that Lipka had acted alone. The only one who might contact Lipka about an FBI interview, the team thought, was Pat, his ex-wife.

6

Date: February 11, 1994
Location: Baltimore, MD

SA Brennan had conducted a background investigation of the former Patricia Lipka and had determined that she was living in Columbia, MD, and working as a nurse in a local hospital. She'd married a fireman after divorcing Robert Lipka, but the marriage never worked out. As of 1994 she was married to her third husband, and based on all Brennan could discover, was happily married. She didn't seem to have any children beside her daughter with Lipka, Kelly, who was living nearby. Her life looked to be going well, and perhaps deservedly so. But SA Brennan knew that contacting her would necessarily change that significantly.

SAs Brennan and Whiteside decided it would be best to interview Pat at her house. Once the date was set they would meet again and plan the interview; it might be the most important of the entire investigation. Every good agent knows that in a delicate situation like this there's only one chance to succeed. A good agent also knows that every interview should have a goal, and the interviewer shouldn't let the interview end until that goal is met, no matter how long it takes. Sometimes it's easier to give up rather than to stay at it with the subject until all the facts come to light, but leaving things unfinished gives the interview subject more time to protect him- or herself from admissions by developing subsequent alibis. Brennan and Whiteside knew this interview with Pat would take several hours.

They also decided to put a little psychological pressure on Pat by scheduling the interview with her in advance. It would give her time to anticipate and dig up memories, and it would let the agents know when she'd have a day off; as a nurse, her schedule was often confusing. They would give her a day or two between her first contact with them to dread the always-feared interview.

On Friday, February 18, 1994, SA Brennan drove to the hospital where Pat was employed. He arrived at her floor and asked one of the nurses to speak to her; he had a brief wait before she appeared at the desk. Asking Pat to step away for a private talk, SA Brennan showed her his FBI photo ID, or what agents refer to as "credentials" (the gold badge they usually only show for quick identification in raid and arrest situations).

Once they were out of the other nurses' earshot, Brennan started the conversation. "Pat, the FBI is involved in an investigation of your ex-husband, Robert Lipka, and we are interviewing former associates of Lipka's. The investigation has to do with some money laundering issues involving Lipka's coin business that he operated in Lancaster in the 1970s. I'd like to interview you about that. Can we meet somewhere away from the hospital? Because I don't know how long the interview might take."

Pat, seeming to maintain her composure, agreed to an interview and checked her schedule. "I'm off on Tuesday, February 22, and that would be a good time. We can meet at my home at 11:00 AM."

"That will work out fine," SA Brennan replied. "Thank you for cooperating and I'll see you next Tuesday. By the way, please don't contact Robert Lipka before we conduct the interview. He's not aware of the investigation at this time."

"I won't call him. I don't even know where he lives now."

***

Monday was a damp, cloudy day; SA Whiteside saw remnants of snow along the ground as he traveled to Baltimore. It had snowed the previous weekend, and then warmed up slightly, creating a foggy mist that made driving miserable on Interstate 95. Whiteside was becoming so used to this trip that he thought he could do it in his sleep. During the past year and a half, he made several trips a month to meet with the investigative team at NSA, or at the Baltimore Division of the FBI. Still, he was looking forward to the interview and to what he hoped would be a confession from Pat when she realized that espionage was the FBI's real interest involving Robert Lipka.

Whiteside felt good all the way around about this next step. SA Brennan had done a great job of setting up the interview, and the two agents got along well. Whiteside hoped this interview would seal Robert Lipka's prosecution. It seemed like a good possibility—although there was simply not much else to go on.

At approximately 10:00AM Whiteside was lulled from his driving reverie by a special report on the radio. The news had just broken that a major spy had been arrested that morning in Washington, DC named Aldrich Ames. Whiteside slammed the dashboard with his fist. "No! Not today!"

This was the last thing he wanted to hear before the incredibly sensitive interview planned for the next day with Pat. The rest of the announcement said that the arrest of this CIA case officer had been in the works for some time, and that the damage he was suspected of causing was extremely serious. Whiteside wondered if Pat had heard the news. Surely it would be spread all over the news channels. Would this arrest have any effect on the outcome of his interview with her? There was nothing he could do about it, though. He'd have to go forward and hope for the best. There was always the possibility that in learning of the arrest, Pat might be reminded of the seriousness of espionage allegations. The more Whiteside thought about it, the more he suspected it could possibly help with the interview the following day.

Whiteside met up with SA Brennan at a local hotel, where Whiteside had booked a room. Together they went over their interview plans and discussed the facts of Pat's divorce from Bob. The interview, or "interrogation" in FBI agent talk, plan relied on a slow build-up of tension. They wouldn't simply go over a timeline, or a specific event in Pat and Bob's life together, but they'd take their time and go slowly and methodically over everything. Subsequent contacts after the divorce, and any custody battles over Kelly, were also on the interview plan. Whiteside and Brennan wanted information on everything from the day Pat first laid eyes on Bob until their last contact with each other. Bob's coin business would be a running theme in the interview, but the goal would always be a confession from Pat of Bob's espionage.

Both Whiteside and Brennan felt sure that Pat knew about her ex-husband's spying. It appeared that she'd met him just as he began his treacherous activity, then, a year into his spying, they married. They spent another year together as a young married couple while he completed his spy work. It was hard for the investigators to believe that Pat would have had a relationship with Bob for two full years without knowing a thing about his contact with the KGB.

***

The following morning Brennan and Whiteside went over the interview scenario again at breakfast to iron out any last minute details. They decided SA Brennan would take the lead since he'd made the initial contact, and would be available for future contact since he lived closest.

Walking through the wet slush on Pat's sidewalk made for a dismal start to the day. Pat herself answered the doorbell and invited the agents inside. As she took their coats she introduced them to her husband, Bill. Bill shook hands with the agents, and the four of them settled into the two love seats in the living room, facing each other across a large glass coffee table.

SA Brennan started the interview on a light note, telling Pat and Bill about the nature of the interview, and that they certainly were not in any trouble. He simply wanted to learn more about the person of Robert Lipka, and hoped Pat could shed light on the subject. Brennan started by asking Pat for a little background information, such as where she was from and where she grew up. Pat appeared a little tense at first, but answered the questions freely.

As SA Brennan moved the interview to her first contact with Lipka, she said she couldn't remember the exact dates. During their discussion of her early years with Lipka Pat seemed confused and her answers were incomplete, as though she was afraid to talk about him. During those moments, her husband rubbed her back. SA Whiteside could see that the interview wouldn't be productive as long as Bill stuck around. When someone supportive is present the interviewee feels comfortable, but the interrogation is designed to place pressure on the person being interviewed. Third parties are sometimes also confederates of the interviewee, or make comments that disrupt the flow of information.

In this particular situation, it seemed apparent that Pat had asked her husband to stay with her. It was possible that Bill knew nothing about the espionage activity; if so, it was highly unlikely Pat would spill the beans in his presence. However, neither Whiteside nor Brennan could think of a way to get Bill to leave. After all, Bill probably suspected it was going to be a traumatic interview with the FBI and he wanted to provide Pat with all the support a husband could provide in such a situation.

Nonetheless, SA Brennan pressed on. He took the interview to the time that Bob and Pat moved to Lancaster, PA. Whiteside noticed that whenever Pat was questioned about events between September 1967, and her divorce in 1974, she recalled every minor detail. But whenever SA Brennan referred to the period from September 1965 to August 1967, when Bob was spying, Pat had difficulty remembering things.

As SA Whiteside observed her nonverbal responses to Brennan's questioning his FBI training kicked into gear. He sat wishing he could video this interview because it was beginning to look like a classic one.

Whenever Brennan asked about Lipka, regardless of the topic, if the date was at any time during the Lancaster period Pat answered fully and with direct eye contact, remembering the smallest details. However, when Brennan would go back to the time Lipka worked at NSA, she would look up, bat her eyelids, say she couldn't remember, or provide a vague answer. After watching this behavior for an hour or so Whiteside was convinced that Pat was covering up. She knew about Lipka's espionage activities. It was simply the clearest example of nonverbal communication Whiteside had ever seen.

To some extent it reminded him of the meetings between Droujinsky and Lipka. Whenever Lipka was confronted with direct questions about espionage he would either feign memory loss or change the topic. None of those characteristics were noted when Lipka was talking about mundane subjects unrelated to his espionage activities.

Whiteside saw no way out of this game with Pat. The interview had lasted at least ninety minutes, and no mention of espionage had yet been made; Bill continued to sit on the sofa next to Pat and caress her back and shoulders; and Whiteside was dealing with a moderate allergy attack from the presence of two cats, while his feet were wet and cold from the walk to the house. But it's always been said that it's often better to be lucky than good in conducting investigations, and this interview was no exception. The telephone suddenly rang and Bill got up to answer it. When he returned he said, "That was the hairdresser. They're ready for my hair appointment, so I'll have to leave."

As he put on his jacket, SA Whiteside said, "It was nice to meet you, Bill. We shouldn't be too much longer. We only have a few more follow-up questions to ask." Bill shook hands with Whiteside and Brennan and left the house. But Whiteside turned back to the living room ready to put on the real pressure.

SA Brennan continued to move the interview back and forth, from their time at NSA, to the time of their divorce. He maintained the steady line of questioning as planned; Pat's husband leaving wasn't enough of a reason to change tack. It was still going to take time, and patience was most important now. Pat spoke freely of the physical and mental abuse that Bob had put her through in their marriage; more freely, in all probability, then if her husband had still been sitting there. However, her demeanor had not really changed. She still remembered clearly the details in her post-espionage life, and little during the espionage phase.

As Pat described it, the abuse had started slowly with Bob refusing to drive her to the hospital for her night shift, forcing her to walk dark streets alone. But then Bob started gambling over games of chess. He started coming home late, then, eventually, not at all. On one memorable occasion Pat came home from work to find baby Kelly left by herself. Lipka's debts piled up, his absences grew longer, and his temper grew shorter. At the slightest provocation he would scream at Pat. Then he started hitting her. Pat also mentioned sexual abuse, although the agents didn't pursue that matter.

A substantial amount of the information Pat gave them would prove useful later in the investigation; the anecdotes showed Whiteside and Brennan what kind of person they were dealing with in Lipka. Pat explained how Lipka had threatened her, in midnight phone calls, that he would fight the divorce and get custody of Kelly. On one occasion he sounded out of his mind with regret and threatened to kill himself if Pat went through with the divorce. Pat had simply said, "I'll see you in court," but then she heard a gunshot rip through the line. She was so upset that she vomited. But fifteen minutes later the phone rang again—and it was Lipka, laughing hysterically. After all that he never showed up at the divorce hearing.

She also spoke about an instance after their divorce when Lipka had showed up at Kelly's elementary school and asked the receptionist to get her so he could take her home. Fortunately, the secretary had checked Kelly's file before anything else; she'd seen the note saying that Pat had to be called before Kelly's father could have contact with her. When the secretary went back to confront Lipka, he'd already fled. It seemed that he was the type to put up a lot of bluster, yet when challenged he would avoid the actual confrontation.

Even Lipka's courtship of Pat had involved deceit. They met innocently enough, at an Army-sponsored dance at Fort Meade, but soon thereafter Lipka had convinced Pat to sneak out and see him outside of her dorm's visiting hours. At the time Lipka was living in the Army barracks and working at NSA; Pat was studying nursing at a nearby women's college, Union College. Lipka would call her at all hours, and she would often sneak out to see him. That turned into furtive hotel visits, and eventually they moved in together. They decided to marry the day Pat blurted out to Lipka at the breakfast table, "I'm pregnant!"

Pat was totally enamored of Lipka, but her parents weren't happy with their situation. They'd always been disappointed in her, though; she'd been the black sheep of the family. It seemed that everything she did disappointed them. And here she was, marrying because of a pregnancy, and dropping out of nursing school.

Pat also recounted that Lipka had actually never graduated high school. Like his classmates he left in 1963, but he had no diploma thanks to a failing grade in English. Lipka claimed that the teacher had purposely flunked him after he'd had an affair with her. It was only later, in the Army, that Lipka earned his GED.

But despite the interesting anecdotes another forty-five minutes or so expired while Pat's nonverbal cues continued. Whiteside knew she was holding back the information about the KGB. Brennan finally finished the questioning they'd so carefully planned the day before, then asked Whiteside if he had any additional questions.

Whiteside looked at Pat and paused for a moment. Then he said, "Pat is there anything we haven't asked you that you think we should know about Bob?"

She put her head down, and after what seemed like an eternity, but was probably no more than ten seconds, lifted her head and replied, "Well, he was selling secrets from NSA to the Russians!"

"I guess you knew that we knew that, didn't you?" Whiteside replied.

"Yes," she replied, and began to sob softly. All the tension in the room immediately dissipated. It was definitely time to take a break. Pat went to the kitchen for a soda and Whiteside went to the bathroom to wash the cat dander out of his itchy eyes. Allergies aside, Whiteside was thrilled: Pat had admitted Lipka's espionage!

After a few minutes the interview recommenced. In response to questioning, Pat said that her husband Bill knew nothing about the espionage. She denied contacting anyone about the interview with the exception of a girlfriend, who she said she had to call because she couldn't stand the stress of the impending interview. She hadn't said anything to her girlfriend about the espionage, though. When Whiteside asked if she had any contact with Robert Lipka, Pat said her last contact with him had been about twenty years ago, and that she had no reason to ever call him. Pat looked the agents straight in the eyes and said she had never discussed Lipka's espionage activities with anyone.

"When did you first learn that Bob was in contact with the Russians?" Brennan asked.

"I don't remember," Pat replied.

Whiteside was disappointed. "How is it that you cannot remember when you first learned that your boyfriend or husband was selling secrets to the Russians? How could you ever forget that moment? Do you recall what you were doing? Were you sitting at home, or out on a date? Can't you remember something?"

Pat thought about it and said, "I may have been sitting at the kitchen table."

"What did he say to you?"

"I don't remember." For the next hour or two, it was nearly impossible to get anything of substance from Pat about Bob's espionage. She did say he referred to the Russians as "Ivan." She also recalled him mentioning that there was a girl involved, and that the KGB had pictures of him; she'd thought he was being blackmailed in some way.

Whiteside asked her how she'd reacted when Lipka told her about his contacts with the Russians. Again, Pat replied that she couldn't recall. When Whiteside asked her if she cried upon learning the news, she said she probably did.

Rather than going into the specifics of Pat's knowledge of her ex-husband's espionage, SAs Brennan and Whiteside decided to switch to a softer approach. They had Pat discuss how she first met Robert Lipka at the dances she used to go to as a nursing student, put on at the Army's Fort Meade, where Bob had been serving. They talked about her daughter, Kelly, and the agents were amazed to learn that Lipka had had no contact with her for years. They also circled back to the marital problems that had developed, and Robert Lipka's abusive nature. Next they switched to Pat's life since leaving Lipka. She talked about her second marriage to a fireman. The marriage simply did not work out and had only lasted a few years. She subsequently married Bill, her current husband, and was happily married. She never had any more children; Kelly is her only child.

After another hour or two had passed the investigators warned Pat that she'd be asked a lot of questions about Lipka's espionage activities in future interviews, even though they knew it would be painful for her to recollect some of the issues. They impressed on her that the smallest details were of extreme importance; she pledged her assistance. Pat seemed willing to meet again that week when she had another day off, and set up an interview with SA Brennan. As he and Whiteside finally left, Brennan asked Pat not to discuss this issue with anyone, including her husband.

Whiteside drove back to Pennsylvania with a smile on his face; he was thrilled Pat had confessed to the knowledge that Robert Lipka was a spy for the Soviet Union, and specifically, the KGB. But he was still troubled about her apparent reluctance to provide the details of

Lipka's espionage activities. Still, Whiteside was amazed that Pat had kept this secret for nearly twenty-nine years. Pat had said that when SA Brennan appeared at the hospital and introduced himself to her as an FBI Special Agent she absolutely knew it was about the espionage secret she'd kept all that time. Whiteside realized her stress level must have been unbelievably high, and knew she needed time to recover. But he needed to get more testimony from her before she decided to get a lawyer and stop talking.

Whiteside also needed to discuss the interview details with the legal team in case Pat decided to change her mind. To that end, SA Whiteside contacted AUSA Barbara Cohan the following day and gave her a full briefing of the interview with Pat. Cohan was thrilled, and shared Whiteside's hope that more information on Lipka's activities would be forthcoming. Together, they telephoned Departmental Attorney Michael Liebman and shared the good news.

SA Brennan was scheduled to meet Pat again the following day, and everyone anticipated continued success. AUSA Cohan confirmed that Pat wasn't a target in the investigation, and absent any earth-shattering news about her culpability, she wouldn't be prosecuted. Robert Lipka was the person who'd had the clearance and access to classified information, and the one who'd removed it from the confines of NSA. He committed the espionage, and he would be the one prosecuted. The team agreed that it was crucial to pass that message to Pat in future contacts so she would feel more comfortable giving information.

The following day SA Brennan showed up at Pat's house after her husband had left for work. Brennan told Pat that he hoped she'd slept better after getting her secret out. She replied that she was still very nervous meeting with the FBI, and was ashamed of what went on years ago with Robert Lipka. Brennan attempted to console her by letting her know that no prosecution was being taken against her. "The FBI simply wants to know as many facts as you can recall from your days with Lipka, when he was involved in espionage with the KGB," Brennan said.

Pat responded that it was difficult to recall specific incidents so she needed Brennan to ask questions that might trigger her memory. Brennan started right off, asking her if she ever went on any meets with Robert Lipka. Pat stated that she had, and recalled a place she called "the fishing spot" where she'd gone several times with Lipka to meet "Ivan." She described a spot along the Patuxent River, off Highway 108, between Howard and Montgomery counties in Maryland. She also said she'd accompanied Lipka to a restaurant, name unrecalled, where he'd pointed out "Ivan" and later put something wrapped in plastic in the men's room for the Russian. After that they'd driven to a wooded area where Lipka was supposed to pick up his money. It had been dark, and Pat had held a flashlight while Lipka searched around some rocks for his money. He couldn't find it, though, and had become agitated, and scared; he'd thought something had gone wrong.

Pat was able to describe how Lipka took documents out of the NSA building: He would take them out concealed on his person, either wrapped around his leg or against his stomach, under his shirt. He did this because NSA security would search packages or briefcases, but would never search a person's body. Pat also described seeing money in the packages that Lipka retrieved from the Soviets. When asked what they did with the money Lipka received, Pat said they bought Ethan Allen furniture, in their Early American style—but only on occasion, so they wouldn't show too much affluence.

The interview was very productive, although Pat continued to say that there were many details that she couldn't remember. Brennan could plainly see that she was still quite nervous. Pat was clearly continuing to hold back some details. However, her husband was expected home soon, and SA Brennan decided he'd learned enough for one day.

Later that day SA Brennan contacted SA Whiteside by secure telephone to relate the details Pat had given in their interview; Whiteside, in turn, passed the information along to the prosecutors. Needless to say, they were all very happy with Brennan's progress. However, AUSA

Cohan wanted to personally meet with Pat to ask some questions of her own. Cohan told Whiteside that she was a very good interrogator, and had a lot of experience in that area. Whiteside would have preferred to wait on that introduction; he hadn't met a prosecutor who could conduct an interview better than an FBI agent, and didn't expect she would be any different. Besides, it was early in the investigative phase with Pat, and there didn't seem to be any hurry to get new faces involved. But since AUSA Cohan would hopefully be prosecuting Lipka at some future date, he knew she would need to meet Pat anyway. What harm could be done?

Brennan made arrangements and the following week Whiteside and Cohan went with him to meet Pat again. Pat was off from work and her husband wasn't home. AUSA Cohan had barely been able to contain her excitement on their way over; she'd be having her first actual contact with a person involved in an espionage case.

After some small talk, SA Brennan went over some of the previous questions he'd asked, and the responses Pat had given. Then he turned the floor over to AUSA Cohan.

Pat appeared more tense during this session than even the first time SAs Whiteside and Brennan interviewed her. Whiteside didn't know what her demeanor had been during her second interview with SA Brennan, but he thought it must've gone better than this interview. Pat seemed very concerned, and despite numerous assurances by AUSA Cohan that she wasn't a target of the investigation, Pat was suffering again from a significant case of "I don't remember" syndrome. AUSA Cohan compared her own first failed marriage to Pat's failed marriage with Lipka at one point, saying, "You married an asshole just like I did." Hoping to build some confidence and a bond with Pat, AUSA Cohan tried to paint herself as an understanding victim like Pat. Unfortunately, Pat's body language—her arms crossed tightly across her chest—indicated she remained scared to death.

AUSA Cohan did ask Pat at one point in the interview, "Does the word 'Rook' mean anything to you?" SA Whiteside sat quietly, but was surprised at the question. He would have preferred to approach the matter by generally asking Pat about her knowledge of a code word Lipka might have been given, and if she said yes, then ask what it was. Whiteside thought it would've been far better to have Pat say she knew the code word, and then provide it, rather than give the word directly to her.

Pat replied, "That was Bob's code word."

SA Whiteside hoped he would have the opportunity later in the investigation to ask her again about the code word, having her say "Rook" without prompting, considering it was unlikely she would remember any of her comments in this interview. He simply wanted to see if she was able to give the word up on her own.

The interview concluded after an hour or so. AUSA Cohan had simply wanted to get to know Pat so that future contacts might go smoother. On the ride back to Perryville, she and SA Whiteside discussed plans for continued investigation in this case. Cohan suggested offering Pat immunity in exchange for her full cooperation, since it was clear she was holding back. Whiteside agreed to the idea. Cohan volunteered to contact Mike Liebman to see if he would agree, too.

***

No news had come from Lipka in several months, so the investigative team decided to respond to his letter sent to "Nikitin" on January 24, 1994. SA Droujinsky drafted a short note acknowledging receipt of Lipka's letter, and stating that no meeting was possible at this time. He told Lipka that "previous instructions remain in force," and signed "Carl Max."

Later that week, SA Whiteside contacted Rod Weidner at NSA to start organizing interviews with Robert Lipka's former colleagues. Whiteside learned that about half of these people were still NSA employees. In addition, NSA gave Whiteside a list of chess club members in case they might have information about Lipka. SA Weidner and Whiteside decided on a list of NSA employees to interview. FBI SAs Whiteside and Brennan would be present at all of them, along with either NSA SA Weidner or another NSA investigator, depending who was available on a particular day.

Having an NSA investigator present was critical to the success of each interview. In the agency culture of the time, employees cleared to access the Sigint world were reluctant to provide any information, of any kind, to any outsider, FBI included. The presence of NSA security personnel could soothe or overcome any clearance issues that might arise between the NSA employee with special clearances and the FBI interviewers. This would keep the employee in the hot seat talking and make the interview more productive.

Another crucial reason for having NSA investigators in the interviews is that they knew how things had been set up in the past. This would let them steer questions or call out deceptive answers. In addition, the fact that NSA was the direct victim of Lipka's treachery also meant NSA SAs could best ascertain the extent of damage Lipka had caused to the security of the United States. As the team planned all of this Whiteside contemplated how lucky he was to have such good cooperation among people and across agencies. There were plenty of stories about interagency infighting, but Whiteside was thankful that his team had none of that.

Before Whiteside got a chance to start those interviews, though, he had other news. AUSA Cohan announced over the phone that she and Michael Liebman agreed that Pat should be offered immunity in exchange for her full and honest testimony about Lipka's espionage. Though Pat had admitted assisting Lipka in the recovery of a dead drop by holding the flashlight while he searched for an envelope of money, there was no desire on behalf of the Federal Government to prosecute her: She wasn't the one stealing documents from NSA, didn't initiate contact with the KGB, and didn't have a security clearance she was violating. Her testimony against Lipka was far more valuable to the Government than a conspiracy charge and no cooperation from her. Michael Liebman also wanted to meet Pat, so they arranged another conference with her.

When Whiteside's group arrived at the Baltimore Office of the FBI, Brennan introduced Mike Liebman and the NSA investigators, who were also joining the meeting, to Pat. AUSA Cohan described the formal "use immunity" to Pat and allowed her to read the document. Pat signed.

Michael Liebman was eager to ask a few questions of her, so everyone else let him have the stage. And, despite his peppering Pat with interruptions, she confirmed the time she'd held the flashlight while Lipka searched for his money, and recalled that that had happened on the first meet she'd accompanied him on, around January of 1967. She also recalled another time when she'd remained in the car, and at Lipka's direction she was to honk the horn if anyone approached the area he'd walked to. Liebman also got her to talk about a third occasion, within a week or two of their daughter Kelly's birth, when Lipka had insisted that Pat go with him to a face-to-face meeting and bring the baby. She remembered that this meeting was near the place where she, Bob, and her parents would go to fish—the "fishing spot" she'd mentioned before. Lipka had told her to make sure that no one wandered down the path and stumbled on his meeting with "Ivan."

Eventually the meeting disbanded. Pat was asked to wait around to talk to the investigative team as the legal team left. The NSA SAs promised to begin interviews the following week with their employees. Soon only SAs Brennan and Whiteside were left with Pat. Brennan and Pat made plans to meet regularly so she could give more information. Brennan also planned to take her to locations she remembered Robert Lipka meeting with "Ivan," so that they might jog her memory and bring new information to light.

Brennan and Whiteside left relaxed. In sum, the investigation was going well, and a solid prosecutable case was forming against Robert Lipka.

7

Date: July 1994
Location: Baltimore, Maryland

The summer day dawned brightly and just a bit warmer than the day before as SA Whiteside headed to Maryland. There he would meet with SA Brennan and the former Patricia Lipka for a trip to the "fishing spot," the popular spot where Pat had described Lipka having face-to-face contacts with his Soviet handlers. Photographs of the site weren't the kind of evidence that would put Lipka behind bars, but it was one more thing against him. Whiteside and Brennan also thought it important to take Pat to all of the drop sites she could recall, hoping it would prompt her memory for additional details. The "fishing spot" was the only exact location she remembered because she had also fished at the same place with her parents years ago.

Pat directed the agents to drive along state highway 108 to the intersection of Howard and Montgomery counties. As they crossed a bridge over the Patuxent River, she told them to pull over off to the side of the road. Pat announced that this was "the fishing spot," a drop site where they had in fact fished in the past. The black macadam road surface, edged on both sides with wide gravel shoulders, was outlined with dense trees. Although the traffic was moderate at the time, it was clear that the woods would provide full concealment of any activity happening at the river's edge.

All three exited the car and Pat led the way down a dirt path to the bank along the river. At the bottom of the dirt trail, where it met the river bank, was a small area of smooth ground good for setting up a folding chair and throwing a fishing line in the river. Pat said it was here that Lipka had met with "Ivan" for a face-to-face conversation. She also recalled that the actual drop site, used infrequently, was about seventy-five yards down a dirt trail to the left, running along the river bank. She walked the agents down the trail until she pointed out a large tree halfway up the side of a small rise, leading to the highway.

"There it is, that's where Bob would put his information for Ivan," she told the agents. "I saw him put a message in a Marlboro cigarette box, and he told me he would leave it at the base of the tree. He'd go back to the fishing spot and wait about fifteen minutes or so, then go back again to the tall tree. That's where he'd find his packet of money and directions for the next drop site. After that he'd walk back to the fishing spot, dangle his fishing line in the water for a few minutes, and then we'd go back to the apartment and count the money. There was usually $500 in the packet. I'll never forget sitting on the couch, counting the money with Bob—it was just like James Bond! Sometimes we actually threw it up into the air!"

After leaving the site and heading out for lunch, Pat recalled other instances when Bob went out alone to leave NSA documents at pre-arranged drops and then pick up his money. She always worried that he wouldn't make it home safely. After Kelly was born those feelings of worry intensified significantly; Pat remembered holding the baby and pacing the floor of their apartment until he got home. When Lipka stepped through the door a feeling of exhilaration would flow over her, and they would all sit on the sofa and count the money together. Lipka always received new instructions regarding the location of his next drop sites in the packet with the money.

Since Pat seemed to be opening up more to the FBI agents they kept up the meetings. After arriving at a local restaurant and ordering food on another occasion, Whiteside decided to revisit the code word that Barb Cohan had discussed with Pat in their first meeting. He wanted to see if Pat would actually offer up the code word that had worked so well when SA Droujinsky used it on Robert Lipka. Having the information straight from her would hold much more weight in court than simply asking her to agree that Lipka's code word was "rook," which in essence gave her the answer. "Pat, do you know if Bob ever had a code word he used with the KGB?" Whiteside didn't think she would remember that AUSA Cohan had asked her straight out if his code word was "rook."

But Pat was a little cagey. Pat answered Whiteside's question by saying that Lipka did have a code word. When SA Whiteside asked what it was, she replied, "It was one of the chess pieces."

Whiteside, who knew how to play chess, acted like he didn't understand and replied, "Chess pieces?"

Pat said, "Yes, you know, like the king, queen, bishop, and knight."

Whiteside noticed that the only chess piece she didn't mention was the Rook, and asked, "Which one was it?"

Pat answered, "It was the Rook."

Whiteside asked her when she learned this was his code word. Pat recalled that they had been out to a James Bond movie together; she couldn't recall the title but remembered that there was an international chess tournament onscreen when Bob leaned over and said his code name was "rook." As later investigation would find, that chess scene was the opening of *From Russia with Love*. Whiteside felt a bit vindicated that Pat had supplied the code word; it seemed to him that this response was far better than leading the witness with the code word itself.

Pat talked on, telling the agents that "Ivan" had taught Lipka how to play chess and that Bob was a good chess player. She also remembered that Lipka's handler told him to take Russian language lessons in case the KGB ever had to get them out of the United States. She said Bob had bought some Russian language records but never put much effort into it. Pat herself had been scared they'd have to move to Russia someday.

But for all Pat knew about Lipka's espionage, she was evidently still in the dark about some things. On another occasion SAs Whiteside and Brennan were having lunch with Pat when she suddenly asked, "It's true that Bob was being blackmailed by the Russians, isn't it? I mean, it isn't like he walked in and volunteered to pass information, is it?"

Both Brennan and Whiteside were amazed; Pat somehow still believed Lipka's cover story about KGB photographs that would compromise him unless he passed NSA secrets.

After a moment of silence, SA Whiteside looked at Patricia and said, "No Pat, it isn't true. Bob walked into the Soviet Embassy and volunteered to pass secret information from NSA."

At that Pat lowered her head in shame and began to cry. The full extent of Lipka's betrayal had just sunk in, and she seemed totally devastated by it all. Once she composed herself, she began talking about all the shame that her daughter, parents, and family members would be facing in the future. She believed that her life had finally turned around with her recent marriage, and things were fine with her daughter and family. Now, once again, they would all be forced to endure an embarrassing and painful experience as a result of her relationship with Lipka.

The agents tried their best to comfort Pat with the knowledge that she was doing the right thing in working to punish Lipka for his betrayal. After all, it wasn't Pat who'd had access to the classified documents; she wasn't the one who'd walked into the Soviet Embassy with an offer to betray her country. If there was any fault on her part, it was maintaining the secret for all these years. Yet even with that, she had always believed Lipka was blackmailed into doing what he did. No, all the fault was Robert Lipka's, and his alone. He used her like he used everyone else to accomplish his own ends.

In subsequent meetings with Pat, she also discussed Lipka's receipt of a post card in the mail after they moved to Lancaster. She remembered how excited he was to receive it as he walked into the apartment, waved it around in the air and exclaimed, "We're back in it!"

Despite Pat's pleading with him to stay out, Bob had snapped, "I have to keep my options open," then slammed the bedroom door on her.

***

NSA had put together a formidable list of current employees who'd been assigned to the same unit as Lipka, including his former supervisor. In addition, the list also named seven current NSA employees who'd been members of the NSA Chess Club from 1964 to at least 1967. Finally, there was a supplemental list of individuals in the same categories who no longer worked for NSA, but who'd been there when Lipka was employed.

The investigative team met and decided it was time to begin interviewing former workmates of Lipka in earnest. The investigation had gleaned all it could from Lipka through the undercover work, and, thanks to Pat's memories, more solid evidence of Lipka's espionage had been documented. There was little risk to the investigation should the interviews result in Lipka learning about it. He couldn't stop the interviews, and the possibility that he would flee to the Russian Embassy seemed slim. Lipka appeared convinced that the statute of limitations for his crime had passed, and that he was free and clear. Nonetheless, the team took the precaution of warning employees after the interview not to tell coworkers, and particularly Robert Lipka, about the investigation. Though the warnings were only verbal, each employee was well aware of the penalty for discussing NSA business with outsiders.

For the first interview they targeted Lipka's former supervisor. He remembered Lipka as a marginal employee who didn't seem to work up to his potential. Lipka had been able to grasp the requirements of the job at hand, though, and didn't require monitoring. The supervisor also remembered Lipka embellishing stories he would repeat over and over for anyone who would listen. Overall, Lipka seemed self-centered to his supervisor, acting like he was the only person who mattered, and that he was better than his coworkers. But unfortunately Lipka's old supervisor hadn't seen any subversion on Lipka's part.

Another coworker recalled that Lipka usually worked the early shift, coming in at 6:30 AM and leaving at 2:30 PM. He remembered that Lipka was in the Army, and that he'd lived in the military barracks on the premises. He identified Lipka's roommate and said the roommate was no longer working at NSA. This former coworker didn't know any former or current employees to whom Lipka was especially close, or maintained a friendly relationship with at the time. But he knew that Lipka had been dating a nurse, and that he'd married her sometime prior to leaving NSA.

The remainder of the employees who'd worked with Lipka remembered him to varying degrees. Most could only remember a few details after viewing his high school yearbook photo or his old military ID. None of the employees admitted to any contact with Lipka after he'd left NSA, and none witnessed anything unusual or suspected him of any wrongdoing at NSA.

Only two former employees remembered Lipka in more detail; they were two men who'd socialized a little with Lipka and Pat. One man recalled that Lipka loved music sung by Bobby Goldsboro. The other friend recalled helping Lipka and Pat move from their place in Maryland to Lancaster, PA. This second friend also confirmed some information Pat had given in interviews: She remembered this particular man owning both a motorcycle and a hearse, which both she and Lipka had found amusing. To Whiteside it was important that more of Pat's information was supported by evidence. Unfortunately, both friends denied any knowledge of Lipka's contacts with the KGB.

Agents asked members of the NSA Chess Club whether Lipka had been a member. As it turned out, there were actually two different chess clubs: One was a more informal group that would play at NSA during lunch; the other was a formal group that was part of a large league, including the Soviet Embassy team. While none of the seven NSA chess club members remembered Lipka playing chess at NSA, several recalled meeting Lev Zaitsev, a master chess player who'd been on the Soviet Embassy team. One recounted a time when Zaitsev played against all the other players, moving from chess board to chess board, and won every game. Two NSA employees had actually played Zaitsev, and both lost. They were well aware of the opportunity both the Americans and the Soviets had to recruit each other as spies in this chess league, but both sides respected the game and tacitly agreed to leave business behind.

Whiteside was disappointed with how little the interviews yielded. Still, they had concrete confirmation of Lipka's assignment, the sensitivity of his job, and his access to information of the most critical nature. There was no way he could ever deny that he'd had access to the kind of documents Vasili Mitrokhin claimed Lipka had passed to the KGB.

***

Another bolt from the blue hit the investigative team in August, 1994, when a book came out by Oleg Kalugin, a former General in the KGB, who claimed to have been involved in the Lipka espionage case. *The First Directorate: My 32 Years in Intelligence & Espionage against the West* was a thrilling read about the career of one of the KGB's finest intelligence officers. It hit the Lipka investigation like a bombshell. Beginning on page 82, Kalugin wrote:

> "Another spy who came to us and passed on reams of top-secret material was a soldier who worked at the National Security Agency (NSA), which monitored and controlled communications throughout the world. Though not as famous or as valuable as John Walker,

the young American handed over a significant amount of material to the KGB. The NSA, based in Fort Meade, Maryland, was not nearly as well known to the public as the CIA. Nevertheless, it was an enormous agency, crucial to America's espionage and counter-espionage efforts. It monitored and decoded communications from around the world, including those of the Soviets, the Warsaw Pact, NATO, and other American allies. The young soldier was a 'walk-in' who came to us in the mid-1960s, explaining that he was involved in shredding and destroying NSA documents and could supply us with a wealth of material. His motivation, too, was money and we set up a system—soon to be used again in the John Walker case—whereby the NSA soldier would leave his materials at 'dead drop' sites in Maryland and Virginia. When he left the documents at a remote, prearranged rendezvous point, the soldier would pick up his payment—usually $1,000 per drop—as well as instructions on when and where the next drop would take place. Such 'dead drops' enabled us to receive and pass material without ever risking the NSA man being seen with one of our officers."

"The soldier's documents were highly classified; some even came to us partially shredded, as he obviously had to occasionally make a show of feeding the documents into the shredding machines. He handed us the NSA's daily and weekly top-secret reports to the White House, copies of communications on U. S. troop movements around the world, and communications among the NATO allies. He gave us whatever he got his hands on, often having little idea what he was turning over. A good deal of the material was of little value, and I spent countless hours poring over it in my cramped office in the Soviet Embassy, chucking out what we didn't need and translating valuable material to be cabled to head-quarters in Moscow. I never once met the NSA soldier. Both his case, and the brazen espionage of John Walker, showed us how incredibly lax security was at some of the United States' top-secret installations."

"The NSA soldier eventually left the agency and went to college, using the money he had received from the KGB to pay for his education. Eventually, he was handed over to the highly secret Department Sixteen of the KGB's Intelligence Directorate, which dealt with spies who had access to signal intelligence information, known as 'sigint.' For all I know, he may still be working as a mole inside the NSA or CIA."

For Whiteside's team this was an incredible confirmation of all they knew from Vasili Mitrokhin, and the team was jubilant. However, SA Whiteside wondered if Lipka had seen it, and wondered how it would affect him. Others in the investigative team suggested that "Sergey Nikitin" should mail a copy of the book to Lipka. This would let Lipka know that his secret was out and he was in danger of arrest. The team wanted to see Lipka reach out to "Nikitin," or try to seek asylum at the Russian Embassy. Such a move would provide damning evidence against Lipka.

Everyone liked this plan, so SA Buckmeier bought a book and made several hidden markings that would identify this copy in case Lipka ever claimed he purchased it. SA Droujinsky penned a short note on an index card to slip inside the front cover of the book; it read, "Bob, please refer to pages 82 and 83. Please activate instructions for emergency contact if needed. Carl Max." The book was mailed on September 15, 1994.

***

A week passed without Lipka visiting his post office box. The SSG surveillance team was poised to tail Lipka if he ran for the Russian Embassy: Necessary paperwork had been filed for an emergency arrest, and Lipka would be stopped before he ever reached the gates. No one wanted to lose another spy; the FBI had already lost Edward Lee Howard, a former CIA employee who'd outsmarted a surveillance team and fled to the Soviet Union in 1985.

After a second week without Lipka checking his box SA Whiteside called the postmaster there. "I've sent a book to a friend," Whiteside told the man. "His name is Robert Lipka, and I sent it several weeks ago. Did it ever arrive?"

"Let me check, sir." The postmaster put Whiteside on hold. Finally he returned. "Yes, yes, we do see a package in his box about the size of a book."

"Thanks. You know, I really want to make sure he gets it, since it's a present. Could you possibly call him and let him know it's there?"

"No problem. We can call him today."

Lipka arrived at the post office in Mountville within fifteen minutes of the postmaster's call, under the watchful eye of the FBI SSG surveillance team. SA Whiteside suspected that Lipka was only using this post office box for correspondence with "Nikitin;" since there'd been none in recent months, Lipka didn't bother checking the box. However, when he learned that a package awaited him he must have assumed, correctly, that it was from "Sergey Nikitin"—although this time it didn't contain any money.

Lipka entered the post office, signed for the package, and returned to his car. He drove about a mile, then pulled off. Surveillance picked him up delicately opening the package. After reading two pages, he put the book down and looked around, slowly peering from side to side, as if looking for surveillance or considering his options. But he picked up the book again. It seemed he was engrossed for several more minutes until he abruptly put the book on the passenger seat and drove to Penn National Race Track. There he locked the van and went inside for an afternoon of horse racing. If the receipt of the book had disturbed him, it wasn't showing to the surveillance team. There would be no hasty trip to the Russian Embassy this day.

Date: December, 1994

Location: Millersville, PA

The SSG continued periodic surveillances on Robert Lipka to ensure his whereabouts. On December 12 they reported that Lipka and his family had moved from their cramped, duplex house on Williamsburg Drive to a comparatively opulent house at 17 Dublin Drive, Millersville, PA. This home, a ranch on a half-acre with a full basement and three-car garage, was a far cry from the tiny place he and Deb had previously owned. They'd stayed in Manor Township but moved to the quiet Penn Manor development; real estate records revealed they'd paid $168,000 for the home. Despite the new purchase, Lipka still hadn't gotten a job; he continued visiting racetracks and spending his wife's day off with her. Meanwhile, surveillance teams familiarized themselves with the new property's entrances and exits.

In February of 1995 SA Whiteside's secure STU III telephone rang with a call from FBI Headquarters Supervisor Michael Rochford. Vasili Mitrokhin was visiting the United States for the first time, he said, and had met with senior officials of the CIA, the FBI, and the Department of Justice; everyone was praising Mitrokhin's efforts. There was going to be an FBI-sponsored dinner for him in Alexandria, VA, and Rochford invited SAs Whiteside and Brennan to meet the still highly classified defector. There would be no business on Mitrokhin's trip, Rochford said;

it was simply a courtesy visit to establish goodwill between Mitrokhin and U.S. government officials.

Good will was something the U.S. badly needed to establish with Mitrokhin. He'd risked his life for each of his three unsuccessful visits to the American Embassy in Latvia. Mitrokhin had made these attempts shortly after his retirement from the KGB archives, and only a few months after the Soviet Union's collapse. Smuggling his notes to the CIA was something he'd waited his whole career to do. Mitrokhin traveled by rail to Riga, Latvia, and crossed the border without incident, despite the fact that the KGB boarded the train at the border to check passengers' passports. Mitrokhin had carefully disguised himself like a typical peasant: plain wool trousers missing a crease, and a work shirt made of inexpensive flannel that looked as if it needed a good washing. He didn't bother to shave.

That morning he conducted a lengthy surveillance detection route before he approached the embassy; they buzzed him in through the embassy gates, and past the Marine guard, then he was escorted through the metal detectors and asked to wait until someone from the State Department could see him.

A young man wearing a dark pinstriped suit and a crisp, white, French-cuffed shirt eventually came out of an inner office. Mitrokhin's English was poor, so he attempted to communicate with the young man in Russian. Mitrokhin tried to explain that he had documents of interest to the U.S. government. However, the young State Department officer didn't seem interested. He told Mitrokhin there were hundreds of people like him trying to flee the former Soviet Union every day, and there was simply nothing he could do. He didn't take even a brief look at Mitrokhin's documents, but simply told Mitrokhin to come back another time when it wasn't so busy.

Mitrokhin got up and left the embassy in absolute shock. He'd risked his life for the past twenty years, collecting information that would devastate the evil government of the Soviet Union, only to be brushed off by the U.S. like one would brush off a bothersome gnat. He decided he would try again early the next morning, hopefully meeting a different State Department employee under less crowded conditions. Mitrokhin simply couldn't understand why his effort was ignored. He had one of a kind material.

The following day, Mitrokhin woke early and showered. He wore the same disheveled clothing as the day before, plus—as extra protection, and a tribute to Riga's cold March weather—a wool hat pulled down to conceal his face. He tried his best to appear physically different than the day before, and even faked a slight limp in case the Latvian authorities saw him entering for a second time. He again entered the U.S. Embassy after a lengthy walk to check for surveillance, and this time specifically asked to see a representative of the Central Intelligence Agency. But he didn't even make it past the receptionist. She informed Mitrokhin that there were no CIA officers assigned there (a standard retort to any such request), and that it was too busy for him to meet with any State Department officers. Once again, he was asked to come back some time when it wasn't so busy. But there didn't seem to be a crowd present.

What's going on here? Mitrokhin had wondered as he left the embassy a second time. Sitting on the sagging bed at his hotel, he pondered his situation again. He didn't trust the security of the telephone system in Riga but he seemed to have no other choice. He decided public telephones were at least a little more secure than the hotel telephones, although he knew he was risking everything by calling the embassy.

Mitrokhin left the hotel a third time that afternoon and walked to a public telephone box several blocks from the embassy. When the receptionist answered he used a fictitious name. "I'm a Russian national who has significant intelligence information," Mitrokhin said, in Russian, "and I need to show the information to someone in a position to evaluate it. I will arrive at the embassy in one hour. Please have someone there to meet me and review my material. You will see how important my information will be to your country." The operator assured him there would be someone to talk with him when he arrived.

Mitrokhin walked around in Riga for an hour to ensure no one was following him. When he felt safe again he made his way to the embassy to finally meet with someone who would take the time to look at the priceless notes he'd smuggled out of Moscow. Mitrokhin was led to a small room away from the embassy's main entrance. By this time, he'd been recognized by embassy security officers as someone who'd been to the embassy the day before, as well as earlier that morning.

A man Mitrokhin hadn't seen before walked towards him and he was encouraged by the new face. "How can I help you sir?" the State Department employee asked, feigning politeness.

Mitrokhin tried to explain that for the past twenty years he'd worked as an archivist for the KGB and that he'd copied notes from their files. The young man seemed interested in Mitrokhin's tale, so he pulled his precious documents from under the ratty overcoat he had on. The State Department representative, who still had given Mitrokhin no indication whether he was affiliated with a U.S. intelligence service, quickly flipped through Mitrokhin's material then handed it back.

The officer must have been thinking that Mitrokhin represented just another one in the crowds of people who feared the downfall of the Soviet Union. Everyone tried to produce something of value so they could get emergency refugee status, but a lot of it was fake, or essentially worthless. The officer probably thought that Mitrokhin's notations were copied from some library and had little or no intelligence value. Had he read and recognized their importance he would have immediately secured Mitrokhin and his material, then set in motion a plan to smuggle Mitrokhin and his notes to the West. But it simply didn't happen. The officer did not recognize the value of what Mitrokhin had handed him.

"I'm sorry sir," the young man said, his face betraying no emotion, "but the U.S. government isn't in a position at present to accept your notes. We're overwhelmed with the number of Russians seeking asylum. I wish you luck, but there isn't anything we can do for you."

Mitrokhin was stunned, and walked back to his hotel room like a zombie. He would need to get back home soon or his absence might be noted by the Moscow authorities, whoever they were at this chaotic time. Over a glass of vodka and loaf of black bread he thought about his next move. The largest part of his archive collection dealt with the United States; he'd identified hundreds of former Soviet agents who conducted espionage operations of some kind against the U.S. for the KGB. But it was clear the U.S. wasn't interested. Disgusted with the Americans, he went to the British Embassy the next day. MI-6 recognized the value of his notes right away and Mitrokhin had been dealing with them ever since.

But now that MI-6 had put Mitrokhin in contact with the Americans, it was crucial that the Americans gain his trust. Whiteside, personally, was thrilled to finally meet the man who had supplied so much information (though he knew nothing of Mitrokhin's ordeal), and happily agreed to attend the event.

Several days later, SAs Whiteside and Brennan met at Union Station in Washington, DC. After a quick powwow at the FBI office with SAs Buckmeier and Droujinsky about next steps against Robert Lipka, they traveled to Alexandria, Virginia for Vasili Mitrokhin's dinner. A host of FBI managers from the Russian Section at FBI Headquarters were present, as well as several key agents from the FBI Washington Field Office. Justice Department attorneys John Martin, Section Chief of the DOJ Internal Security Branch and a member of the group that originally met Mitrokhin in England, and John Dion, head of the DOJ Espionage Unit and Whiteside's colleague on the Lipka case, also joined the dinner.

Mitrokhin himself was a small, older man with graying hair and glasses who spoke little English. Yet, despite his age, he seemed surprisingly spry and well-muscled. He also seemed quite cheerful, smiling at people who'd come up to shake his hand. He smiled even more when

FBI Section Chief Steve Dillard formally began the dinner by raising his glass and simply saying, "To a very brave man!" The room reverberated with applause.

Naturally, any Soviet intelligence officer who is willing to defect and provide thousands of pages of classified information to his former enemy is very brave. And it is always admirable. When CIA case officer Aldrich Ames was recruited by the KGB, he gave them the names of ten KGB officers selling information to America; all ten were killed. Mitrokhin faced the same threat of death for his betrayal of the Soviet Union, should another Aldrich Ames name names. His personal bravery was without question. Years of slipping information from KGB files out of the office and keeping them at his home, only to later translate those in code, showed his boldness. His journey with top secret KGB information to Riga, Latvia was further proof of his courage and determination to accomplish his goal. He was a man possessed of an inner strength few knew he had.

During dinner FBI members renewed old friendships and people expressed considerable interest in the Lipka case to Whiteside and Brennan. This was the only U.S. espionage investigation presently being conducted as a direct result of information provided by Mitrokhin. Everyone hoped it would prove successful because it was the litmus test for hundreds of cases that could be opened in the future from Mitrokhin's information.

To that end, Whiteside and Brennan started planning a time for debriefing Mitrokhin in detail about his knowledge of Lipka's espionage. SA Whiteside returned from the upbeat dinner excited for this meeting. He only knew a few Russian phrases from having hosted two Russian exchange students, so he planned to learn as much as he could. Whiteside also devoted his work time—slowing down the actual investigation for a month or two—to make arrangements for Mitrokhin's meetings.

But Whiteside found out later that a meeting in Philadelphia had decided, with FBI Headquarters' agreement, that lead prosecutors

AUSA Barbara Cohan and Departmental Attorney Michael Liebman should have the chance to fully debrief Mitrokhin. They would meet him in London, in April. FBI personnel would be there, but not Whiteside or his investigative team.

The attorneys were taking the trip to check whether Mitrokhin fulfilled the legal requirements that would allow him to testify. The primary concern was whether Mitrokhin had simply reported heresay—or second-hand information—to the FBI, or whether he had direct knowledge of the Lipka KGB file. Heresay wouldn't be admissible in court, so if Mitrokhin's information was secondhand the prosecutors couldn't ask him to testify if Lipka came to trial. At this point neither Whiteside's team nor the attorneys knew what access Mitrokhin had had—or not had—to Lipka's KGB dossier. In England Cohan and Liebman planned to fully debrief Mitrokhin to find out.

The attorneys would be in MI-6's hands, though. Mitrokhin was their witness, so they had the right to set the rules. It was up to them to say where and when the prosecutors would see Mitrokhin. One thing Cohan and Liebman knew in advance was that Mitrokhin spoke little English, so a trusted translator would be part of all proceedings.

SA Whiteside was not happy about being excluded. While he understood the importance of letting the prosecutors understand exactly how Mitrokhin could help them at a trial, he knew far more about Lipka than any of them. He was also eager to know if Mitrokhin had been involved in handling Lipka. But Whiteside tried to put it in perspective: The trip wasn't about Lipka per se; it was about the suitability of Mitrokhin as a government witness.

Therefore SA Whiteside diligently met with AUSA Cohan several days a week to go over details of the case and make lists of potential trial witnesses. Cohan was particularly interested in meeting with the retired FBI agents who'd conducted the investigations of Peter and Ingeborg Fischer, as well as the agents who'd investigated the activities of KGB Illegals Support Officer Artem Shokin. His covert assignment was to furnish clandestine support to any and all Soviet illegals assigned in the U.S.

Shokin had been a registered diplomat for the Soviet Union, based at the United Nations in New York City. But he'd been involved with the Fischers on at least one red-letter occasion. One Saturday in April 1968, the Philadelphia Division surveillance team had been in place for its usual surveillance when the lookout radioed that both Ingeborg and Peter were leaving in their white Plymouth Valiant. The FBI had suspected they might be taking a trip based on intercepts from the previous day. Agents also knew that the KGB preferred to conduct their operations on weekends, when they thought the FBI didn't have a full staff. But the FBI was aware of this, so agents worked weekends watching the Fischers' activities.

The Fischers made their way to U.S. Route 1, the major highway from Maine to Florida at the time. Several surveillance units followed, but in a relaxed way, while the Fischers kept a slow pace that wouldn't draw attention. There were enough FBI vehicles to switch off frequently so the KGB-trained couple wouldn't remember them. The surveilling agents would also change hats, add or take off jackets, and do other small things to change their appearance. The trip was longer than expected, but fortunately all the FBI cars were gassed up.

Eventually the Fischers ended up taking the New Jersey Turnpike to New York City. Once the Fischers entered Manhattan they drove like they were having difficulty finding a location. Still, the FBI agents thought the Fischers might be practicing surveillance detection maneuvers. Whatever the reason, the Fischers drove up and down Riverside Drive, along the east side of the Hudson River. They were in the vicinity of Grant's Tomb, which they drove past twice before returning and parking.

By now it was 7:10 PM and nearly dusk. Both Peter and Ingeborg exited their car and walked north. Suddenly they split up, with Peter disappearing from view and his wife moving around Grant's Tomb, momentarily out of view. The next thing the FBI agents could see was Peter Fischer exiting from a line of woods in Riverside Park and walking toward Ingeborg, who appeared to be serving as a lookout. They joined each other and returned to their car hand in hand. Peter Fischer opened his trunk and took out what appeared to be a walkie-talkie: He extended the silver antenna, pushed several buttons, and then put it back in the trunk. He and Ingeborg promptly pulled out and drove back to Upper Darby.

Earlier in the day, FBI Philadelphia had alerted the New York office to the fact that they were tailing the Fischers, and agents from the New York office were assisting that night. The New York agents stayed near Grant's Tomb while the Philadelphia FBI teams trailed the illegals back home. The New York agents had a quick reward: At approximately 10:07 PM, Artem Shokin, who was officially assigned to the United Nations Secretariat as a diplomat—but in truth served as an illegals support officer for the KGB—was observed parking his car at the exact spot where Ingeborg Fischer had been standing. Shokin and his wife both exited their car and lit cigarettes, seemingly enjoying the cool spring air. But their movements suggested to the FBI they were checking for surveillance. Sure enough, a few moments later Shokin disappeared into Riverside Park at the exact point where Peter Fischer had slipped in several hours earlier. He was in the woods about ten seconds before returning to his wife and quickly driving off.

Agents on the scene had radioed ahead to have a surveillance group stationed at Shokin's apartment. Shokin arrived home a few minutes later. He walked to the rear of his car, briefly opened his trunk, then snapped it closed. He entered his apartment building with a trench coat draped across his arm, covering his hand.

These Special Agents had just witnessed Soviet intelligence officers filling and clearing a drop, something as rare in the intelligence world as seeing pigs fly. But the FBI agents didn't attempt to recover the drop material so they wouldn't interfere with, or otherwise prematurely end, this Soviet intelligence operation. Meanwhile, agents in Upper Darby were collecting even more evidence from the mics in the Fischers' apartment:

"Think about our success!" Peter said joyfully.

Ingeborg replied, "Our success!"

"You did it very good."

"Yes, the Russians always have it secure. It makes a difference, doesn't it?"

Peter stammered, "I—I. . . drop it. We did it right, didn't we? So quick—we did it so quick."

A few more minutes passed and Peter said, "We drink to our success, sugar. I didn't hunt for it. I found it immediately."

"I wonder if they found it?" Ingeborg replied.

Twenty-five minutes ticked by before Peter spoke, again referring to the drop sequence in New York: "Today we had luck. We drove there and found it fast. Almost drove away, sugar. We drove right by it on the Riverside." After a pause Peter continued, "Naturally it was Riverside. It was 122. The place where we were was exactly 122 Riverside. They should explain that there are two Riversides, one in this direction and one in this direction. They should have said Riverside in the southerly direction."

Apparently the illegals did not know that Riverside Drive is separated into two separate roads around 122nd Street, near Grant's Tomb.

"Yes, yes," Ingeborg replied.

"It was also right the first time we got out," Peter said.

"Must have wondered what we were doing."

"Very good. . . take it away this time. . . lost so much because of stupidity." (Whiteside concluded that Peter was referring to previous drops missed due to inadequate information).

Ingeborg asked, "Now they have found it, this chrome thing, don't you think so?"

"Found it—122." (Peter was clearly convinced that his drop was placed in the exact location, and that it surely had been picked up by their Soviet handler, Whiteside reasoned).

"It was two and one half hours later after we put it there that we got home," Ingeborg said. "But we are never certain."

"It was so good. . . It is always something," Peter said.

After this the Fischers started talking about dinner, so Whiteside put this transcript aside. One by one, he reviewed all the transcripts of conversation from the Fischers' apartment and identified those FBI personnel who monitored the mics. Whiteside also identified all of the retired agents who had participated in surveillances of the Fischers in Philadelphia and during the New York trip. Unfortunately, many of these same agents were currently in their eighties, in various stages of failing health, and might not be able to testify at Lipka's trial.

SA Whiteside began the task of reaching out to each of these former agents. Subpoenas would have forced them to meet with him, but not one former employee, regardless of distance or health issues, declined his informal request to meet in Philadelphia for a conference on this case. In particular, former Philadelphia counterintelligence Supervisor Norris Harzenstein was thrilled to attend, despite very poor health. After AUSA Cohan complimented him on the detail his former agents kept in their reports and surveillance logs, Harzenstein beamed and said, "That's because they were Harzenstein trained!"

Retired agents came from as far away as Utah, Nevada, Texas, and Florida, simply in return for the cost of airfare. Not only were they dedicated FBI Special Agents thirty years ago, but still in retirement they answered the call of duty when their country needed them. These men embodied the motto of the FBI: "Fidelity, Bravery, Integrity." Despite their ages, health issues, and the length of time that had transpired since their work against the Fischers, they could still recall even the smallest details of the case and the roles they played in the investigation.

In addition to their sharp memories, several of these retired agents also had furniture from the Fischers' former apartment. The Fischers had fled the country under the pretense of visiting sick relatives in East Germany, then later asked their postman to sell off their furniture and empty the apartment. This same postman, Ned Hecht, had been feeding information about the Fischers to the FBI, and several agents bought pieces out of sheer curiosity. When Whiteside spoke with these retired agents he found out that the living room bookcase, a coffee table, a lamp, a shortwave radio, and the same walkie-talkies the Fischers had used in the park near Grant's Tomb were still in these agents' possession. If needed, the Fischers' apartment could be re-created the same as it had been in 1966.

9

Date: June 1995
Location: Washington, DC

Attorneys Cohan and Liebman returned from their London trip, and months passed. Whiteside and his team had kept busy reviewing the pen register of Lipka's home telephone and identifying new callers. He and his colleagues also took the opportunity to go back over the Lipka files and make sure that no leads had been missed. They kept in touch with NSA, and SA Brennan, to follow up on any new information developed from reviewing NSA records or contacts with Pat. The surveillance team occasionally checked in on Lipka to watch for any new patterns of behavior. But finally Whiteside received the call from FBI Headquarters he'd been hoping for: MI-6 had agreed to another full week of debriefing sessions with Vasili Mitrokhin in London, and Whiteside was asked to participate this time.

The invitation wasn't extended just because someone liked Whiteside, though. The attorneys' trip had been unsuccessful: Mitrokhin had refused to meet with them. The Brits were embarrassed that Mitrokhin was so vehemently opposed to the meeting that the Americans had traveled so far for, and they couldn't provide a reason for it. Later people found out that Mitrokhin was simply being Mitrokhin: He hadn't seen any value to the meeting, so he'd refused it. Whiteside was secretly pleased that Mitrokhin didn't meet with the attorneys.

It hadn't made sense to cut case investigators out of the contact with Mitrokhin.

AUSA Barbara Cohan, Departmental Attorney Michael Liebman, and Washington Field Office Russian speaker Special Agent Terry Monahan would make the second trip with Whiteside. MI-6 had assured Rochford that this trip would meet with more success than the last.

Whiteside's team was scheduled to convene at MI-6 Headquarters on Monday June 12, 1995, at 10:00 AM. Directions would be given to Mitrokhin's secret location there, and interviews could begin that afternoon. Whiteside hung up the telephone and made his reservations immediately.

The morning of the twelfth, following a full English breakfast complete with blood pudding, the group of four hailed a cab for the fifteen-minute ride to Vauxhall Cross, on the banks of the River Thames, where MI-6 Headquarters was located. At the time MI-6 officially did not exist to the public. To maintain that security, Barb Cohan gave their minicab driver only the street address for their destination—but the cabbie immediately replied, "Oh, you want to go to MI-6!" So much for secrecy!

Upon arrival, each person showed their identification at the front desk, then the visitors were allowed through state of the art rounded, heavily tinted security doors that had room for only one person at a time, like something out of *Star Trek*.

On an upper floor they were seated in a tasteful conference room with blue, fabric-covered chairs and plush carpeting. Glass trays sitting on the conference table contained ample amounts of tea, coffee, and biscuits. Shortly thereafter, two senior MI-6 officials entered and made introductions around the polished mahogany table. Discussion centered on which topics the American group hoped to explore regarding the espionage activities of Robert Lipka. The leading Brit urged patience and caution in dealing with Mitrokhin. They didn't want his short temper to flare and cause him to walk away again.

Since the group planned to meet with Mitrokhin all week, an MI-6 representative would be at the safe house every day at around noon to prepare lunch for everyone. It was dangerous for Mitrokhin to be seen in the local area too often, plus he preferred simple food. In addition, Wednesday would be an off day for everyone: Mitrokhin tired easily and needed to rest in the middle of the week. Everyone agreed to the plan, and the Brits invited the Americans to a dinner on Thursday night, hosted by MI-6. Things seemed to start off well.

When the Americans arrived at the safe house after lunch that same day only Mitrokhin's translator, Harry Spencer, had arrived. Mitrokhin came in about ten minutes later. After some small talk the group got down to business. For trial purposes, Liebman and Cohan thought it was necessary to have Mitrokhin describe in as much detail as possible the KGB file on Robert Lipka, from the outside top cover to the final page. This would add legitimacy to the fact that Mitrokhin had access to KGB files, including Robert Lipka's dossier. Cohan, Liebman, and Whiteside attempted to discuss the issue with Mitrokhin—through his interpreter—the remainder of the afternoon.

It was exhausting work. By the end of the day everyone was tired, but Mitrokhin especially didn't seem to be too happy. It looked to Whiteside, who was mostly observing rather than asking questions, like Mitrokhin was displeased with the entire process. Despite his giving answers—which were translated by Harry—the answers were short, as if there wasn't much thought put into them.

Tuesday morning dawned brightly with just enough coolness in the air to make it a lovely summer day. After another English breakfast too delicious to pass up, the Americans took a cab to the safe house. Mitrokhin seemed to be in better spirits so they started the questions fairly quickly. Mitrokhin's answers were brief again, though a few were long and obviously impassioned. But after a time it was apparent that little was being accomplished; the prosecutors still hadn't been able to move past the KGB physical file description.

To calm his frustration and pass the time, SA Whiteside had been studying his Russian language book. During a lull in the debriefing he tried saying something to Mitrokhin in Russian. Mitrokhin listened, and then asked to look at the book. Whiteside passed it to him. Mitrokhin looked closely at the cover then opened to the title page. Suddenly he tossed it back to Whiteside exclaiming, "Jew book!"

No one really knew what Mitrokhin meant by this comment, so they ignored it and continued the debriefing until it was time for lunch. The housekeeper had made a salad and sandwiches, and laid out two bottles of wine along with the customary bottles of mineral water. After eating, as was his habit, Mitrokhin took a two-mile walk outside. The Americans and Mitrokhin's translator accompanied him, and while they walked Mike Liebman discreetly asked Barb Cohan if she'd heard Mitrokhin's comment about a "Jew book." Barb ignored the comment; when Mike asked again, she said decisively, "Shut up, Michael."

Respecting people's religious, sexual, cultural, and other differences wasn't a concern in the spy profession, unless it was simply a guise to assist in a recruitment effort. Michael Liebman, who'd never worked in the intelligence and counterintelligence fields, was obviously sensitive to comments about Jews. But if Mitrokhin had a problem with Jews, Liebman would not only have to deal with it, but ignore it until the business at hand was successfully accomplished. And fortunately Liebman was able to find it within himself to drop the matter; interviews continued as usual during the afternoon session. It wouldn't be Mitrokhin's last comment about Jews, though.

But that afternoon there were no further outbursts from Mitrokhin and in all it was a good day's work. By the end of it the team had learned valuable information about how the KGB maintained files on recruited agents. Not surprisingly, it was highly similar to the way the FBI kept files on its subjects. After all, how many different ways were there to maintain investigative files by agencies like these?

The next day, Wednesday, was their day off, and the Americans were able to sightsee without worry. On Thursday the meeting with Mitrokhin began in earnest. He continued to describe the KGB files in detail to the prosecutors. However, at times there seemed to be a disconnect in his specific knowledge of the Lipka file: Mitrokhin had provided voluminous information about Robert Lipka from his notes, but he couldn't describe the physical properties of Lipka's file. Questions about this seemed to frustrate both Mitrokhin and his interpreter, Harry. Tension mounted throughout the day until late in the afternoon, when it was finally resolved: Mitrokhin had never seen Lipka's actual KGB file!

Everyone was shocked. The prosecutors had focused their questions on Lipka's KGB file because those details would be needed in court during a trial. No one thought about the fact that Mitrokhin may not have seen Lipka's actual file; after all, they'd thought, he must have provided the information he did from that file. But surprisingly, that was not the case. Mitrokhin neither saw Lipka's file, nor did he supervise the Lipka operation.

What Mitrokhin had seen, further questions illuminated, was a memo in the file of KBG illegals Peter and Ingeborg Fischer. That memorandum had been prepared by the KGB Center just before the illegals visited Moscow for a conference, a little after Lipka's August 1967 departure from the National Security Agency. That memo contained the background on the Lipka case, Lipka's description and address in Lancaster, PA, and information about Lipka's then wife Pat. It identified the drops he'd filled and the amount of money he'd been paid for the NSA documents that he'd passed. In short, it had all the pertinent information on Lipka and his status so that the KGB could fully debrief the Fischers. It was at this conference that Moscow asked them to contact Lipka with the postcard he'd told undercover agent Droujinsky about.

This new information from Mitrokhin finally directly tied the Fischers into a conspiracy to commit espionage along with Robert Lipka and the KGB Illegals Support Officer, Artem Shokin. Unfortunately Mitrokhin hadn't seen any NSA material and couldn't identify any of the more than 200 documents his notes said that Lipka had passed to the KGB. But even without this evidence, there was at least a conspiracy case that could be pursued against Lipka and the others.

That evening the prosecutors and FBI agents were guests of the British at a favorite restaurant of theirs called Tiddy Dols, in London's Mayfair section. Their lamb was perfectly broiled, and everyone loved the gingerbread dessert. Singing piano players kept the place lively. As people were leaving, full and happy, the Americans promised to return the hospitality when the Brits visited.

Everyone was more relaxed Friday morning, and plans were made for Mitrokhin to visit the United States again. The prosecutors wanted him to see the courtroom where the trial would be held, and they wanted Mitrokhin to undergo some mock trial training so that he wouldn't be surprised by anything when he testified.

During their final lunch everyone was jovial. To separate himself a bit from the prosecutors, SA Whiteside attempted to develop a more personal bond with Mitrokhin; he felt he could serve well should Mitrokhin seek a friend when upset or concerned about future issues in the Lipka matter. To that end, Whiteside tried out some of his new Russian words and phrases, much to the mirth of Mitrokhin. Mitrokhin also used some English words, showing he'd probably understood their questions better than suspected.

The prosecutors asked just a few more questions after lunch, and all seemed well. Mitrokhin had agreed to return to the United States. But just before people were ready to say their good-byes Mitrokhin suddenly erupted in rage. His face turned scarlet, and he began a long diatribe in Russian. When he finally finished, Harry translated his outburst into English. Simply put, Mitrokhin had said that "one doesn't use a king to kill a cockroach, and that it was not his responsibility to convict Lipka. That was the responsibility of the FBI and the Department of Justice, not Mitrokhin's, and he didn't feel he had the responsibility to testify in court against Lipka. He had provided the information about Lipka, and now it was the responsibility of others to prosecute him."

The entire group was shocked. This sudden setback threatened to destroy all they'd accomplished. But the team had to depart, so they tried to leave with happy thoughts and good wishes for Mitrokhin, hoping that future contacts, if any, might make him more willing to help. Mitrokhin calmed down too, and seemed gracious in saying good-bye to the agents and prosecutors. At the hotel the Americans had a final meeting and decided that Mike Rochford should still contact his liaison person in the British Embassy to try to get Mitrokhin to the United States. If Mitrokhin didn't testify the case might be impossible to try.

***

Throughout the intervening months, investigators Brennan and Weidner had continued to meet with the former Patricia Lipka. They scheduled weekly or biweekly meetings with Pat because, little by little, she would remember additional details that might have value in court.

At one meeting Pat spoke about three cameras that Bob once brought home in a shirt box. One was a rollover camera, a new KGB invention at the time, which opened like a checkbook and worked like a miniature photocopying machine: To photograph a document, Lipka would simply roll the camera over it—a speedy process that allowed a spy to photograph many documents quickly. They also gave him a Minox camera built specifically to photograph documents. It was equipped with a chain at one end that, when extended, showed how far above the document to hold the camera before sliding the sides together and then apart to capture the image. Lipka had showed all these cameras to Pat, saying, "Look what Ivan gave me!"

"These are great, Bob! Do you think James Bond used something like this?" Pat remembered asking.

"Probably not," Bob had answered. "I can't actually use the things. They're too big. Someone would see them. Besides, it's easier to just use the documents from Milt Robey. I should just give 'em back to Ivan."

SA's Brennan and Weidner were also meeting regularly with Pat in the hope that she could recall specific documents Lipka may have passed to the KGB. They hoped she could pick out what she'd seen, since she may have simply found Lipka's documents sitting on the dining room or kitchen table. In earlier interviews, where NSA investigators had shown only a few templates, Pat had remembered that there were warning notices on the cover sheets of documents she'd seen at the apartment. Therefore Brennan and Weidner had selected a wider variety of items for her to review—differing somewhat from each other—from the period Lipka had been assigned to NSA.

But while Pat said the documents generally looked similar to what Lipka would pass to the KGB, she was unable to remember specifics.

"I'm sorry I can't remember what I saw on the table when Bob was putting the documents in bags for the KGB," Pat said. "This all looks vaguely familiar to me, but there's nothing I can say for certain that I specifically recall. I can remember seeing the words 'Top Secret,' and remember there was often a lot of writing on the documents, but not more than that."

Whiteside and his team had hoped that Pat would recall code names or markings on documents Lipka had packaged for the KGB in her presence. Still, her information at least provided confirmation of the class of material Lipka had passed. It was possible that Lipka hadn't shown her many documents.

"It wasn't like he read the documents to me or discussed them at any length," Pat continued. "He never told me what it was that he was passing. He usually worked fast and didn't appreciate me being too close to him while he was preparing his drops. I was lucky enough to see something only if he stepped away from the table for a brief moment. I'm sorry, but I cannot remember any specifics about the documents."

This was hard for the investigative team to accept because they knew that an espionage charge and conviction depends on telling the court exactly what a spy gave to the enemy. They would continue their efforts with Pat, then, while the other half of the team worked to get Vasili Mitrokhin to agree to testify in Federal court against Robert Lipka. Each hoped the other would hit on something concrete.

***

Meanwhile, in Philadelphia, AUSA Barbara Cohan worked diligently day after day to review evidence, read lengthy FBI documents from both the Fischers' and Lipka's investigations, plot timelines, and write court documents. During her few off hours she began building her own personal library of espionage and intelligence/counterintelligence books, based on Whiteside's recommendations. At that time her shelves held over forty titles.

During this time Cohan and Whiteside were in touch fairly often, trading information and discussing the espionage books. Whiteside drove into Philadelphia, often several times a week or whenever necessary, in order to meet with Barbara Cohan or to review files maintained in the FBI office. He would also brief his superiors there on the progress of the Lipka investigation. But one afternoon in mid-July while in the city, SA Whiteside walked across Market Street to Cohan's office in the next block with something different to discuss: He'd just received a call from Mike Rochford with the good news that the Brits had finally secured Vasili Mitrokhin's willingness to travel back to the US and meet with the prosecutors again. No one could make promises about Mitrokhin's level of cooperation, but everyone thought that by agreeing to the visit Mitrokhin may have been signaling a change of heart. It was up to AUSA Cohan and SA Whiteside to plan his August 1995 trip to the City of Brotherly Love.

10

Date: August 1995

Location: Lancaster & Philadelphia, PA

When Mitrokhin arrived, August in the Delaware Valley also arrived, with its characteristic pressure of heat and humidity. The ground rules for his meetings were similar to those in London in that meetings would only occur on Monday, Tuesday, Thursday, and Friday, with Wednesday off.

On Monday morning at 9:00 AM Mitrokhin stepped into the United States Attorney's Office in Philadelphia, and over the next two days Barb Cohan and the rest of the team went over Mitrokhin's information on the Lipka case. While he may not have realized it at the time, these debriefings were also preparing Mitrokhin for court testimony. He seemed to be relatively calm early in the day, but would usually let his anger get the best of him by the end of each afternoon. It was likely that he still couldn't grasp the significance of putting a "cockroach" like Lipka in jail, and probably still thought it was beneath all the risks he'd personally taken for the free world. In fact, Whiteside's team quickly found that they were spending most of their time convincing Mitrokhin that his testimony would inform still more people about the evils of the former Soviet Union. Fortunately Mitrokhin's English had improved considerably in the two months since the group had last met, and it was much easier to hold a conversation with him. His translator, Harry, was still part of the group, though.

As Mitrokhin sipped his tea late Tuesday afternoon Barb Cohan told him that on Thursday morning he would face another AUSA who would be acting like Lipka's defense attorney, to practice cross-examination. People held their breath for Mitrokhin's reaction while Harry Spencer translated Cohan's words into Russian.

"Yes, yes, I can meet with him."

Whiteside's team shared smiles, and smiled at Mitrokhin as he continued to nod his head in agreement while Harry translated further. Some people doubted that Mitrokhin really understood what he was about to face, but they were relieved that he would make the effort.

Nonetheless Mitrokhin's agreement made for a congenial day off. Wednesday of that week SA Whiteside took Mitrokhin on a drive to see the Amish and Mennonite farms along the beautiful country roads of Lancaster County, where Lipka still lived. SAs Whiteside and Terry Monahan, along with Mitrokhin and his translator, plus a representative from the British Embassy, piled into Monahan's rented Cadillac and headed out. Mitrokhin sat in the front seat while Whiteside drove.

This trip was a far cry from the city life Mitrokhin had been used to in London and Moscow, and it reminded him of his *dacha* in the Russian countryside; Mitrokhin would often comment about one area or another being similar to his hometown. He was thrilled to see Amish and Mennonite farmers working their fields using only horse-drawn equipment. He marveled at the immense farms, and the richness of the fertile soil. He asked SA Whiteside to stop at one of the roadside small wooden sheds offering shoofly pies and other Amish delights to get a closer look, though he didn't purchase anything. When Mitrokhin talked about his favorite passion—mushroom hunting—Whiteside mentioned that neighboring Chester County was considered to be the mushroom capital of the United States.

The group stopped for lunch at a local Amish restaurant that served genuine Pennsylvania Dutch food. Mitrokhin savored his stuffed pig stomach and even had dessert: hot apple fritters smothered in fresh vanilla ice cream. Whiteside took another country road on the return trip to Philadelphia, while Mitrokhin continued to be enthralled with the scenery. It was the first time that SA Whiteside had seen Mitrokhin so at peace.

Nearing the Newtown Square Resident Agency on the way back into Philadelphia, Mitrokhin needed to stop to use the restroom. Whiteside drove to the FBI office and asked if anyone else needed to use the bathroom, but the others said they would wait in the car. After Mitrokhin was done, Whiteside asked if he'd like to see his office. Mitrokhin said yes, so Whiteside showed him around the FBI space and led him to his own office, which he shared with another agent. Mitrokhin looked at the photographs of Whiteside's children on his desk, and looked out the window at the open fields and white pines. When he spoke, Mitrokhin said his office in Moscow had been similar to this one. Looking once more at the photos, he commented on Whiteside's children, and spoke about his son being so ill. Mitrokhin told Whiteside that all he wanted out of life "was a house made out of wood, with a place to grow vegetables." He truly was a simple man who ate kasha every morning and was thankful to have something to eat every day.

Whiteside gave him his home telephone number, telling Mitrokhin that he was always invited to stay at his place if he wanted to come back and look for a "house made out of wood."

Mitrokhin replied, "This is the first time since I left Russia that anyone ever gave me their home number."

It was one of those magical moments between former enemies, and one that Whiteside hoped would serve to better cement a trusting friendship between them for months to come. When Whiteside dropped Mitrokhin off at his hotel with the rest of his group, he couldn't thank Whiteside enough for the day's activities.

On Thursday morning AUSA Carl Lunkenheimer joined the meeting to play opposing counsel. The team was pleasantly surprised to see that Mitrokhin grasped the concept of the mock trial and got through the morning with high marks. During their lunch break, SA Whiteside took Mitrokhin and the Brits on a walk to Washington Square Park in Philadelphia, where hundreds of anonymous dead from the Revolutionary War are interred, and an eternal flame burns for deceased Revolutionary War heroes. Mitrokhin seemed very interested, though the Brits didn't!

After lunch, the group went on a tour of the Federal courthouse that AUSA Cohan had arranged so Mitrokhin wouldn't feel too uncomfortable if he testified. He sat in the witness chair and AUSA Cohan asked him a few questions. She also explained the jury's function, as well as the fact that during Mitrokhin's testimony it might be necessary for him to wear a disguise, or to have the spectators blocked off, so that only the defendant and jury could see him. These were issues of great importance and no one had any idea how it all might play out in the future. Mitrokhin was still considered a Top Secret project; even the prosecutors and FBI still hadn't learned his true name at this point.

Following the courthouse tour, the group returned to Barbara Cohan's office. She and Mike Liebman wanted to meet privately with Mitrokhin's handlers; when they excused themselves Whiteside and Mitrokhin were left together. As soon as they were alone, Mitrokhin, without any warning or prompting, said, "John, the problems in the Soviet Union are the fault of the Jews. Lenin was a Jew; Stalin was a Jew, Khrushchev a Jew. All Jews!" Mitrokhin grew louder and louder as he continued his ranting, his face growing scarlet. Whiteside worried that the Jewish prosecutors would hear him when he finally bellowed, "The Holocaust: big Jew lie!"

But Whiteside, who'd attended Cheltenham High School, a predominately Jewish public school where Jonathan and Benjamin Netanyahu had also been educated, stopped Mitrokhin and said, "Vasili, the Holocaust has been pretty much confirmed as the loss of six million Jews."

Mitrokhin replied, "Maybe three million, but not six. It is a big Jewish lie." Just then the prosecutors entered, and thankfully Mitrokhin calmed down as they entered the conference room.

Whiteside pondered Mitrokhin's previous anti-Semitic remarks while the others talked, and he recalled that Mitrokhin had once been posted as a KGB officer in Israel. Whiteside wondered if Mitrokhin's anti-Semitism had something to do with his posting in Israel, after which he was sent back to Moscow and demoted to the archives. But that was a question that would never get an answer. In the meantime it was obvious that the religious faith of the prosecutors was bothering Mitrokhin, although Barb Cohan didn't practice her Jewish faith and had been very kind to Mitrokhin. Whiteside hoped it would be something that would pass and Mitrokhin would get over. Nothing was easy in this investigation, despite the progress that seemed to be getting accomplished.

That night it was the FBI's turn to treat the Brits, and Mitrokhin, to dinner. The Brits' assistance with Mitrokhin was truly remarkable, and without their help the case against Robert Lipka simply would not have been possible. Barb Cohan's husband was a chef at a well-known Philadelphia restaurant and she made arrangements for a wonderful dinner there, including an appearance by the chef himself.

Before the meal, customary cocktails were ordered. But before anyone could give a toast, Mitrokhin took his glass, raised it, and said, "I toast to our success!"

It was done! Mitrokhin, with that simple toast, had agreed to testify in Federal Court against Robert Lipka. It was the last major piece necessary in the case against Lipka. The meal, already delicious, tasted a whole lot better after Mitrokhin's gesture.

The following day the group held one last session in the U.S. Attorney's office with Mitrokhin, which finished by noon. Though no one knew it, this was the last time they would see Mitrokhin in connection with the Lipka investigation. Good-byes were said—this time without any outburst—and Mitrokhin headed back to Washington, DC with his British escorts. Everyone's expectations were high.

11

Date: December, 1995
Location: Philadelphia, PA

As Christmas 1995 arrived the investigative team hoped it would be the last one Lipka celebrated in freedom for a long time. He had almost certainly deprived others of freedom—and probably their lives—by selling secrets. A grand jury had been formed to listen to the Lipka evidence; an advance indictment would lend more weight to the case than a simple complaint in an arrest warrant. Everyone could sense the case was coming to a head.

Since it was impossible to show in court a specific document that Lipka had passed to the KGB, the best and only approach to charging him with espionage was under a conspiracy statute. Conspiracy was defined as two or more individuals who conspired to commit espionage, in this case for the Soviet Union. Had the team been able to identify any of the 200 documents Lipka passed to the KGB, there would have been that many counts of espionage charged against him; instead, the prosecution would have to settle for one count of conspiracy to commit espionage. The coconspirators in this case were Soviet KGB illegals Peter and Ingeborg Fischer, and KGB Illegals Support Officer Artem Shokin. Prosecutors Cohan and Liebman were able to craft a brilliant complaint against Lipka and his coconspirators, and continued to present witnesses before the grand jury in the case. As the New Year began, it seemed that everything was falling into place.

The team planned to finalize the investigation of Lipka during the last week of January. SA Whiteside planned a one week exercise for his team designed to place additional pressure on Lipka. They wanted to see, one last time, whether they could scare Lipka into reaching out for protection from the Russian Embassy or from his contact, "Sergey Nikitin." The plan involved three specific parts: In the first part, on Monday, Lipka's ex-wife, Pat, would contact Lipka and say that the FBI wanted to interview her. The intent of this contact was to bring them together in a safe place and have him discuss some or all of his past espionage. Then, on Wednesday of the same week, SAs Whiteside and Brennan would introduce themselves to Robert Lipka and officially interview him. Depending on how the interview went—that is, whether the agents got a denial or confession—Lipka would be given another day alone with his thoughts, and a day to seek whatever help he might need. On Friday, if he hadn't confessed, they would arrest Lipka and search his residence.

But as the best laid plans sometimes go, this one didn't quite work out.

Only a week or so before Whiteside meant to put his final plan into action he ran into Assistant Special Agent in Charge (ASAC) Sheila Horan at a retirement party for a colleague. While chatting with Horan Whiteside asked, "Sheila, will you be traveling with us to Lancaster to be a part of the final arrest plan for Robert Lipka?"

"No, John boy, in fact that whole plan has been put on hold by FBI Headquarters."

"What?" asked Whiteside, raising his voice. "When did this nonsense come about and who's responsible for this decision? What the hell is going on here, and why hasn't anyone said anything before now?"

ASAC Horan replied, "I simply cannot comment about it at this time. I only know that your operation has been placed on hold for an indefinite time."

Whiteside was incensed that he was learning this information for the first time. He had not been including the ASAC in the planning, although she was briefed frequently about the Lipka case. Possibly this information was just received, but from whom?

Whiteside tracked down Special Agent in Charge (SAC) Bob Reutter at the party and asked him the same thing. "Bob, I just learned from Sheila Horan that my arrest scenario on the Lipka matter has been put on hold. What the hell is going on?"

Again, Whiteside met with a stonewall: "She's correct, it's been put on hold for an indefinite amount of time," Reutter said. "I can't tell you any more than that."

"Who made this decision and why wasn't I told about it? What if I hadn't come to this party, would you have let me know?" Whiteside persisted.

"There's nothing else I can tell you right now," Reutter answered as he walked away to greet other party guests.

Whiteside fumed for the rest of the evening, not able to enjoy the camaraderie offered to a retiring Special Agent. Whiteside had worked with Sheila Horan in the mid-1970s in the Soviet Division of the New York Office. She had been assigned to a GRU squad while Whiteside worked on a KGB squad. Several years later, he'd also worked for Bob Reutter in a Brooklyn, NY organized crime team. He trusted them both and knew them well. However, this event was completely shocking after all the work he and his team had put into prosecuting Robert Lipka. The worst part was not even learning what the problem was, or if Lipka would ever be prosecuted. No one was giving answers that evening, but SA Whiteside returned home determined to find out what the sudden end of his case was all about.

The following day he called a confidant at FBI Headquarters. While this friend didn't exactly name a case, he let Whiteside know about Headquarters' concern for another espionage matter, and that arresting Lipka in the next two weeks might hurt the success of that other case. However, he said that the Lipka prosecution would continue, and suggested that plans should be made for an arrest in February.

Nonetheless Whiteside wanted the full story. Eventually he learned that just as the Lipka case was approaching an end the FBI was heavily involved in an espionage investigation against one of its own employees, Earl Edwin Pitts. Pitts, an FBI Special Agent stationed at the FBI training complex in Quantico, VA, was being investigated for selling FBI secrets to the former Soviet Union. At the same time that the Philadelphia Division planned to initiate the weeklong arrest scenario against Robert Lipka, the FBI in Washington, DC was planning a false flag operation against Earl Pitts similar to what Whiteside's team had conducted against Robert Lipka three years earlier. FBI top brass believed that the scheduled arrest of Lipka might spook Earl Pitts so that Pitts wouldn't buy into the planned false flag operation. But in typical FBI style, and certainly in keeping with the "need to know" mindset of the National Security Division, none of the Lipka investigative team members were made aware of these concerns.

Knowing the full story calmed Whiteside down. It was reasonable the Lipka arrest scenario be put on hold until the Pitts investigation stabilized. After all, Whiteside reasoned, it had been more than thirty years since Lipka first betrayed his country; another few months' delay wouldn't make a difference.

In the intervening weeks Whiteside and the investigative team planned the arrest scenario for the week of February 19, 1996; the date was approved by FBI Headquarters. A week before the date the team met in Philadelphia in the office of SAC Bob Reutter to review the plan and make any necessary refinements. Representatives of the SSG, the FBI Special Agent surveillance team, a technical squad supervisor, SAC Reutter, ASACs Horan and Tom McWade, and the FBI's Legal Counsel Representative were all present. The only major difference was that some team members questioned whether the scenario should play out over a three-day period rather than a five-day period. Although SA Whiteside argued that shortening the time frame would cut the probability that Lipka might reach out to "Sergey Nikitin" or the actual

Russian Embassy, SAC Reutter was concerned that Lipka might escape like Edward Howard, a former CIA officer who eluded FBI surveillance and escaped to the Soviet Union.

While Whiteside was debating the length of the plan, SA Brennan was preparing the first stage in Baltimore. The Baltimore SSG and agent surveillance teams, plus Special Agents from the Baltimore counterintelligence squad, all were assigned to be on duty at a restaurant where the team hoped Lipka would meet his ex-wife, Pat. Brennan met with Pat and they plotted to lure Lipka to the Hunt Valley Mall in Maryland, where she would meet him in the eatery section. Brennan even supplied an agent to pose as Pat's husband in case Lipka tried to follow her out of the mall and hurt her. After all, as best Lipka knew, Pat was the only witness to his espionage activity. And, for the most part, he was correct in that belief.

***

At the meeting in Philadelphia SAC Reutter had the final say, and he ordered that the arrest scenario take place over a three-day, rather than five-day, period. Whiteside had no choice but to follow the directions of his boss. He contacted the NSA team and asked them to put secure communications in place at the command post in Lancaster, PA for the arrest scenario. They would also be present during the operation in case their knowledge of NSA documents, systems, programs or other specific topics might come into play during interactions between Robert Lipka and Pat, or subsequently between Lipka and his interrogators. The volume of information about Lipka's tenure at NSA that these agents had amassed was a critical part of the investigation.

The FBI Laboratory committed to using their special search unit, specifically used in espionage cases, to perform careful searches at Lipka's residence after the arrest. They would use a variety of special techniques, including x-ray, to search walls and floors for any false openings concealing classified documents. They would also search for microdots, microfiche, and other items commonly used by spies, like secret writing and concealment devices.

In addition, SA Whiteside put together a group of Special Agents to conduct the overt search of Lipka's residence. The group was headed by Whiteside's former New York City partner, Greg Auld. SA Auld would supervise the search team that would use conventional search methods to both locate evidence confirming information from Vasili Mitrokhin and Pat, and to uncover any classified documents from NSA. Two other FBI Special Agents from Whiteside's Newtown Square office, Jef Feehery and Donna Kibbie, were ready to conduct an interview of Deborah Lipka at the post office where she worked immediately after they got the message that Lipka had been arrested.

Lastly, Whiteside informed SA Buckmeier, in the Washington Field Office, that the arrest scenario would proceed on February 21, 22, and 23, 1996, a Wednesday, Thursday, and Friday. Whiteside asked Buckmeier to ensure that there would be FBI Agents stationed near the entrances of Russian diplomatic establishments in Washington, DC in case Lipka attempted to flee there to avoid arrest. Additionally, Whiteside asked Buckmeier to make sure SA Droujinsky would be prepared to receive any calls for help Lipka might make to "Sergey Nikitin" in desperation.

Barbara Cohan and Michael Liebman thought it best to remain at their respective offices during the arrest scenario so they could respond if any legal problems or questions came up. Everything was planned as carefully as possible to ensure that this final effort might unearth even more incriminating evidence of espionage against Robert Lipka. Now all the team had to do was wait.

***

The day before the arrest scenario finally arrived—a Tuesday afternoon. Heavy snow had fallen over Lancaster a week before, and with rising temperatures fog from the melting snow began to get thick and soupy. It made driving miserable as FBI and NSA personnel arrived at the Comfort Inn in Lancaster.

A command post was set up by the technical squad, which included the pen register on Lipka's home telephone. Other technical squad members had been out to Lipka's new neighborhood the day before seeking locations for surveillance cameras that would keep a constant watch on Lipka's residence. They also found a cooperative neighbor to assist with surveillance by providing space for FBI technical equipment. The neighbor was surprised when the FBI knocked on his door, but he agreed to help his country in a matter of national security; the agents didn't tell him who the target of the investigation was.

Cameras were installed in carefully selected places, and a mobile command post was set up to monitor the cameras. Additional SSG surveillance units from the Detroit and New York Divisions of the FBI arrived at the hotel to assist; with all these elements in place Whiteside's team could track Lipka twenty-four hours a day from Tuesday evening until the anticipated Friday morning arrest.

Later that afternoon, with all surveillance personnel present, SA Whiteside conducted a final briefing to reinforce the importance of the case, and to be clear that under no circumstances were they to lose Robert Lipka if he left his residence. He was to be followed at all times, unless it appeared that he was about to board an airplane or in some other way leave the United States. If that happened it was likely that they would receive immediate authorization to arrest him. Should the surveillance teams observe Lipka driving near any Russian diplomatic establishment they were to promptly report the details to the command post so that Lipka could be intercepted on the spot, if necessary. There were few questions from the group; everyone understood the importance of finally seeing justice brought to Robert Lipka, a man who'd gotten away with espionage for thirty-one years.

Following the briefing, SA Whiteside went to the command post and called SA Brennan on the secure line NSA had set up. Whiteside felt confident about the preparations he'd made, but now everything depended on Pat. Brennan reported that he'd been with her all day, and they'd rehearsed the phone call she would make to Robert Lipka the following morning. Brennan felt she was prepared, although he knew she was nervous about the whole idea. Brennan and Whiteside both agreed that it was crucial Pat insist on meeting Lipka at the Hunt Valley Mall, and refuse any place he might propose. Both agents knew that she could only be protected if she met Lipka in the presence of numerous FBI Special Agents. Everyone working the Lipka case was well aware of Lipka's controlling manner, and it was important that Pat hold her ground on the meeting place. Brennan was satisfied that they were ready to execute the call, and said he would wait for the "go ahead" from Whiteside before having Pat telephone. Whiteside hoped the call would be made as close to 10:00 AM as possible, when surveillance usually reported that Lipka was at home and alone.

That night the SSG team radioed that the fog made visibility only a few feet. But they'd managed to see Robert Lipka exit his garage and drive his green conversion van to a neighbor's house—not the one who'd agreed to help the FBI. Lipka brought a large black garbage bag, which looked full, inside this neighbor's home. He returned to his own house shortly thereafter, without the bag. This was the only time that surveillance observed Lipka leave his residence that night. It was strange, but later the investigation found out that the garbage bag contained only soccer uniforms his boys had worn in a local youth soccer league. Soccer season had ended and Lipka was returning items to the coach. Still, it raised everyone's anxiety and presented the unsettling idea that Lipka might be preparing something.

Shifts running the command post and surveillance changed at 8:00 AM, with the exception of a few shifts that overlapped the usual eight-hour pattern. That morning surveillance reported that Lipka was at home with his wife and sons. The boys were expected to leave shortly for school, and Deborah was expected to depart for work. SA Brennan called to say that he was with Pat and they were ready to go. Surveillance soon called in that Lipka's sons and wife had departed. The moment had arrived.

SA Whiteside called SA Brennan at 9:55 AM. "Good luck," he said.

Pat was a bundle of nerves at the thought of calling her ex-husband. It had been so many years since they'd talked, and she never thought this day would come. But SA Brennan had an easygoing personality, and he helped her relax.

The telephone rang at 17 Dublin Drive, Millersville, PA, interrupting Robert Lipka as he sat at the kitchen table reading the *Daily Racing Form*. He got up and walked to the wall telephone, answering it, "Hello."

"Bob?"

"Yes."

"This is Pat, your ex-wife."

"Yes," Lipka replied, clearly on guard.

"Yeah," Pat said. "I want to know why you sent the FBI to talk to me?"

There was a brief pause as Lipka answered, "I did what?"

"Sent the FBI to talk to me."

Lipka said simply, "No."

"Well, an FBI agent showed up at my job yesterday and wanted to talk to me about you, and I figured who else would send him but you."

"No!"

"Well, why do they want to talk to me?"

There was a long pause. Finally Lipka said, "Can we meet some place Pat?"

She replied "Okay. Can't we just. . . no, I have to meet with them this afternoon" her voice growing a bit hysterical.

"No—do not do that," Lipka ordered.

"They're coming back. I mean I can't say no to these people. This is the FBI, Bob. What am I going to say to them?"

"Uh. . . get a lawyer. Hold on. Just do me—do me a favor. This phone—this phone is obviously tapped."

"No, no, this is okay. I—I went to a friend's house. I thought about that."

"Yeah, but you. . . but—but I'm not at a friend's house. Tell you what..."

Pat interrupted him: "Why did they tap your phone; why would they tap my phone; why do they want to talk to me, Bob?" Her acting was outstanding, and even enhanced by her actual nervousness.

"Are you off work today?"

"Yeah, I called in sick. I couldn't go to work with this on my mind."

"Okay, I'll tell you what, drive up Route 83 to York, PA."

"I'm not coming up to York. Why can't you just talk to me now?"

"Well, if the FBI is involved in something, do me a favor."

"Okay, what's that?"

"Okay, and do yourself a favor, and meet me in person so we can talk privately."

Pat replied, "All right, but I'm not coming to Pennsylvania. I don't want to travel over the state line. Let me think of some place that's in the middle, here. Cause I've got to be back at my house by 4:30 PM. I mean that's when they're going to be there. And they expect me to be there or else, you know. . . they know where I work. They're not going to just disappear out of my life. Um. . . okay. . . I'll meet you but it has to be some place public." Bob agreed, and Pat suggested the Hunt Valley Mall. Lipka asked if there was a Days Inn there, and claimed not to be familiar with the place. Pat told him that it was a big mall and that he couldn't miss it. Lipka was heard to sigh loudly, possibly realizing what was waiting for him in the not-so-distant future. He asked Pat again if there was a Days Inn there.

"Look," she said, "I'm not meeting you at some place like a hotel. I want to be out in the open. I would just feel safer."

Lipka replied with a quavering voice, "Well. . . ah. . . you know. . . okay. I. . . um. . . that's fine. What is the name of the mall?"

"Hunt Valley Mall," she said, as Lipka repeated the name again.

"Okay, and where—where in the mall?"

"How about the eatery?" Pat answered. "They all have those areas where you can buy food and sit at tables in the center of the mall."

Lipka asked for directions again, obviously confused as he was trying to comprehend all that had suddenly happened to him in the space of just a few minutes. After confusing the route to the mall, and not understanding whether to turn east or west at the exit, he tried again to press a different meeting place: "Well, it's much easier. There's a Denny's right at the Timonium exit, right next to the Days Inn."

Pat held her ground, telling him that it would be easy to find the mall and that she would feel better in a big place. Lipka finally agreed to meet her there, and noted that it was 10:00 AM. "How about noon?"

"About noon or 1:00 PM? How about 1:00 PM?"

"1:00 PM?"

"Yeah. . . okay. . . I'll see you there at 1:00 PM."

"All right," Lipka replied, and Pat said, "All right, bye," and ended the call.

Moments later SA Brennan called the Lancaster command post and filled them in on Pat's call. Brennan said he'd seen many Academy Award-winning performances in his time, but nothing that rivaled the performance Pat had just given. The meeting was on.

Shortly after Brennan's debriefing one of the SSG units watching Lipka's house reported that he'd left in his conversion van. Surveillance followed him to an off-track betting parlor where they observed him exit the van and go inside. The team was tensely watching to make sure he'd make the meeting with Pat. At 12:30 he finally departed. Still, no one could be sure whether he'd meet Pat or just go about his business. But surveillance soon reported that the van was heading south on PA route 83 toward the Mason-Dixon Line.

The SSG lead vehicle, operated by Judy Lee, reported back to the command post that Lipka had taken an early exit from Route 83 and was sitting at the exit, obviously looking for surveillance. Those units warned in advance were able to pull off until he resumed his journey. Others simply passed him and set up again, a bit farther down the highway, ready to join in the surveillance when he passed their position. What made this surveillance easy was the fact that they knew where he was headed, so long as his destination wasn't the Russian Embassy in Washington, DC.

At about the same time, at a local motel, Pat was being wired up with a hidden tape recorder by the Baltimore FBI technical squad for her meeting with Robert Lipka. She told SA Brennan that she was very nervous about meeting Lipka. Brennan assured her of her safety, and let her know that most if not all of the patrons she would see in the food court would be heavily armed FBI Special Agents.

Pat was then introduced to the FBI agent who would pose as her husband. "Tony" would drive to the mall with her in the unlikely, but possible, event that Lipka had someone watching the area. The two of them would walk together to the mall and locate the eatery. At 1:00 PM, Tony would walk away, but stay within sight of Pat at all times. If Pat felt threatened at any time she was to tell Lipka that her husband was sitting nearby and offer to introduce him; if she didn't feel the need for "Tony's" help she would simply walk over to him at the end of the meeting, return to the car with him, and ride back to the motel, in case Lipka followed her out of the mall.

Brennan assured Pat that her safety was of paramount importance, then they went over points she was expected to cover with Lipka.

Specifically, if she was nervous, she could tell Lipka that the contact by the FBI had totally unnerved her.

At 12:45 PM SA Brennan heard from Judy Lee that Lipka was nearing the Hunt Valley Mall. Tony and Pat headed out.

Lipka parked the van and walked to the mall. As he entered he was observed looking around a lot. He continued walking to the food court.

At the same time, the command post received the surveillance message that Lipka had arrived. Judy Lee contacted SA Brennan, who was at a table near Pat, that Lipka had entered the mall. Brennan alerted all of the FBI personnel on scene, tested that Pat had turned on her microphone and tape recorder, then moved a little farther away and joined a female agent at her table nearby.

12

Date: February 21, 1996
Location: Hunt Valley Mall, MD

Pat recognized Lipka immediately as he walked over even though it had been more than twenty years since they'd last seen each other. His hair was still very dark, with no gray in it. However, he'd gained a significant amount of weight. Lipka's face looked the same to Pat but the rest of him looked quite obese.

Pat raised her hand as Lipka entered the eatery to signal him. He walked over to her table, eyeing the other diners, and sat down. Pat greeted Bob, "I'm sitting here thinking, 'oh God, would I recognize him again?' "

Lipka responded that he had gained a lot of weight after several operations; Pat told Lipka that he really looked like his dad. Lipka ignored the comment and got right down to business. "So what did they say to you?" he asked.

"They said they wanted to talk to me, and they wanted to talk to me about you. They couldn't talk to me then because I was in the middle of a shift."

Lipka then asked Pat if the FBI had mentioned a friend of his named Gerry Weinberger—the same man Lipka had insisted that "Nikitin" invite to Russia. Pat said she barely remembered Weinberger but asked Lipka why the FBI would want to talk about Gerry. Lipka dodged the question and said, "Why are you shaking?"

"Because I'm really nervous. I'm not real happy with FBI people showing up on my doorstep."

"Okay, first of all I haven't seen you in how many years?"

"Oh, God, twenty-some."

"Right, and I haven't bothered you. I let you live your own life, and you've let me live mine, and I'm happy for both of us. That's about the way we both built new lives and have probably been very happy—which I am."

"Yeah, and I don't want the past to come back and destroy this life."

"Let me say something about it. There's no physical evidence of anything. You have nothing, okay? And since you have nothing, I have nothing. The only evidence they would ever be able to put together would be you against me."

"But they must have something else. How did they get your name? Pull names out of a hat?"

"I have a good idea of how. I was reading this book and evidently someone—it's just a recently written book, about a guy who defected—was fingering people. But they have not been able to even make one arrest because there's no evidence. He could have gone down through the phone book and picked out names. Okay? You don't know the whole story about it. You never knew the whole story."

"I knew what you told me and that was it."

"Anything that I did was to advantage Milt Robey. At the direction of Milt, okay?" Pat said she didn't remember that name at all, and Lipka said he'd never mentioned Milt Robey to her. He then drifted onto his limited memory issue, the way he had whenever Droujinsky put pressure on him. Lipka finally ended with a comment about his limited memory of the time he spent in the Army.

Pat asked, "Well, why, after almost thirty years, would these guys show up and only mention your name?" Lipka asked her how long they'd talked to her and she told him only five or ten minutes.

Pat started to cry and Lipka said, "Well, here's how I would handle it if I were you."

Pat blurted, "We're talking espionage!"

Lipka immediately cautioned her with a loud "Ssshhhhhh!"

"I don't think anybody can hear. I don't think there is a minimum. I mean they came after you thirty years later."

"Hold it, hold it, hold it! Ssshhhhh! There's no statute of limitations on anything we've done," Lipka said.

Pat replied sarcastically "Yeah, I know, obviously thirty years later they're knocking at my door."

"The only thing, the only way anything can happen is if they intimidate either you or me into saying anything."

"Well, this morning you said 'get a lawyer.' That certainly made me feel good."

Lipka ignored the comment and repeated that he'd never told Pat anything about his work. Pat agreed that he'd never talked about his work at NSA, his legitimate work. But Lipka began stuttering a bit and finally told her, "All I ever did with this thing was at the direction of a guy named Milt Robey. Okay? That's it. I did what he said. I put things where he said, you know, those kinds of things. That I can remember his name and rank of Colonel. I can remember his face clearly. And I can remember him at NSA taking me behind this whole big row of file cabinets and said I was replacing another person. I know his first name was Jack but can't remember his last name. And I can remember him saying to me, 'If you turn out to be a spy for the Russians, I'll shoot you myself.' "

Pat told Lipka that those words were scary, but Lipka steamrolled on with instructions for Pat in the FBI interview. He told her to say that she didn't remember anything and that he'd never told her anything about work, or things like that, to this day. He told her that the FBI would try to scare her and say they already talked to him, though no one had. Then Lipka said, "This is important. Every day except Tuesday, Saturday and Sunday, I go to a York off-track betting parlor. Let me tell you where it is. If you ever need to call me, don't call me ever again at home. I don't mean that as any slight."

Pat said, "Well, I kind of worried and hoped that nobody would answer the phone but you."

Lipka asked her if she was married now, and after she said yes, he said, "Well, then you don't want me calling there, or anything like that. But is that where they are going to meet you?"

"Yes, but my husband won't be home. That's why it's okay that they come to the house. But I don't want him to know, and God forbid Kelly ever finds out about any of this."

"Well, that's true. That would wreck them. I have two boys. Let me show you. They're ten and thirteen." Lipka brought out photographs of his sons from his wallet. "And one just discovered girls (laughs). I've lived a very happy life, you know. That's my little one, his name is Tom. And this one is James." Pat told him they were nice-looking boys. Lipka said, "Well, they are, and I wouldn't want anything to happen to ruin their lives."

Pat said she understood that and "the most important thing in the world is protecting Kelly. She has a very good life right now, with a good husband and a little girl; I don't want anything to ruin that, least of all her mother going to jail."

"These people are vicious. Years ago, they gave me a card at NSA to call a number if anything ever happened. I threw it away and have no idea what the number is. If you think it's that out of hand, I could call the Director of Security. I'm not so sure he was in—in on this whole thing."

Pat asked if they would still help him out today if he called them. "I mean, at one time you said they'd get us out," referring to the Russians. "I can't afford a lawyer," she added. "I don't make that much money and I don't want my husband to know about this."

"No, no, no, no. . . yes you can. I'm going to give you a hundred dollars. Put it some place and don't spend it betting. If they. . . if these guys bother you for longer than a couple of questions, and then your answer is, 'Bob never did tell me anything,' and I never did. Okay? If they go

196

beyond that, you just tell them, 'Enough's enough. I want to talk to a lawyer.' They can't question you after that. Okay? So you answer two questions and maybe three. Don't be nervous."

"Easier said than done."

"All right, all right. You should understand that I missed filing income taxes two years, right around the time of the end of our marriage. Now, since then, I've become a millionaire. I got that way in the coin business and made out like a bandit when people lined up to sell their silver. So, this is not a matter of money. If you need money, the amount, although I can't just go willy-nilly."

"I don't plan to need a lawyer."

Lipka asked Pat to repeat where she should contact him if she needed him; he was quizzing her for some reason. After she parroted back the information about Lipka's off-track betting parlor in York, Lipka gave her driving directions to get there. Then he asked Pat if she had a business card with contact information, because he had no idea where she lived, or what her last name or Kelly's last names were. "Well, no offense, but that's okay," Pat answered. Lipka said he kept his name in the telephone book for Pat, in case she ever needed anything, but she answered that she wasn't expecting this kind of circumstance.

"Well, we're not sure that this is gonna amount to a hill of beans, because with no physical stuff..."

Pat interrupted him saying "Well, it was enough to scare me."

"That's what they want to do. The thing you should be scared of is if you talk too much, or say one thing they can misinterpret, you're dead. Make the thing short and to the point and say you don't know anything about this, which you don't. And you can say that honestly because you really don't." For several minutes Lipka went off again trying to convince Pat that she wasn't aware of his espionage, and insinuating that she would be the one punished if she said anything wrong.

"Okay, I don't," Pat replied. "I don't know anything about anything."

"Once you go down that road, then we can't protect Kelly, we can't protect Tom, we can't protect anybody. And I'm telling you it would be all over the newspapers." Pat told him she'd thought about that a lot since yesterday and the contact from the FBI. "Don't be talkative," Lipka continued. "The only thing you need to say is he never told me anything about his work. His motto was 'never say anything'. NSA: never say anything. And—and I used to tell you don't tell people where I work and what I did. Okay? See, this. . . you just—you don't know, you don't know anything about what I did there. Unless of course, there is this long story that I don't want to ever get into, but, you know, I was recruited out of high school by these people, by the Army Security Agency. They came to me and they recruited me. That's all. You know, I can remember that. Beyond that I can't remember anything."

Pat didn't say anything and Lipka abruptly changed the subject to his access to information at NSA, saying, "I only had access to whatever they gave me access to. But I have no idea what the deal is here. And I think that should be your tactic. Okay? That's. . you know, that's the way it is." Finally Lipka paused, reached into his wallet, and handed Pat one hundred dollars.

"Just put that away in case you ever need it," he said. "Then—then you know if you have to go to a lawyer and just sit there and. . . ah. . . bet the long horse (*laughs*). And then buy a couple of—go to the windows and buy a couple of horse races. That's what I do now."

Pat accepted the money, and Lipka started to ramble on about his expertise at betting on horse races. He even claimed that he'd won a quarter of a million dollars at Delaware Park one day. He also boasted that money "snowballed" into a lot of money in the coin business. Of course, no mention was made of the thousands he actually earned from the KGB for committing espionage against his fellow citizens. Instead, he painted a humble picture, telling Pat that he lives a very quiet life: He doesn't bother anyone or let anyone bother him, and compared his life to that of a retired man.

"So was mine until I had a visitor," Pat said, bringing Lipka back to the issue at hand.

"Well, the thing you say to them is you thought it was about income taxes. If they say, you know, 'it's espionage,' and honestly, you don't know anything. You don't have to be nervous about that. There's nothing that you know and believe me, this is the country that I love, this one right here. You have to calm down. I would not let them bluff you or say that I sent them. Okay? I wish I could tell you more about this operation but believe me, there are others who know about this operation and a lot of people who don't. Believe me; the stuff that was fed to those people on the other side was fed to mislead them. Okay? And there were lots of people that were trained at Fort Holabird to do stuff like that, understand?" Lipka was again trying to put everything on Milt Robey as being responsible for whatever contact Lipka had had with the KGB.

"All right, I'll play dumb," Pat replied. Lipka took the opportunity to change the subject, talking about a mutual friend they'd had a long time ago. He told Pat he has no bitterness toward her and that "it just didn't work out." They both agreed that newspaper exposure would kill their parents and destroy their children. Pat showed him a baby picture of Kelly's daughter and asked him if his mother talks about Kelly to him; Lipka replied that his mother doesn't tell him anything about Kelly because Kelly asked her not to.

Lipka suddenly turned serious and told Pat that he has two pills. "I don't have them with me right now," Lipka said, "because I wasn't sure if this was a set-up or just what it was. If it ever came to that, I'd take them. I wouldn't take them except for the reason to protect my kids."

Pat asked how that would protect them since information would still come out. Lipka replied, "No, it wouldn't. That's the end. How could it come out? From you? From us?"

Pat said, "Oh, not going to come from me."

Once again Lipka changed the subject to his health problems; Pat patiently sat through another long diatribe about his surgeries. Then

Lipka started anew on all of the alleged riches he made at his coin store. Finally he told Pat the interview could all be about his friend Gerry Weinberger, and his own trip to Vancouver.

Pat finally replied, "I don't know, but I'm going to find out real soon."

"Well, don't worry about it." Pat agreed and said that she didn't know anything. Lipka said, "You really don't. You can say that truthfully. Are you sure you don't want to give me your last name or your telephone number?"

"Yeah, I'm sure. If I need you I'll come up to that place in York." Lipka said that was good enough. Pat replied, "Hopefully this will be the end of them, and I can put it in the back of my mind for another thirty years, and then I'll be senile, and who'll care?"

"I'm senile now, honestly," Lipka said. "You had to literally tell me where to go and how to get here."

Then Lipka shifted conversation to his sons' Cub Scout meetings at his house. "I have a big, big house. You could land a Piper Cub in the basement on either side. It's a hundred and twenty feet long." Then he went back to talking about his surgeries. After another of his now famous digressions, he told Pat, "Well, I hope everything works out; if not, the only losers are our kids."

"Well, that's what I'm worried about."

"Don't get wordy, just say, 'I don't know anything about that. He never said anything.' And you don't; I never said anything to you about anything. If they start putting documents or pictures, especially if they say, 'Do you know this guy or that guy,' don't even touch the photographs. That is extremely important. Now, the other thing is they will be wired, also. They record everything you say even though you won't be able to see it. So don't say anything. Just say, 'I don't know anything about Bob.'"

Then, reversing direction again, Lipka mentioned looking up an old friend they both knew, who had owned a motorcycle and a hearse. Next he moved to problems between himself and Pat's mom after the divorce; Lipka thought his ex-mother-in-law was more upset about it than the two of them actually were. Lipka ended their meeting saying, "You know, that's just the way it is. I don't regret our coming together and I don't regret our kid. I would have liked to have known her. But that's never going to happen now. You know? I have long since come to that realization. Okay, I'll see you."

Lipka stood up and began walking away as Pat replied, "Okay. Well, drive carefully."

It was over at last: The long-awaited meeting between the only two people who were aware of Lipka's espionage since 1965, until Vasili Mitrokhin shared his notes in 1992. They hadn't met since the mid-1970s and, incredibly, neither had disclosed a word about their espionage for all those years to another soul.

Pat got up from her table and slowly walked in the direction of her waiting "husband," Tony. A few minutes later, Judy Lee with the SSG team reported that Lipka had entered his van and departed. She and her team would loosely surveil Lipka to ensure he returned to the Lancaster area, and not toward any Russian diplomatic establishment.

"Tony" drove Pat back to the command post motel where the tape recorder was removed from her person. She sat a while with SA Brennan to calm down before returning home. Brennan received a quick verbal debriefing from Pat, while the Baltimore FBI technical squad made copies of the recording for Brennan to take to the investigative team, awaiting the results, in Lancaster.

Pat apologized for several instances in the conversation where she agreed with Lipka that she knew nothing, when in fact she knew almost everything. She regretted not reminding him that she'd helped him on dead drops and even saw "Ivan" on occasion. She'd counted the money, and worried about him getting arrested every time he went out on a dead drop alone. Pat wished she could've thought quicker on her feet in the meeting, but she'd felt somewhat intimidated by Lipka. Brennan recognized the fact that Pat missed some golden opportunities to better implicate Lipka in his espionage, but, all in all, the meeting went as well as could be expected under the circumstances. Brennan congratulated her on a great job, and promised to let her know if and when Lipka was arrested so that she could be the one to break the news to Kelly.

***

After SA Brennan arrived at the command post in Lancaster, the investigative team and the Philadelphia Special Agent in Charge Bob Reutter listened to the tape recording of Pat and Lipka's conversation. They were impressed at how savvy she was talking to Lipka, and how her personal nervousness only added to what Lipka perceived as her fear of her upcoming interview with the FBI.

The conversation also revealed more of the mysterious ways of Robert Lipka as well. Listening to Lipka telling Pat that the FBI secretly records interviews, and not to touch anything, especially photographs they might display to her, the investigators realized that Lipka had followed his own advice during his meetings with "Nikitin:" He'd turned the television on to try to defeat any recordings, and had never touched any of the photographs displayed to him. He only entered the hotel room on one occasion, always refusing all future attempts to go back into a hotel room. Lipka was clearly extremely cautious. In fact, this was causing a small problem with the interrogation Whiteside and Brennan had planned to conduct with him the following day.

Any FBI Special Agent with basic interview and interrogation training knows that a major subject of interest should be interrogated away from his or her residence, at a neutral site. Additionally, the best time to begin the interrogation is late in the day, after the investigators have had a long rest and the subject has been awake all day. The logic is that the subject will be tired and hopefully more psychologically willing to confess. Being in unfamiliar surroundings also makes the subject less comfortable, and prevents him or her from diverting interrogation pressure to familiar items in the home. However, the Lipka interrogation presented problems in both of these aspects: time and place.

First of all, Lipka had refused all but the first request to go to a hotel room for an interview. It was quite possible that he feared he was being monitored, and he'd made it clear that he didn't feel comfortable going to a hotel room. The investigative team couldn't think of a plausible scenario that would convince Lipka to meet a self-identified FBI Special Agent in a hotel room for an interview. They also didn't want to give Lipka advance warning of the interview so they could at least catch him off guard. This would prevent Lipka from contacting an attorney right away, which would let investigators gauge Lipka's willingness to talk.

Secondly, Lipka was only available during the day because his wife would return from work in the late afternoon, and his sons would return from school before that. Therefore, just at the optimal time of day for an interview, Lipka would be surrounded by his family. He certainly wouldn't talk then, although even if he agreed to, as Pat had while her husband was around, it would be counterproductive.

But even without optimum interrogation conditions the team decided to interview Lipka at his residence, once his wife had left for work and the boys had left for school. This option left them with the most time to conduct the interrogation, and the possibility would still exist that a lengthy interrogation could be moved to a hotel room if Lipka wanted to keep his family unaware. There simply seemed to be no other viable option.

13

Date: February 22, 1996

Location: Lancaster, PA

The next morning, the surveillance team radioed that Lipka was at home alone. This was the signal; SA Whiteside rang the doorbell and Lipka answered, dressed only in a white T-shirt and black, knee-length, spandex underwear. Whiteside identified himself and Dan Brennan as Special Agents of the FBI and told Lipka they wanted to talk to him about some problems at NSA during the time he was assigned there. Lipka replied that he had to go slip on a pair of jeans, and closed the front door.

Whiteside and Brennan took simple defensive precautions, stepping away from the front door slightly, using the brick front of the house to protect themselves in case Lipka returned to the front door with a gun or other weapon. However, he quickly returned and invited the FBI agents into his home. He suggested that they sit at the dining room table because his living room was sparsely furnished. There was only one chair and a large electric piano on a stand in the living room. Interestingly enough, the music book sitting on the attached music stand was opened to a song entitled "Russian Waltz."

The dining room was furnished with a wooden, pecan-colored table and matching chairs. A large matching breakfront complemented the set. SAs Brennan and Whiteside steered Lipka to one end of the table, where they formed a triangle position. Whiteside looked around him, thinking that a search of Lipka's residence would be easy if the rest of the house was furnished so sparsely. But he didn't know how wrong he would turn out to be.

The long-awaited interrogation began. "Bob, as I mentioned to you when we arrived, we want to talk to you about some issues that took place at NSA," Whiteside said, "about the time you were assigned there in the Army. We've been conducting a lengthy investigation about the loss of some classified information, and are trying to interview every employee who may have had access to the missing information. We certainly appreciate your willingness to talk to us. You are one person on a long list of former employees we hope to talk to about this breach of security."

"I have no idea what this is about."

"Well, before we can discuss this matter in detail, I want to provide you with your rights so that you know you can stop talking to us whenever you desire to do so. Let me read these rights to you, and then I'll give you the form so you can read and sign to show you received and understand your rights under the law."

Whiteside read aloud then handed Lipka an "Advice of Rights— Warning and Waiver Form" to read and sign, if he agreed to be interviewed. This document was the Miranda rights in writing, something Whiteside decided to give Lipka in case they needed to arrest him immediately. Lipka took a very long time to read over the form, forcing Whiteside and Brennan to sit and wait. He also insisted on adding several sentences to the form; none of them affected the agreement, but the request clearly demonstrated that Lipka wanted some degree of control. It was classic Lipka, as seen in his dealings with undercover agent Droujinsky.

At the beginning of the interview the agents asked Lipka to provide personal information about himself and his reasons for enlisting in the Army. He willingly discussed his intelligence training at Fort Holabird and subsequent assignment at NSA. He also discussed his duties in the

Priority Materials Branch, and life in the barracks. Next he moved on to his first marriage, and gave some personal information about Pat. But Lipka said he hasn't seen her for twenty years, and had no idea what she was up to. The obvious lie was noted, and certainly came as no surprise to the agents.

About an hour into the interview the front doorbell rang. Lipka got up to answer what turned out to be a five-gallon water bottle delivery, and hung around making small talk with the delivery man before closing the door and returning to the agents. This small interruption destroyed the flow of the interview/interrogation. Unfortunately it would prove to be the first of several interruptions Whiteside could have avoided if he'd been able to interview Lipka away from his home.

Lipka was more composed when he sat down again. Brennan and Whiteside continued to push Lipka, though. Eventually his stress was visible: Small streams of perspiration starting running from his temples. The more the interview focused on knowledge Lipka might have about a possible espionage suspect, the more he perspired. Finally, his stress seemed to get the best of him. "Bob, we can show that the missing documents occurred during the time you were assigned to NSA. Surely you must have some idea as to who may have been responsible for contact with the KGB," Whiteside pushed. "I mean, the documents didn't just walk out of NSA."

Lipka's reaction to the stress of the moment was to stand up and tell the FBI agents that he'd been the victim of serious neck and back surgery, completely ignoring the question. He began to lift his T-shirt over his head, to show his scars, but as he reached his pudgy arms up his jeans slipped down over his spandex underwear. Here he was, an American spy, standing with his jeans around his ankles and his shirt in his hands, showing his back scars to the FBI. It was difficult for the agents to keep a straight face while Lipka put his clothes back on and sat down; it was sad, but it was also a once-in-a-lifetime way to relieve some of their own stress.

During the rest of the interview Lipka returned to his surgery every time the stress level went up, saying he'd almost died. It was the same pattern of stress deflection he'd used in his meeting with "Sergey Nikitin," and during his last meeting with Pat. Listening to Lipka one would think he was the only person to ever have back surgery.

But Brennan and Whiteside didn't let up on the intensity of the interview/interrogation. They pressed closer to the issue of Lipka's access and why he thought someone might sell classified information to the KGB. They discussed the penalties for espionage. When Lipka started showing visible signs of stress again Whiteside asked him if he had any suspects in mind. They asked Lipka what type of information he'd had access to at NSA, and Lipka replied that he wasn't permitted to ever discuss the items he'd had access to. In fact, Lipka pressed on and said he couldn't discuss anything about NSA without getting permission in writing. Whiteside thought it was just another dodge Lipka was using to relieve his stress. But when Lipka asked if he could call NSA for their permission to cooperate with the FBI, Whiteside and Brennan told him to go right ahead. *We'll call his bluff*, Whiteside thought.

Lipka got up from the dining room table and walked into the adjoining kitchen, looked up a number in his wallet, and placed a call. With that call, one of the most amazing moments in the Lipka case occurred. Through some twist of fate, Lipka was eventually put through to Larry Contrella, the very man supervising Lipka's investigation at NSA. Contrella, involved in the investigation since the start, would later say how shocked he was to pick up the telephone and hear the caller identify himself as Robert Lipka. At first he thought it was a prank. But he managed to listen as Lipka explained that he was being interviewed by two FBI agents and he needed written NSA authority via fax to answer their questions about NSA. After getting past his own amazement, Contrella naturally agreed to fax his authorization.

Lipka hung up, entered the dining room, and told Brennan and Whiteside he was waiting for a fax from NSA. At that time neither

Brennan nor Whiteside had any idea Lipka had spoken to their associate, Larry Contrella; they had heard only Lipka's half of the conversation, but knew that the pen register at the command post would identify the number Lipka had called. They both found it obvious that Lipka was groping for ways to reduce his stress. He must have known he was the focus of the investigation, especially after meeting Pat the previous day.

While they all waited on the fax from NSA, Lipka's telephone rang again. The caller asked to speak to SA Whiteside; it was Whiteside's immediate supervisor, Sid Pruitt, calling from the command post. The technical squad had just identified Lipka's call to NSA via the pen register, and they were understandably confused about what was happening at Lipka's house. Pruitt wanted to know if Whiteside was aware of this call, or if he'd made it himself. Whiteside knew that Pruitt was trying to help, but he really wasn't. Pruitt's call was just one more interruption in a series that would force the interview/interrogation to start building the pressure on Lipka all over again. Whiteside could only say that he and SA Brennan were in the middle of an interview, and that he was fully aware of what was going on. He couldn't say anything more with Robert Lipka sitting about six feet away.

A few minutes later, Lipka's fax machine came to life, and an NSA cover sheet arrived, along with a letter giving Lipka permission to speak to the FBI signed by Larry Contrella himself. The FBI agents were shocked when they realized that Larry Contrella had actually received the message from Lipka. The day was getting more and more bizarre. But they had to continue the interrogation.

By now Lipka was attempting to distract Whiteside and Brennan by talking about the lack of security at NSA. When they tried to bring Lipka back to the investigation he claimed his memory problems prevented him from recalling much about his work at NSA so many years ago. But Whiteside suddenly had an inspiration. "Mr. Lipka," he asked, "have you ever read *The First Chief Directorate* by a KGB General named Oleg Kalugin?"

"Yes, I bought the book and read it," Lipka said. Whiteside suspected another lie, because he knew the undercover agent had mailed a copy to Lipka. But Whiteside decided to sidestep the issue for the time being and took out a copy from his own briefcase. He asked Lipka to read, beginning around page 83, with the passage that provided information about the identity of the NSA spy.

Lipka began silently reading the page that Whiteside showed him. When Lipka reached the part that noted the KGB often received documents partially shredded, Lipka looked up briefly and said, "I never shredded anything." *What an amazing admission* Whiteside thought. Of course Whiteside knew that Lipka never did shred anything because there were no shredders when he'd been at NSA; all document destruction back then was done with burn bags. Still, Lipka looking up and making a comment at that moment was a clear indication that knew he the passage was directed at him.

As Whiteside and Brennan continued to narrow their questions to focus on contact Lipka had had with material that disappeared from NSA, Lipka began perspiring again. Suddenly, for the second time that day, he stood up and took off his shirt, attempting to show his scarred back. Mercifully his jeans didn't slip down this time. SAs Brennan and Whiteside could tell Lipka was really feeling the pressure and were getting hopeful about a possible confession. That hope increased after Lipka put his shirt back on, sat down, and finally said, "There was a man that I put things out for. His name was Milt Robey."

While this was just Lipka's old alibi, the same one he'd told the undercover agent he would use if he was ever confronted by the authorities, as well as the cover story he'd told his ex-wife just the day before, the agents knew they were getting close. Although Lipka blamed the events on Milt Robey, he might feel compelled to identify the documents he put out for Robey, and how, where, and why he did so.

"What do you mean you put things out for him?" SA Whiteside asked, eager to press the admission Lipka had just made. But at that moment, Lipka's telephone rang again. The tension they'd worked so hard to build up dissipated immediately.

Lipka left to answer the phone. He returned to the dining room, still talking, saying, "Right now I have two FBI agents sitting in my dining room, accusing me of being a spy." He walked back into the kitchen and in a moment or two ended the call. When he walked back into the dining room he said, "That was my lawyer, and he advised me not to talk to you."

SAs Whiteside and Brennan told him that since his lawyer told him to stop talking, it was his right to do so; therefore the interview was over. Lipka made attempts to continue, in his controlling way, to talk about related topics like security matters at NSA, but the agents told him in no uncertain terms that the interview was over. Once a subject has been advised of his rights and takes the lawyer option, an interview must be concluded. Any additional interrogation without the presence of the lawyer would make any statements inadmissible in court.

Brennan and Whiteside were upset with the last call. Just when they were close to getting Lipka to confess his espionage, even on the behalf of Milt Robey, this second telephone call had done them in. Plus, they found out later that the "lawyer" was simply a real estate lawyer who'd helped Lipka purchase his house; this person had no known experience in cases with criminal charges.

It was time to leave. The agents packed up their briefcases and headed toward the front door, bitterly regretting that they hadn't been able to interrogate Lipka away from his house. But it was clear that Lipka didn't want them to leave: He didn't know what would happen next, but he did know that he hadn't satisfied their investigation. As SA Brennan started to walk out the front door Lipka said, in a quaking, almost tearful voice, "I love my country."

SA Whiteside told him they would see him soon and joined SA Brennan for the ride back to the command post.

Despite the agents' regrets about conducting the interview /interrogation in Lipka's home, the interview had gone well. Lipka didn't give them a full confession but he did give out a few key pieces of information. SAs Brennan and Whiteside briefed the investigative team and FBI Philadelphia Division officials at the command post, then placed a conference call to AUSA Barbara Cohan and Departmental Attorney Michael Liebman, bringing them up to date on the interview with Robert Lipka. AUSA Cohan had prepared a criminal complaint charging Robert Lipka with one count of Conspiracy to Commit Espionage, a violation of Title 18, Section 794 C, U.S. Code. A warrant was issued for his arrest the following day; a search warrant was prepared for a complete search of his residence, seeking any evidence confirming his military service and association with NSA, items removed from NSA, and items used in the furtherance of conducting espionage. Most of the team hoped Lipka would try to flee to the Russians because such an overt act would bolster the case against him. However, the interview proved that Lipka continued to think he was smarter than everyone else, would use his alibi, and trust his own instincts.

As night fell the fog rolled in thicker than ever, defeating the capabilities of some of the surveillance cameras around Lipka's residence. SA Whiteside directed the surveillance team to get closer in order not to lose Lipka, should he leave. At this point in the case it wouldn't matter if he saw that he was being surveilled. He had only a few hours of freedom left.

PART III
ENDGAME

"Justice is incidental to law and order."
J. Edgar Hoover, Director, FBI

1

Date: Friday, February 23, 1996
Location: Millersville, PA

The new day dawned overcast and extremely foggy. At the command post in the Comfort Inn, the technical squad was beginning to dismantle equipment that would no longer be needed. The out-of-state surveillance teams began leaving for their respective field offices. Only the Philadelphia surveillance teams, investigative team, and a search team were left to have breakfast together. The NSA investigators would travel to Philadelphia, after Lipka's arrest, to be in the courtroom for his initial appearance later that day. The special search team from the FBI Laboratory was standing by.

Thirty-one years after Lipka had walked into the Soviet Embassy to sell Top Secret national security information obtained from NSA, he was about to meet justice.

At 7:45 AM the search-and-arrest teams pulled out and drove to Lipka's residence, parking on a street behind his house. Surveillance reported that Deborah Lipka had left for the post office, and that their older son had already boarded the bus for middle school. Younger son Tom Lipka was still at home, but would be leaving shortly.

After a few minutes sitting behind the Lipka residence, SA Whiteside watched Tom Lipka walk through the snow in the backyard, carrying his backpack. In that moment the devastation that would come to Lipka's family after his arrest hit home for Whiteside, who had children of his own. The brown-haired little boy walking through the snow, seemingly without a care in the world, would return home that afternoon to find his whole world destroyed. It would probably take a while for the real damage to finally sink in. Because of the actions of his father, Tom's life would never be the same. There was quiet in the FBI car as they waited for the young boy to depart. It would be a long day.

Nonetheless, the time for action had finally arrived. At 8:30 AM SAs Whiteside, Brennan, and Auld, Whiteside's old partner in charge of the residence search, along with Auld's team, arrived at Lipka's home. They rang the doorbell, and when Lipka answered SA Whiteside said he had a warrant for Lipka's arrest on a charge of conspiracy to commit espionage. The agents moved inside and directed Lipka to sit down at the dining room table. Lipka quietly complied with the orders as SA Auld handed Lipka a copy of the search warrant and began to direct his team to begin.

Lipka asked Whiteside if he could write a brief letter to his wife, and was granted permission. As usual, Lipka wrote a copious amount— almost a full page and a half— before SA Whiteside told him to end it. Next Lipka said he needed to use the bathroom. He was escorted by SAs Whiteside and Brennan to ensure he didn't take any pills, try to escape, or hurt himself or others. Walking back to the living room Lipka asked SA Whiteside if Whiteside had talked with Milt Robey from NSA. Whiteside, sick of hearing stories about Milt Robey, spat back, "Bob, Milt Robey is dead!"

Lipka brought his hands to his chest dramatically and tossed his head back, exclaiming, "Oh no, there goes my only witness!" Once again, Lipka unknowingly verified what he'd told the undercover FBI agent years ago: That if he was ever caught he would blame it all on Milt Robey. This comment and others like it would surely play well in court.

SA Whiteside prepared to handcuff Robert Lipka, but Lipka, as usual, tried to control the situation. He asked if he could be handcuffed in front because his size prevented him from keeping his hands behind him. Whiteside knew it would be almost impossible to handcuff Lipka behind his back anyway, so he complied. But Whiteside didn't do it gently; he fumed that yet again Lipka was manipulating the situation by putting up a meek facade. Finally Whiteside and Brennan led Lipka to the rear seat of a beige Ford Crown Victoria police interceptor, where Lipka claimed the seat belt wouldn't fit around his immense girth. He had to be transported without wearing it.

SA Brennan entered the rear seat of the car, next to Lipka and behind the driver. As SA Whiteside walked to the driver's side of the car, he saw Kemp Ensor, Deputy Director of Counterintelligence at NSA, watching the arrest from the street. Whiteside gave the thumbs up to Ensor. As they drove to Philadelphia SA Brennan again read the required Miranda advice of rights to Robert Lipka. It was now 8:50 AM.

Whiteside radioed the command post and the FBI in Philadelphia that an arrest had been made and that the prisoner was being transported, then turned to an AM news channel. At approximately 9:25 AM, Lipka began to complain that his arms were falling asleep, but several minutes later he closed his eyes and tried to sleep. His rest was short lived, however, because just a few minutes later he started talking about NSA. Whiteside and Brennan hadn't planned to interrogate Lipka in the car since he had a lawyer and had decided not to talk. But they listened as Lipka babbled. He told the FBI Special Agents that he'd been under orders for everything that he'd done, and blamed his actions on a code-named case at NSA. He said he needed to talk to the Director of Security at NSA. But eventually he circled around to his back problems, telling the agents how he was represented in a law suit for $500,000.

At 9:50 AM, the first radio broadcast came across WKYW reporting the espionage arrest of Robert Lipka. He listened quietly to the report. Thirteen minutes later, another news broadcast announced his arrest.

At 10:27 AM the agents and the spy Robert Lipka arrived at the Federal Building garage in Philadelphia where the FBI is housed. Lipka, in handcuffs, was taken by elevator to the FBI space on the eighth floor.

After gaining entry to the secure area, Lipka was allowed to use the bathroom and given a drink of water. After a few minutes Lipka was photographed by the FBI and his fingerprints were taken. At 12:10 PM, after another bathroom break, he was taken to the Federal courthouse in an adjoining building for transfer to the U.S. Marshals Service. Finally, at 12:15 PM, Lipka was officially turned over to the Marshals' office for booking.

***

Back at the Lipka residence, SA Auld's search team had divided up for room assignments. Each team member would search the open areas and plain view contents of his or her assigned room. At the same time a team from the FBI Laboratory initiated x-ray searches to locate hidden compartments and concealment devices.

Despite the fact that sixteen different Special Agents were used in the search of Lipka's residence, the search lasted until nearly 10:00 PM. While Whiteside and Brennan had only seen sparsely furnished rooms during their interview with Lipka, such was not the case in the rest of the house. Lipka had saved newspaper articles by the hundreds. It was a long and tedious process for the agents to check all of the records and notes maintained in the residence. And as Lipka had told his ex-wife, Pat, one could almost land a Piper Cub airplane in his basement. It was huge, and filled with all sorts of objects, including the Ethan Allen furniture Pat had carefully described them purchasing with KGB funds long ago.

While the search began in earnest, Special Agents Jef Feehery and Donna Kibbie went to the post office where Deborah Lipka worked. They were able to take her to a small room and interview her about her husband. When they told her that her husband had been arrested for espionage she was stunned. After regaining what little composure she was able to muster, she explained to the interviewing agents that she was not aware of Lipka's espionage and swore that he'd never discussed it with her. The agents took her back to her residence after telling her it was being searched for evidence of espionage. She was told she may want to get her boys from school since the news of Lipka's arrest would soon be all over the Lancaster area. They also advised her to stay with relatives for a few days because news trucks and reporters would surely be arriving at her home all day. Deborah took their advice, returned home, packed a bag for herself and her boys, and left the house.

Shortly after Lipka was taken away from his residence one of the NSA investigators contacted Pat and told her that Lipka had been arrested. She seemed relieved, at least temporarily, until she remembered that she would have to call her daughter Kelly and give her the news. She dreaded that moment, plus she knew that her parents, who were both alive, would be disappointed in her again. Here, too, another entire family would be devastated by Robert Lipka's espionage. How many others had paid a terrible price as a result of his treachery was yet to be determined.

At approximately 1:30 PM an initial appearance before a U.S. Magistrate Judge was held for Robert Lipka and several other prisoners wearing bright orange sweat suits. AUSA Cohan was present to represent the government's interest. When Lipka's name was called, Lipka dramatically limped to the desk in front of the judge. There had been no limp discernable during the past three days of investigation, nor when he'd been on his way to be photographed and fingerprinted; did he think the Magistrate would feel sorry for him and release him?

In any event, Lipka said that he didn't know any of the coconspirators named in the complaint against him. Based upon the nature of the charge, he was held without bail until Lipka could obtain counsel and the next hearing scheduled.

At the bang of the gavel attorneys Cohan and Liebman, SAs Brennan and Whiteside, NSA SA Rodney Weidner, Whiteside's supervisor Sid Pruitt, and Cohan's secretary, Sharon, all proceeded to Old Bookbinder's

Seafood Restaurant for a celebratory lunch. It had been a long and complicated investigation, but everyone's hopes had reasonably come to fruition. It now rested in the able hands of Barbara Cohan and Michael Liebman to prosecute Robert Lipka to the fullest extent allowed by law.

Just as they all disbanded, full but exhausted, Whiteside and Pruitt received a call from SA Auld at Lipka's residence. In the lengthy search of the house no hidden compartments had been found. Still, there was a lot of work to do at the search site and Auld wanted them to help the photographer identify specific items of interest. It was another two-hour drive back to Millersville, and by the time they arrived it was dark. Most of the search team had gone home.

As Whiteside walked through the house he saw for the first time what a nightmare the search through Lipka's piles had been for the team. He accompanied the photographer to each room of the house and had pictures taken of all the furniture Pat remembered buying with KGB money: There was the cannonball bed and a brass lamp with an eagle mounted on top of the shade. Every item Pat had recalled was located and photographed. Lipka had kept every piece from his failed marriage, even though some was disassembled in the basement.

The search team had found old address books with Lipka's father's address in them, confirming an address provided by Vasili Mitrokhin from the KGB files in the 1970s. Proof of Lipka's military service and posting at NSA were also located. During the search of a bedroom, a copy of *The First Directorate* by Oleg Kalugin was found on the bed. It seemed that Lipka had returned to it after his interview with the FBI the day before. And sure enough, hidden markings showed that it was the book "Nikitin" had sent Lipka. A set of Russian language learning books and phonograph records were also located, verifying Pat's assertion that Lipka had been told to learn Russian by his KGB handler. The only items of value that the search didn't locate were documents from NSA.

***

By Saturday morning the Lipka arrest had made it to the front page of the local, and many national, newspapers.

Meanwhile Lipka was making connections with fellow prison inmates. He probably presented little threat since he wasn't a violent person, and certainly was in poor physical condition. It was possible that if he ran into any Vietnam veterans, and they learned that he may have been responsible for military deaths based on the information he'd given the KGB, things might not go too well for him. But apparently the other inmates accepted him, and several suggested criminal lawyers they'd used from the Philadelphia area. One in particular was mentioned a lot: Ronald Kidd. Lipka finally got through to Ron Kidd, and they agreed to terms.

On Tuesday, February 27, 1996, the Federal grand jury that had been meeting monthly to go over the evidence and hear testimony in the Lipka case, delivered a true bill. Their indictment charged Robert Lipka with one count of conspiracy to commit espionage in violation of Title 18 U.S. Code, Section 794c.

Barbara Cohan got the news and began getting ready for a long trial. She discussed her preparations with the investigative team, but said she was waiting to hear about the name of the judge who would be appointed to their case. As everywhere, there were good judges to work with and very difficult, if not impossible, judges to work with.

About an hour later, while Whiteside was still in AUSA Cohan's office, her telephone rang with the news that a judge had just been selected: Charles R. Weiner. Cohan hung up and looked at SA Whiteside with color rising in her fair cheeks. "Well, Charlie Weiner has been appointed to hear this case," she said.

Whiteside wasn't familiar with Judge Weiner, so he asked, "Is that good news or bad news?"

Whiteside could sense that Cohan wasn't too thrilled. But she looked at him and said, "We could have done a lot better, and we could have done a lot worse." Those weren't the words Whiteside was hoping to hear, but as Cohan went on about Judge Weiner, she seemed to talk herself into being content with the selection. By the time Whiteside left her office, she'd talked him into it, too: He was convinced that Judge Weiner was a fair pick.

***

On March 6, 1996, AUSA Cohan, Departmental Attorney Michael Liebman, and SA John Whiteside walked from the U.S. Attorney's office to the Federal courthouse on Philadelphia's historic Market Street. They passed through security magnetometers and took the elevator to the sixth floor, where they entered the courtroom. A few minutes later, Ronald Kidd, Lipka's attorney, arrived.

Kidd, a balding, white male, exuded confidence and experience in his crisp pinstripe suit. But he was personable enough to introduce himself to Whiteside and shake his hand. Whiteside was impressed by Ron Kidd's grasp of the facts during his initial statements to the court; it was evident that he'd already done research in this case. However, Whiteside wondered whether Lipka was telling Kidd the truth about his espionage. If he was a betting man, Whiteside would've put money on more lies.

A few minutes later Robert Lipka arrived in his bright orange sweat suit, for which the press nicknamed him "the Great Pumpkin." Whiteside was surprised to see that Lipka was being pushed in a wheelchair by a deputy marshal.

After Judge Weiner entered the courtroom the proceedings began. Because of the seriousness of the charge, the judge asked if the government was going to pursue this case as a death penalty case. AUSA Cohan replied that they were not. After completing her statements,

Robert Lipka was asked how he wanted to plead to conspiracy to commit espionage. "Not guilty your honor!" He said loudly.

Lipka was pushed over to see his wife momentarily. Deborah Lipka's brother had brought her all the way from Millersville so she could view the proceeding for herself. As they quickly embraced she broke down in tears. They spoke briefly, and then Lipka was wheeled off, back to prison. Judge Weiner set the detention hearing for March 21, 1996. Until that time Lipka would remain in the custody of the U.S. Marshals.

_2_

Date: March 1996

Location: Lancaster County, PA

Although Lipka had finally been indicted, the investigation didn't stop. There were still interviews to conduct with his former associates, some of whom had been identified through the pen register on his phone. These interviews could still provide evidence for the prosecution and help them all better understand Lipka.

One of the first interviews took place with Lipka's older brother. He lived in Lancaster County, and the team thought it was worth a try to contact a family member. SAs Whiteside and Brennan initiated the contact without calling first to prevent a fast rejection. A knock on the door brought Lipka's brother to the front of his home. There was no question he was related to Robert Lipka: They shared a similar distinctive upper lip and dark wavy hair.

"Mr. Lipka, I'm Special Agent John Whiteside from the FBI, and this is Special Agent Dan Brennan," Whiteside said, showing his credentials. "We'd like to speak with you about your brother, Bob, and about his recent arrest."

Lipka's brother invited the agents into a well-kept, energy-efficient home built partially into the side of a hill for ecological reasons. "Before I answer any questions, I'd like to know two things," Lipka's brother said. "First, can you assure me that the evidence against my brother isn't only his statements to the undercover agent?"

Whiteside answered, "I can promise you that the evidence against Bob is not only from the undercover operation; there are other sources of information that haven't yet been disclosed."

"My other question is whether you're totally relying on Bob's ex-wife to prosecute him in this matter?"

"Again, Mr. Lipka, we have solid evidence from other sources, not just his conversations and information from his ex-wife. Why do you ask?"

Lipka took a deep breath and launched into a story: "When my brother was younger, he would always come home from school with a bizarre tale about something that happened to him, or someone else. There was never any substance to his tales, although he would take a small bit of fact and weave an incredible story around it. Once my parents separated, it was one of the reasons that Bob went to live with my father. When I learned that Bob was arrested, and read newspaper stories about the investigation and the undercover contact with him, I thought to myself that he probably spun some lengthy yarns about his background and activities. Knowing Bob, most of what he said was probably untrue. And my question about his ex-wife involved a difficult divorce. I'm sure she wouldn't say many nice things about him. I was just worried that if those two sources were the bulk of your case, you may have the wrong man."

"As I told you, there's a lot more evidence that has not been disclosed to the media. You can be assured that we are confident the charge against your brother is legitimate and can be proven in court."

The interview continued for a bit, although it was determined that Lipka's brother knew nothing about his espionage activities and had little to offer the investigators. Still, Whiteside and Brennan left the interview with a better explanation of some of the stories Lipka had spun to the undercover agent. His penchant for making up tales was certainly believable, and at the same time difficult to understand. To understand better the agents decided to drive to

Harrisburg, PA and interview Lipka's father, since they were only a short distance away.

Armed with the address for Lipka's father found both in KGB records and the papers in Lipka's house, the agents found a run-down apartment in a seedy neighborhood of Pennsylvania's capital city. The tin-faced mail holder indicated he was residing in a second-floor apartment. Whiteside and Brennan climbed the stairs and knocked, unannounced, at the apartment door. In a few moments the door was opened by an elderly man with unkempt graying hair, dressed in a worn sweater and cheap cotton slacks. There was no reason to ask if he was Gust Lipka; the resemblance to Robert Lipka was striking.

Agent Brennan asked "Mr. Lipka?"

"Yes," he replied. He showed little emotion, almost as if he was expecting the visitors.

"We are Special Agents from the FBI and would like to ask you some questions about your son Bob."

"Come in then."

Brennan and Whiteside entered the small, sparsely furnished apartment. It looked like it could use a good cleaning. There wasn't any place to sit, so the agents remained standing. "Mr. Lipka, are you aware that your son, Robert Lipka, was recently arrested for espionage?"

He replied, "Are they going to kill him?"

"Well, he hasn't gone to trial yet, but I don't think that will happen."

"Are they going to kill him?" he asked again. It was fairly clear to the agents that this interview wasn't going to be productive in terms of developing any additional evidence to be used in trial. SA Whiteside was pleased that Gust Lipka continued to reside at an address on file with the KGB in 1976, which served to at least validate some information and close a loop in the case.

Out of the blue Mr. Lipka pointed to his military discharge paper, hung on his apartment wall, to show he was a veteran. His actions seemed rather disjointed and Whiteside suspected that Gust Lipka was having some sort of mental difficulty. He didn't seem to grasp the essence of the interview; Whiteside could see that interviewing Gust Lipka wouldn't provide anything useful. The agents thanked him for his time and left the apartment.

As the days progressed, SA Whiteside decided he would contact some of Lipka's associates in the Lancaster area by himself. There was little reason to have SA Brennan travel from Maryland for minor interviews that wouldn't create new witnesses or yield bombshell information. This set of interviews was basically a mop-up exercise to close a few holes remaining in the case. They also introduced Whiteside to the interesting cast of characters Lipka had gathered in his life.

His first effort took him to the residence of Bruce Jefferson. Bruce Jefferson operated a coin shop in town where Lipka had worked before divorcing Pat, and for some time thereafter, prior to opening his own shop. Whiteside rang the doorbell and waited. No answer. He rang a second time, before the door was opened by a scantily clad young female about twenty years old. Whiteside asked if this was the residence of Bruce Jefferson and she answered "*Da*," the Russian word for "yes." She opened the door and pointed to a chair in the living room for Whiteside to take. She said in broken English with a heavy Russian accent that she would get Bruce. She went back upstairs and was not seen again. Several minutes later, a man in his sixties came down the stairs; he shook Whiteside's hand and introduced himself as Bruce Jefferson.

"Mr. Jefferson, I'm here to ask you some questions about your knowledge of Robert Lipka," Whiteside said after they'd both sat down. "My understanding is that he used to work for you in the coin shop. He was recently arrested on a charge of espionage. What can you tell me about him?"

"I'm glad you aren't here about my Russian girlfriend!" Jefferson exclaimed. "I was worried she might be here illegally, and you were here to take her in, and possibly arrest me. There's nothing like having firm flesh to hold when you're my age."

"I'm not here about the Russian girl. I want to know about any knowledge you have about Robert Lipka."

Jefferson said he no longer operated the coin shop, but, "I remember him well. At one time he opened his own shop and was a bit of a competitor of mine. He also wrote a coin column in the local newspaper once a week for a while. When he worked for me, I always thought him to be a bit lazy. He liked to talk, and he always had plenty of stories to tell."

"Do you have any idea where he came up with the money to open his own coin shop?"

"No, I never really thought about it. It wasn't a very good business though. I remember him attending shopping malls on the weekends to sell coins, postcards, old newspapers, and other junk. I don't think he ever made out too well. His store was named Liberty Coin. He didn't operate his shop for too long a period of time."

"Did you see that he was arrested a few weeks ago for espionage?"

"Yes I did. It was in all the local papers. I was a bit surprised, as was everyone else. He had mentioned being in the Army, but he never said a word about being a spy. I really haven't had much contact with him since he got out of the coin business."

Since that seemed to be a dead end, Whiteside thanked Jefferson for his time and the interview concluded.

About a week later Whiteside was scheduled to meet a doctor Lipka had had contact with in the past. He was listed as a family practitioner, but Whiteside wanted to know how this doctor fit into Robert Lipka's life. Though he probably wasn't "the good doctor" Whiteside's team had already identified as Gerry Weinberger, there were enough calls from this second doctor on the Lipka pen register to suggest some benefit might be obtained from an interview.

When he arrived at the address Whiteside was surprised by the large size of the building and apparent size of the doctor's practice. There seemed to be several nurses and office workers in the sprawling, relatively new complex. The receptionist greeted Whiteside, then led him to a small conference room, saying the doctor would be with him shortly. As Whiteside waited he examined photographs of what appeared to be the doctor in foreign countries, giving medical attention to poor people. More interestingly, he noticed a photograph of the doctor shaking hands with Colonel Ollie North. *Could this have been where Lipka met Ollie North?* Whiteside wondered.

The doctor walked into the office and introduced himself, offering Whiteside a seat. Whiteside told him that the visit had nothing to do with Robert Lipka's medical conditions or history, if indeed he was a patient; rather, it was an effort to sort out Lipka's espionage activity.

"I'm Robert Lipka's doctor and cannot provide you with any of his personal or health information," he replied. "What is it exactly you're looking for?"

"In the conduct of our investigation of Robert Lipka, we learned that he was involved with Ollie North and someone whom he refers to as 'the good doctor'. I'm trying to determine what—if any—contact either of you may have with Ollie North. I see a photograph of you with him and believe there's some relationship."

The doctor paused for a moment. "One day when I was treating Mr. Lipka, we were discussing the Ollie North situation. I thought North was a scapegoat for the government and was upset over how he was being persecuted in the press. I decided to throw a fundraiser for him in the Lancaster area. We ultimately raised about $20,000. I remember talking to Mr. Lipka about this event. He didn't attend, nor did he contribute to the fundraiser. We talked about it during that one office visit, but never again. He didn't mention any friendship or contact with Ollie North at that time, at least to the best of my recollection."

The doctor had a full slate of patients and needed to get back to them. When Whiteside pushed for more information the doctor said he didn't know anything about Lipka's espionage and couldn't give any additional information. After that curt response Whiteside decided it was best to leave.

During the next few days Whiteside pondered a couple of unanswered questions that arose during the investigation. One major question involved Pat Lipka, and what she knew or didn't know. In some discussions with her, she seemed to think that Robert Lipka was the victim of a KGB plot that blackmailed him into passing classified material. But she had also once mentioned that there was a girl involved, at least according to Bob. Plus she also recalled how much fun it was to sit on the sofa, count the money he received, throw it up in the air, and believe they were living a James Bond movie.

Whiteside saw inconsistencies in her behavior, or at least in the way she thought about the situation. Perhaps Lipka had used his Milt Robey alibi on her well before their meeting in the mall, convincing her that what he was involved in was an NSA-sanctioned operation. But if that was true, why would she think she could keep the money, and why would she obey Bob's command never to speak a word of this to another soul? Exactly how was she processing this information back when it was happening? Her question to Whiteside and Brennan, asking if Lipka had been blackmailed, and her sadness at learning the truth about Lipka's volunteering, seemed to show that she didn't originally think he was doing something truly evil.

A second matter also really bothered Whiteside: While Mitrokhin had given evidence that Lipka had received $27,000 for his efforts, another long-time FBI recruitment-in-place code-named "Fedora" told the FBI that "Dan" (the same code name Mitrokhin said the KGB had given Lipka) had been paid $150,000 for his efforts. Whiteside had done the math; fifty meets at $500 per meet would be $25,000. If Lipka received another $2,000 as a bonus—which wouldn't be out of the ordinary—this made the receipt of $27,000 very plausible. But if the figure of $150,000 was accurate, where did the additional $123,000 come from, and when was Lipka paid that money?

Mitrokhin had only seen an abstract that summarized the Lipka case at the point when illegals Peter and Ingeborg Fischer were summoned to Moscow for a meeting about Lipka, which was shortly after Lipka had left NSA in 1967. But Whiteside's other KGB source, "Fedora," had worked in the same city as the KGB's ex-head of Washington operations, Boris Solomatin, long after Lipka left NSA; therefore, "Fedora's" information was likely more recent.

Was it possible that the KGB had continued to pay Robert Lipka after he left NSA, hoping Lipka would get his college degree and go back to NSA? Yes! If the KGB thought that a trusted agent would return to NSA, they would gladly support his college education and expenses. An agent who had NSA access like Lipka, and one who successfully made fifty dead drops without incident, was an agent the KGB would love to have return to his original job; Lipka was already carefully trained in intelligence tradecraft, and trusted by the KGB. The sum of $123,000 was a small price to pay if the KGB actually thought Lipka would return to NSA and continue his espionage.

Was it Lipka who had conned the KGB into believing that he planned to return to NSA, even though he had no intention whatsoever to do so? After all, the KGB arranged a meet for Lipka in New York— the same city "Fedora" and Boris Solomatin were working in—as late as 1974. They also kept up with the address of Lipka's father well into the mid-1970s, which clearly shows continued strong interest in this spy. Watching Lipka work undercover agent Droujinsky for money but no product caused Whiteside to believe it wasn't outside the realm of possibilities that Lipka continued conning the KGB into the seventies. But Whiteside couldn't spend time chasing these answers. There was a trial to prepare for and work to be done.

***

AUSA Cohan and Departmental Attorney Michael Liebman worked tirelessly preparing for Lipka's detention hearing, where Judge Weiner would set Lipka's bail—if he allowed Lipka to be released from prison on bail at all. Whiteside's team had no doubt that there was a distinct possibility Lipka would try to flee the United States if released. After all, he was facing a potential life sentence and he had, by his own admission, been given instructions by the KGB in case he needed to escape. Lipka had told "Nikitin" that he didn't have a passport, but the possibility existed that he did. It was also possible that the KGB had given him a forged passport. In addition, Lipka had demonstrated his ability to avoid detection and operate clandestinely thanks to the fact that his contacts with the KGB went undiscovered for so many years. Keeping Lipka in prison until his jury trial had to be a top priority.

March 21, 1996, arrived quickly and found AUSA Cohan, Michael Liebman, and SA Whiteside hurrying to the courthouse for the detention hearing. U.S. Marshals escorted Robert Lipka, who arrived using crutches, to the defense table.

After Judge Weiner sat the detention hearing began. The prosecution presented their case and offered SA Whiteside as a witness. Whiteside testified on the general procedures intelligence services normally take in trying to protect a valued agent, and how an intelligence service would provide emergency instructions and a way to flee if an agent felt his cover had been blown. Whiteside confirmed the tape recordings made between undercover FBI agent Droujinsky and Robert Lipka at four separate meetings. Whiteside also confirmed that his investigation failed to determine any known employment for Robert Lipka.

But Ron Kidd challenged Whiteside. "Agent Whiteside, is it true that you are the case agent in connection with this investigation?"

"Yes it is."

"Does that mean that you know more about the case than anyone else in the FBI?"

"It means that I am responsible for the overall conduct of the investigation. In so doing, I probably have the best overall knowledge of the case," Whiteside demurred.

"Are you familiar with the conversations my client, Mr. Lipka, had with your undercover FBI agent?"

"Yes I am."

"Do you recall any conversation about Ollie North that took place between them?"

"Yes I do."

"Did you check out those comments to see if they were true?"

"No, I did not."

"Do you recall my client mentioning anything about Richard Nixon being a spy for the KGB?"

"Yes, I do."

Kidd shot Whiteside a cunning look, then asked, "Did you attempt to verify if Richard Nixon had in fact spied for the KGB?"

"No, I did not."

"Agent Whiteside, let me ask you why you did not follow up on these allegations and confirm the details."

"I did not follow up on those statements as I believed both were tales made up by Mr. Lipka," Whiteside stated. He was answering everything precisely and honestly; Whiteside could see where Kidd was headed with his questions but didn't have the leeway to react. One doesn't have the luxury of thinking and feeling while testifying; one must concentrate on the questions.

"Well then," Kidd continued while opening his arms in an overdramatized question, "what makes you think that the stories he told your undercover agent about contacts with the KGB weren't tales he made up also? Isn't it true that just about everything Mr. Lipka said were fabrications?"

"No," answered Whiteside.

"No? You just testified that he made up stories. What do you mean 'No'?"

"The comments made by Mr. Lipka about his espionage activities and his contacts with the KGB can be and have been verified by other sources in the investigation, and I know them to be true."

"What about this 'Bandara-style' execution. Do you think my client actually meant to kill someone with poison?"

"The Bandara assassination was an actual event that occurred in October 1959, initiated by the KGB. I have no knowledge of whether Mr. Lipka was serious in his desire to have the source that identified him as a spy assassinated in a similar manner."

"No further questions, your honor."

As Whiteside stepped down AUSA Cohan stood up, smiling over Whiteside's testimony, and asked the court to hold Lipka without bail, since he was both an escape threat and inquired into the means of killing a person. Mr. Kidd countered that Lipka should be granted bail because most of the evidence against him failed to show him as a threat to the community, or an escape risk.

The hearing finally ended and Robert Lipka was returned to prison; he and the government would have to wait on a ruling. Fortunately, it didn't take long. Within the week, the court ruled that the government proved, by a preponderance of evidence, that no condition or combination of conditions would reasonably assure the appearance of Robert Lipka as required. Additionally, the court ruled that the government had proved by clear and convincing evidence that no condition or combination of conditions would reasonably assure the safety of other persons and the community, as required by Title 18 U.S. Code Section 3142 (e). Lipka would not have the option of getting out on bail before the trial.

***

Up to this point Ronald Kidd hadn't been allowed to see any classified information. But with the trial looming, the Department of Justice initiated the security clearance process for Kidd. It would take a few weeks; in the interim a secure safe was brought into the courthouse to hold classified documents so Kidd could work with Robert Lipka to look at the evidence against him.

At this point in the investigation neither Lipka nor Kidd knew the true identity of Vasili Mitrokhin; for that matter, the FBI and Federal prosecutors didn't either. The Brits had kept Mitrokhin's name completely secure, referring to him only by a fictitious name. However, at some time in the court proceedings it would be necessary to provide Mitrokhin's true name to Ron Kidd; the defendant and his legal team had the right to know the true identity of the witness against him. But the U.S. government still had to protect Mitrokhin.

***

Another pretrial hearing—this one to set parameters for using classified information from the FBI investigation in the courtroom—was held in October of 1996. The defense team had to know which material was—and remained—classified, and therefore could not be divulged to any outside people during or after the trial. Judge Weiner ordered that Lipka was not permitted to divulge any of the classified information he would see while preparing his defense to anyone except his attorney. The government had requested this ruling because of Lipka's proclivity to babble; the team was concerned that Lipka might seek revenge for his arrest by spewing classified information from the recent investigation, or from his past at NSA. Fortunately Judge Weiner ruled for the prosecution, and Lipka agreed to abide by this order. Ron Kidd made no objection.

During the next few weeks there was some unexpected difficulty in getting Ron Kidd a Top Secret clearance. The investigative team never found out the reason; this effort was handled by the Department of Justice in Washington, DC, and they kept the facts to themselves. But it began to look like obtaining a clearance for Kidd wouldn't be successful, so AUSA Cohan raised the question of whether Lipka actually would have the right to an attorney of his choice if he couldn't have Ron Kidd. If Lipka was denied using Ron Kidd as his defense attorney simply because Kidd was unable to receive a security clearance, lengthy appeals would likely take place; these could last for years before the trial was ever started. Because many potential government witnesses were quite elderly, and might not live through extended appeals, Barb Cohan was faced with a troubling legal issue: Should she push to remove Kidd as Lipka's attorney, and face possible appellate action, or not worry about Kidd getting a clearance and work something else out?

In the end Cohan opted for the plan that would keep prosecution moving, and prevent Lipka from making appeals. The clearance problem was solved by allowing Kidd to continue as Lipka's attorney while insisting that classified documents could only be reviewed in the confines of a special room in the Federal courthouse. Ron Kidd would have to be trusted, as any American citizen would be, to maintain the confidentiality of the classified documents. Should he disclose any classified information, he would be liable for prosecution under the espionage statutes, just as his client was. It was simply the best of a lot of bad options.

Meanwhile, Robert Lipka was already planning to spill Top Secret information despite the court order against it. Lipka and Kidd had been looking through FBI evidence collected against Lipka when they discovered the open letter Mitrokhin had written to any Western embassy that would accept him in Latvia. Mitrokhin had signed the last page of the communication with a fictitious name; for reasons unknown to everyone but himself, Robert Lipka memorized the fictitious name and assumed, incorrectly, that he had the true identity of a high-level KGB spy who'd defected to the West. Back in prison Lipka met another inmate with contacts at a major television news channel. He and Lipka planned to make a few dollars—and a big splash—by revealing the identity of the Soviet KGB defector. Lipka asked this other inmate to arrange for an exclusive, on-camera interview. Unfortunately for Lipka, his foolish attempt to divulge Mitrokhin's incorrect name was uncovered by the prison authorities through their monitoring of inmate's telephone calls.

Once the government found out about Lipka's plot to expose Mitrokhin—only three weeks after Lipka had been ordered not to disclose classified information—AUSA Cohan filed contempt of court charges against him. About the same time, AUSA Cohan decided against fighting to deny Lipka access to Ron Kidd. It was time to get into the trial phase of this case without dallying over Ron Kidd's clearance.

The question of allowing classified documents in a jury trial still remained, though. The following day, Wednesday, March 26, 1997, Judge Weiner heard arguments behind closed doors on this question. There were no classified documents that the government could prove Lipka'd passed to the KGB, but the government needed to show examples of the type of documents Lipka had had access to. Demonstrating the extent of his access, the importance attached to that information, and the fact that Lipka had had the means to pass it would show just how damaging Lipka's espionage had most likely been.

This closed-door hearing concerned a number of representative NSA Top Secret documents that either had been identified by Lipka's ex-wife, Pat, or documents NSA investigators could prove Lipka would have had access to while working in the Priority Materials Branch. Although prosecutors wanted to use them at Lipka's trial, they were understandably concerned that their contents stay protected.

The government uses a three-tiered classification system to protect sensitive information; anything restricted is referred to as classified. Confidential information is defined as information that, if placed in the hands of an enemy nation or state, could cause damage to the security interests of the United States. The next highest classification is Secret, which is information that if divulged could cause serious damage to the security interests of the United States. The highest level of classification is Top Secret, which is information that if divulged could cause grave damage to the security interests of the United States. Vasili Mitrokhin made it clear that Lipka had passed over 200 documents classified at the Top Secret level.

But it was still a mystery to Whiteside's team exactly what Lipka had passed. There were a number of world events Lipka could have affected. Just before the Army posted Lipka to NSA, the failed Bay of Pigs invasion occurred in Cuba. Shortly thereafter, the Cuban missile crisis occurred, threatening the world with nuclear annihilation. During Lipka's stint at NSA the Vietnam conflict escalated, and the 1967 Six Day War between Israel and the United Arab Republic (now Egypt) took place. A NSA unarmed observation ship, the USS *Liberty*, got attacked by Israel and numerous Navy and NSA personnel were killed. In addition, another NSA intercept ship patrolling the shores of North Korea, the USS *Pueblo*, was attacked in December 1967, a few months after Lipka left NSA. This ship was actively collecting intelligence for the U.S. government at the direction of NSA prior to Lipka's departure. In 1968 the Soviet Union invaded Czechoslovakia; the planning for this event surely took place during Lipka's employment at NSA.

Lipka had passed daily and weekly summaries that were prepared for the President, according to KGB General Oleg Kalugin's book. Surely many of the above matters—as well as untold others—were reported to the President in those reports. Was Lipka's secret selling related to any of them? Very possibly. Therefore, it was difficult for the government to provide an assortment of documents Lipka had access to for trial because he had access to almost everything.

SA Brennan, a studious yet fun-loving Irishman, was called to the stand during the closed-door hearing and testified to the fact that the documents produced in court were the property of NSA. In addition, he testified to the classified nature of each of the documents and to the fact that all of them passed through the Priority Materials Branch at NSA, where Lipka had been assigned. Brennan admitted that the government couldn't prove that any of these specific documents had been passed by Lipka to the KGB, only that these were authentic examples of the type of documents Lipka had had access to on a daily basis. Brennan stressed that the government wanted to bring these documents into evidence to illustrate the seriousness of Lipka's crime. The documents presented in court by SA Brennan were all classified at the Top Secret level.

Robert Lipka was called to the stand by his attorney. Lipka denied ever seeing some of the documents Brennan had mentioned in his testimony, or having any access to others in that group. But he did confirm that he may have had access to several of the documents.

AUSA Cohan didn't attempt a cross-examination of Lipka at this hearing because she knew that the documents were not directly identified as items passed by Lipka. He'd admitted under oath that he'd had access to a variety of the documents, and this was sufficient for Cohan's case against him.

Following the testimony, the judge said he needed time to consider whether to allow classified documents into evidence for Lipka's trial. Before closing this hearing, however, he asked Barbara Cohan how many days she would need to present the Government's case.

"Three weeks, your honor," Cohan said with finality.

"Three weeks?" Judge Weiner thundered. "You can have three days! How many witnesses do you plan to produce?"

"Sixty."

"Sixty?" screamed the Judge. "You can call six witnesses!"

That was when SA Whiteside realized why Cohan had fumed when she found out Judge Weiner would handle this trial. Now Whiteside could only watch in horror as the case seemed to slip away.

AUSA Cohan replied, "Your Honor, if defense counsel will stipulate to the testimony to be offered by the other witnesses, we will be able to get by with only six witnesses."

Judge Weiner looked at Ron Kidd and asked, "Mr. Kidd, I'm sure you will stipulate to those witnesses, won't you?"

Ron Kidd simply and incredulously replied, "Yes, your Honor." The hearing ended and all awaited a trial date to be set.

Date: April 1997
Location: Philadelphia, PA

B arb Cohan suspected that Ron Kidd knew his client faced a difficult fight if he continued to insist he was not guilty. She imagined Kidd would sit down with Lipka and lay out the government's case against him, beginning with the investigation of the Fischers and ending with the information from Vasili Mitrokhin and Pat, making sure to emphasize the importance of the audio and video tapes of Lipka with the undercover FBI agent, and testimony from many former Special Agents who'd worked on parts of this case. Surely an acquittal didn't look promising. In addition, Cohan thought Kidd would warn Lipka that an unsuccessful fight in court might very well translate into a life sentence in a Federal penitentiary. She wasn't sure whether Kidd would try to work out details for a plea bargain, but suspected it was the best thing Kidd could do for his client. For her part, Cohan planned to prepare for a jury trial seeking a life sentence for Robert Lipka.

During the next few weeks she and Mike Liebman threw themselves into preparing a Prosecution Memorandum for the United States Attorney, Michael Stiles. Stiles had replaced the former U.S. Attorney, Mike Rotko, in this political position, which is appointed by the President. The document Cohan and Liebman were preparing would primarily outline their plan for prosecuting Robert Lipka, as well as point out the possible pitfalls of a trial—especially with Judge Weiner on the bench.

And there were pitfalls looming. The tapes of Lipka's conversations with undercover agent Droujinsky weren't in good shape: Several of the original recordings had developed an annoying screeching sound behind the interviews. The sound would get progressively longer in length as the tape played. AUSA Cohan wrote in the memo that if the judge started listening to the tapes and got frustrated he might just discard them all together, which would throw out many of Lipka's espionage admissions.

A second major issue was the eroding ability of the retired FBI Special Agents to remember clearly, under oath and on the stand, facts involved in the investigation of Peter and Ingeborg Fischer, and Artem Shokin. Previous meetings with these men, who were true heroes, did demonstrate some forgetfulness. After all, many of them were over 75. It was entirely possible that Ron Kidd's sharp cross-examination could create enough confusion in their testimony to discredit them.

The issue of jury appeal was also important. While a spy case usually attracts a lot of interest, this case began more than thirty years ago and it might not have the appeal of a more recent case, like the John Walker case. If the jury thinks that Lipka's crimes are too old to cause damage, he could get away with it.

Nonetheless, one issue overrode all the rest: Vasili Mitrokhin. MI-6 still had him protected in a secure location under an assumed name. No one working on the Lipka investigation knew his true name. Although the Brits had brought Mitrokhin to Philadelphia for practice testifying, in reality they were looking for ways to avoid putting him on the witness stand in a United States court where all of the spectators, jury, and the defendant could view him. They were insisting that if Mitrokhin had to testify, he do so from behind some sort of protective shield so no one could see, sketch, or photograph him. When AUSA Cohan told the Brits that it was unlikely Judge Weiner would go along with completely hiding the witness's identity, they countered that a heavy disguise would be the second-best option. Cohan replied that she'd try, but doubted whether a disguise would sit well with Judge Weiner.

In addition, despite the secrecy, news of a top secret witness had leaked out. News reports were referring to him as a "mystery witness," Fortunately, most people thought the "mystery witness" was actually Lipka's ex-wife, Pat, or Oleg Kalugin, who'd written about Lipka in his book. These were good guesses, but obviously off the mark. Kalugin was out of reach, probably in Russia at the time. He also never identified Lipka by name in his book.

Cohan wrapped up her prosecution memo to Mike Stiles by discussing the possibility of a plea agreement. She wrote, "Here the FBI and the prosecutors disagree. The FBI believes that Lipka will plead guilty and not want a trial, while we believe that Lipka will take this all the way to a jury trial, which might last as long as three weeks." In truth, Lipka was an impossible person to read. However, SA Whiteside ate, slept, and breathed this case for almost four years, and knew Lipka and Lipka's ex-wife much better than the prosecutors. Having heard stories over and over about the times that Lipka acted like a tough guy, only to back down when confronted, the case agent believed that Lipka would do so again, especially when faced with the prospect of a life sentence.

***

The telephone call came to Barbara Cohan: Kidd was offering to plead Lipka guilty if they could work out an agreeable maximum sentence. Kidd was obviously sharp enough to realize that the government didn't really want to surface their "mystery witness," and felt he could use that to Lipka's advantage.

Cohan discussed the situation with Michael Liebman and her superiors, and was gracious enough to include SA Whiteside in the discussions. Everyone wanted to see Lipka receive a life sentence for his betrayal. But there was one problem with a life sentence: During the time of Lipka's known espionage, which was from 1965 to 1967, the sentencing guidelines for the Federal District Court for life sentences mandated that convicted criminals would be eligible for parole after serving ten years. Since Lipka's crimes were committed under those old guidelines, he would have to be sentenced under them. Therefore, even if the government took Lipka through a jury trial and he was given a life sentence, it was probable he'd only serve ten years.

Further, there was also a strong possibility that the judge might impose a lesser sentence on Lipka. In that case, under the old sentencing guidelines, a convicted felon would only need to serve one-third of his sentence before being eligible for parole. To top it off, that convict would also be automatically released after serving two-thirds of the sentence if he didn't create any problems while serving his time. Thus, if Lipka was found guilty and sentenced to twelve years, he would be eligible for parole after four years and automatically released after only eight years. Was it really worth the risk of exposing Vasili Mitrokhin? Was it really worth the trouble of putting together such an involved case?

The chess game had begun anew between the prosecution and the defense. Each could clearly read the other's position and imagine moves in the endgame.

After much soul-searching, AUSA Cohan contacted Ron Kidd and made her offer: A maximum sentence of twenty years if Robert Lipka would plead guilty to the conspiracy to commit espionage charge. The contempt of court charges related to Lipka's attempt to publicize Mitrokhin's identity would be dropped, but Lipka would remain responsible for whatever fine the judge might impose, up to a maximum of $10,000, which was an old sentencing guideline limit. Also, Lipka absolutely must reimburse the government for the $10,000 that undercover Special Agent Droujinsky gave him.

Then AUSA Cohan presented another offer: If Robert Lipka was willing to be fully debriefed by the FBI and NSA investigators regarding his actions with the KGB, and thereafter pass a polygraph examination demonstrating that he had told them the truth, the government would ask for an even more reduced sentence, less than the twenty years she offered up front. Cohan avoided mentioning a specific reduction in time in case Lipka had little information to add. However, a comment from the prosecutor to the judge advising of Lipka's full cooperation in the case would likely have some effect on a reduced sentence. Such a reduction was the purview of the judge alone.

Kidd was thrilled with this news. He was sure he could convince Lipka that he could probably get away with a maximum sentence of five to eight years with cooperation. After all, Lipka had absolutely nothing to lose and everything to gain.

But Lipka wasn't pleased. In fact, he felt that he shouldn't do any more time than what he'd already served, which at that point was a little over one year. Kidd knew that while Lipka had confided some things during their sessions, he'd never confessed completely, which handicapped Kidd in trying to work out the best deal. So Kidd, working as best he could with what he knew, insisted that Lipka was being given a great opportunity for a reduced sentence. Eventually Lipka agreed to discuss his case with the FBI and NSA, but he refused to accept the possibility of a twenty-year sentence.

Thus Kidd called Cohan back with a counter offer calling for a maximum of eighteen years. Cohan, Whiteside, and Michael Liebman immediately got together on a conference call. They realized that, due to sentencing guidelines, the difference between a full sentence of twenty years and a sentence of eighteen years would be only sixteen months of actual jail time. Plus the overriding concerns with witnesses and technical issues, and the huge issue of exposing Mitrokhin, left the prosecutors little choice. Everyone reluctantly agreed to accept a maximum eighteen-year sentence for Lipka, and hoped the judge would sentence him to that full time. However, they kept the deal on the table for Lipka's full confession and polygraph verification in exchange for requesting a lighter sentence from the judge.

Three days later, after discussing the recent plea agreement with Ron Kidd, Lipka agreed.

On Friday, May 23, 1997, Lipka appeared before Judge Weiner in Federal court wearing his bright orange prison garb. Lipka, in tears, stood before the judge soliloquizing: "I've lived a life of terror for thirty years, fearing this would be discovered," he sobbed. "When it happened—when I first got into it—I didn't realize what it all meant. Everybody in this courtroom takes for granted that flag and what it means. Only a person who traveled in my shoes could understand what that means: To know there are people who died for that flag, and that in some way I didn't—that I betrayed that flag. I'm sorry for that."

Lipka then turned his gaze toward the prosecutors and said, "They've done a very good job and I have no animosity toward these people."

Judge Weiner banged the gavel on Lipka's plea and the U.S. Marshals returned him to the Fairton Correctional Facility in New Jersey. There would be no need for a trial in this case. The secret of Vasili Mitrokhin would be preserved, at least for a time.

4

Date: June 1997

Location: Philadelphia. PA

Prosecutors and Ron Kidd arranged to spend at least three days with Robert Lipka to fully debrief him about his espionage. SA Whiteside asked SA Brennan and NSA investigators to join the debriefing sessions; this looked like a prime opportunity both to explore in-depth the workings of the KGB in the mid- to late- 60s, and to identify any vulnerabilities in the U.S. caused by information Lipka had passed to the enemy. NSA investigators in particular couldn't wait to learn which documents Lipka had passed to the KGB.

Two deputy U.S. Marshals brought Lipka to a meeting room in the Federal courthouse building usually used by the AUSAs for interviewing witnesses and conducting business during court breaks. Standard, government-gray, metal furniture and a long, wooden conference table were the only furnishings. The windows were bare and overlooked the city streets; a worn commercial carpet covered the floor. Several empty file cabinets collected dust along the wall. U.S. Marshals unlocked Lipka's handcuffs but left his leg shackles on so that he had to shuffle to a chair—one facing away from the windows that lined the outside wall overlooking Arch Street.

SA Whiteside purposely sat next to Lipka, at the head of the table, and placed a tape recorder in front of him. Ron Kidd sat at the other end of the rectangular table, next to AUSA Cohan. Investigators Brennan and Weidner sat at the remaining places around the table, across the table from Barb Cohan. Before any questioning began SA Whiteside reminded Robert Lipka that he was at this debriefing voluntarily, and obtained consent to record the entire debriefing. Then Whiteside made it clear that the government wanted to hear everything about Lipka's espionage activities, from the time he first thought about committing espionage until his last contact with the KGB.

Ron Kidd also took the opportunity to remind his client that full and truthful cooperation was the key to getting a reduced sentence. Kidd was frank, serious, and firm with his client. "Bob, it's in your best interests to cooperate fully with the FBI and answer all of their questions truthfully during this and any other hearings. You have everything to gain and nothing to lose if you tell the truth. Please cooperate and try to reduce the length of time you'll have to spend in jail."

SA Whiteside turned on the tape recorder and started asking Lipka about his reasons for even considering walking into the Soviet Embassy. Lipka immediately stonewalled: He claimed he couldn't remember details about that, or recall how he actually arrived at the embassy. As the morning session ground on, Lipka kept his concentration focused directly on the tape recorder, rarely looking anyone in the eyes. His answers were vague and usually inched around direct questions. After the first hour or so, he'd given essentially no information about his association with the KGB.

Everyone was growing frustrated, especially his own attorney. Several times Ron Kidd interrupted his own client, who'd been rambling on about something that had nothing to do with espionage. "Bob! Stop lying to these people and tell them the truth!" Kidd would shout, his face turning red. "Start cooperating with them and help yourself. You are acting very foolish and need to answer these questions. Stop wasting everyone's time and tell the truth. And for God's sake stop making up stories."

But Lipka continued to ignore questions and mutter on about his injuries, lack of memory, and the fact that the espionage had occurred so long ago. Finally, after sitting for more than two hours listening to his client rumble on about nothing, Kidd abruptly stood up and shouted, "I can't take any more of this nonsense Bob, and if you don't want to help yourself and take a great deal, then I'm leaving."

Kidd stared at Lipka for a moment as Lipka remained stoic. "Don't you want to stay out of jail and get back home with your wife and sons?" Kidd pleaded. "What's wrong with you? We worked hard to get to this moment, when you have the opportunity to greatly reduce your sentence, and you continue to sit there and make a fool of yourself. Well, I've had all I can stand and I'm leaving. As your attorney, I'll tell you once more that it is in your best interests to cooperate and answer the questions they pose to you. Goodbye."

And, with that, Ron Kidd left the room. No one saw him again until the day of sentencing.

None of this had any impact on Lipka, though. He continued giving incomplete answers. As he'd done before, when he felt threatened he talked about his memory loss and back surgery. The only helpful thing Lipka did was stop talking—sometimes in the middle of a sentence— whenever the tape ran out in the cassette recorder. He would silently point to the recorder and not say another word until the old tape was replaced. Once the new tape was in, he would continue his statement, often picking up mid-sentence.

This game went on for two days. Everyone hoped Lipka would finally see the value in confessing, but it became obvious that that would never happen. Lipka spent his time trying to minimize his espionage activities: While Mitrokhin had confirmed at least fifty drops from Lipka to the KGB, Lipka claimed there were only eight; despite Mitrokhin's evidence that Lipka was paid $27,000 by the KGB, Lipka claimed he was paid only $1,250, and said he could explain the $50. In discussing the number of documents passed, Lipka admitted to only ten or twelve, whereas Mitrokhin had noted over 200. At one point Lipka described himself as "the K-Mart of spies."

Why Lipka refused to cooperate remains a mystery to this day.

On Tuesday afternoon, during a lunch break from Lipka's interrogation session, SA Whiteside was left alone with him while the others went for sandwiches. To pass the time Whiteside starting talking chess to Lipka, remembering his involvement with the game. To break the ice Whiteside said, "Bob, I played in my first U.S. Chess Federation-sanctioned tournament this past weekend." Lipka showed no reaction, so Whiteside went on. "It certainly wasn't what I expected. There were a lot of factors that made this tournament difficult for me: A case of nerves from facing strong competition, plus playing a timed game, and keeping notes of each move was very distracting. Have you played tournament chess?"

"No, not officially. And I've never been rated or ranked by the Chess Federation."

Whiteside replied, "Well, I think I need to work on a strong opening; that was the weakest part of my game in comparison with my opponents last weekend."

"I can help you with that. A good opening for you to use the next time you play would be as follows: When playing white, move the king bishop pawn one space forward to f3. Black will open with a king pawn move two spaces to e5. White's next move is the king knight pawn two spaces forward, to g4. This would be a great start," Lipka smiled.

What Lipka hadn't mentioned was that the next black move would be the queen bishop to h4, putting white in checkmate and ending the game. But Whiteside had been playing chess since he was seven years old, and, like most chess players, was well aware of this opening. Players called it "Fool's Mate" because white plays like a fool: It's the quickest possible checkmate in the game of chess.

Whiteside thanked Lipka for his advice as his colleagues arrived with sandwiches. There was no point in confronting him about his sadistic trick; Whiteside didn't really care what Lipka thought at this point in the case.

***

As part of the plea bargain Lipka was scheduled for a polygraph after two days of interrogation. The debriefing sessions had been a complete waste of time as far as the investigators were concerned. Lipka hadn't provided any new information: He wouldn't identify one NSA document he'd passed to the KGB, or his former handlers, or his drop sites. He wouldn't even provide a reason for his espionage, or why or when he decided to go to the Soviet embassy.

For the polygraph all Lipka needed to do was to exhibit "no deception" to several key questions. "No deception," or truthfulness, is indicated by the absence of change in blood pressure, respiration, heart rate, and galvanic skin response. The test administrator resolves all issues and reviews the test questions with the subject before the test. During the test an extremely accurate instrument measures the subject's physiological responses. A person telling the truth will not react to any questions during the test. If the polygraph showed that Lipka was indeed telling the truth about there having been only a small number of meets, scant payments, and few documents passed, the court would be so advised. But if deception was indicated, then prosecution would recommend a full eighteen-year sentence.

The test was scheduled for first thing in the morning, without any debriefings beforehand. Lipka and the polygraph operator moved to a room apart from the investigators to conduct the test. Several hours passed; the wait for the polygraph to be completed seemed endless. Lunch was ordered and eaten in the conference room. Whiteside was sure his evidence in this case was accurate. But he was concerned that a personality like Lipka's could influence his polygraph charts. Everyone present was experienced in using polygraph testing in other cases, and trusted that the examiner would resolve the matter, one way or another. Still, there was some lingering doubt that Lipka might actually beat the test. At long last, the polygraph operator reentered the conference room and met with the investigative team. By this time, Lipka had already been returned to the U.S. Marshals.

SA Frank Cryan, the polygraph operator, heavily took a seat at the conference table. After a pause he looked at the group around the table and said flatly, "Lipka bombed the test. It was as bad a case of deception as I've ever seen. Lipka was only asked six key questions about his involvement with the Soviet Union, and showed deception on each one."

***

Several weeks before Lipka's scheduled sentencing, AUSA Barbara Cohan received an unusual handwritten letter from his prison cell. Lipka labeled his letter a "Proffer," and wrote that he was enclosing 100 questions he'd created to cover some of the basics of the case. He also said that he'd included his "expected responses." He noted that his reason for preparing this "proffer" was that "the truth should be told and various officials such as NSA people and FBI agents freed up to go on to other cases." Then he added, "I know that it is unlikely that I will live long enough to ever be paroled and quite clearly understand that because of my poor health, my sentence is likely to be a 'life' sentence for me. So this is my one opportunity to get straight with this portion of my life." He went on to say that for the past thirty years he'd tried to live a quiet, peaceful life and avoid any criminal behavior. Finally he addressed Cohan directly, saying he realized that she had the job of publicly demonizing him, but that he would hold no ill feelings toward her for doing her job.

Next he moved on to his family:

"A few years from now the only persons who will truly remember or care about this will be my wife and my two sons. I would hope that as you prepare your speech and presentation for the sentencing that you will keep them in mind."

Lipka complained that he hadn't had a caring father around when he was growing up, nor had his father made any effort to help him get into college. Of course Lipka didn't mention that in fact he himself had failed English, and therefore entered the Army without a high school diploma. Instead, he wrote that "my father's lack of willingness to help me get into college may be part of the answer the NSA people and the FBI agents are seeking and are so curious about."

Then he turned blame to the legal system, saying that children of convicted felons serving long-term sentences have difficulty growing up without that parent. His own sons would suffer, Lipka wrote, because his savings for their college educations will have vanished due to legal fees and expected fines.

Next, Lipka moved to veiled threats:

> "In the final analysis, I am truly just a person who made a mistake as an immature young boy and realized my mistake, got out of it the only way possible, and got on with my life. I want you to seriously consider how easy it would have been for me to sign re-enlistment [sic] papers and continue to do this for many years as others did. Instead I made a deliberate effort to safely end this."

Finally, Lipka wrote the paragraph that might have been the most damaging of all. While trying to paint himself as a victim Lipka provided the only concrete evidence that his espionage efforts were responsible for causing deaths in the 1960s:

> "I know that telling you this will make no difference in my sentence. Mr. Kidd says that is now pretty much locked in stone. So I think you can be certain that what

I am telling you is true. This activity was not something I wanted to continue after I truly thought it out. My impulsive action in 1965 was an immature decision I regretted very much over the years. *There were victims in the 1960's to be sure* [emphasis added] but now a new set of victims, my totally innocent boys, my wife and her family must suffer and have suffered for something they had no hand in. Had I known the extent of damage that this would do to them I might have opted for a final way out to spare them this awful stigma. I have to truly wonder what it is the government gained by dusting off this old case?? [sic] Sure I am in jail and <u>rightly should be</u> but the long lasting damage to so many other persons makes the value of this suspect."

Lipka signed his letter, "Enjoy the day! Bob."

There were eight pages of questions and answers, such as, "Did you ever photograph any classified documents inside NSA?" He then answered his question, "No." Of course the investigative team already knew he hadn't photographed any documents; he'd simply removed them on his person. This list of 107 questions and answers was vintage Lipka: Misleading information of little or no relevance to the case. The true extent of his damage may never be known, but every Vietnam casualty bears that question mark.

✳✳✳

On the day of sentencing Lipka had one last chance to present a statement. He began it by apologizing for his espionage, but descended into ludicrous pleas for leniency. At one point he invoked the Civil War, saying, "Lincoln forgave the Confederate soldiers and allowed them to return home."

Judge Weiner was not moved. He answered that the government had placed a trust in Lipka, which Lipka had betrayed. Judge Weiner also mentioned his own Navy service during World War II, and underlined that even though he may not have enjoyed it he did his duty proudly.

Judge Weiner's sentence was what the prosecution had hoped for: "Mr. Lipka, I sentence you to 216 months in the custody of the Bureau of Prisons. In addition, I am imposing fines in the amount of $10,000, which is the maximum fine for espionage under the sentencing guidelines at the time of your offense. I am also imposing another fine of $10,000 for monies paid to you by the Federal Government in connection with their espionage investigation."

After some thirty-two years, making it the longest-running espionage case ever brought before the Federal court, the Robert Lipka investigation finally came to an end.

5

Date: October 1997
Location: Newtown Square, PA

After successfully prosecuting Robert Lipka, it was a letdown for Whiteside to return to more routine work. While intelligence and counterintelligence agencies work on penetrating hostile intelligence services and developing agents-in-place in foreign countries on a daily basis, espionage work brings a certain special pleasure to those responsible for conducting investigations. Espionage cases, which are partially spin-offs from counterintelligence work, are actually criminal cases and involve the violation of specific statutes. There is an unofficial and unspoken inner circle that consists of only those few who have successfully worked an espionage case. Everyone involved in the Lipka investigation from the FBI, NSA, Department of Justice, and the United States Attorney's Office can stake a claim to be part of that small, proud circle.

Sometimes the members of this circle enjoy comparing espionage agents to debate which spy did the most serious damage to national security. Clearly, this is a subjective exercise. What exactly makes one spy worse than another? Robert Hanssen, a former FBI agent arrested in February of 2001, has been mentioned as one of the worst spies in our history. Perhaps that is an accurate statement, especially based on the type of still-classified material he provided to the Soviets. His information caused the deaths of two KGB agents helping the Americans. Of course, this evidence only came to light as the result of his plea agreement, which both helped him avoid a death sentence and allowed his wife to qualify for a "survivor pension."

Aldrich Ames, a former CIA case officer, has also been acknowledged as one of the most damaging spies in our history. Arrested in February 1994, his access to CIA files, and knowledge of Soviet KGB defectors and recruitments made by the U.S. intelligence services, sentenced many of those people to die from a KGB bullet to the back of the skull. Ames also confessed to his activity with the KGB, in this case to keep his wife from receiving a lengthy jail sentence.

What about the other spies in recent history? Ronald Pelton, an NSA employee, gave up critical communications intercept information to the KGB. John Walker had exposed the communications systems of the U.S. Navy to the KGB for over eighteen years. When interrogated, he eventually cooperated with investigators to obtain a reduced sentence for his son, whom he'd drawn into the espionage web. Clyde Lee Conrad, at about the same time that John Walker was actively allowing the KGB to penetrate our Navy, was himself providing NATO secrets to the KGB in Germany. Some have opined that if open war had broken out during the 1980s, when both Walker and Conrad were active spies, the Soviet Union would have had a devastating advantage over U.S. and NATO forces.

This book makes no claim about the seriousness of Robert Lipka's espionage in comparison with these other spies. His damage to national security is simply unknown at the present time. However, unlike all the other major spies, Lipka had access to literally every document coming into and going out of the National Security Agency. He served in the United States Army at NSA during a time of war in Vietnam, during the most intense period of the Cold War, and during the Soviet Union's quickest proliferation of nuclear weapons. As he wrote to AUSA Cohan, "There were victims in the 1960s to be sure." Lipka knew that at least some of what he passed caused harm either to U.S. servicemen and servicewomen serving abroad, or to innocent civilians.

Lipka's unwillingness to cooperate with investigators is also unprecedented. Nobody—not even Lipka's own lawyer—knows why he threw away a reduced sentence to protect his secrets. But theories have been offered. One is that Lipka didn't trust the prosecutors; in essence, he didn't believe that a full confession would in fact get him a significantly shorter sentence. And though his own lawyer tried to convince him of the government's seriousness, it was clear that Lipka never fully trusted his own lawyer, either.

A second theory is that Lipka's sociopathic personality simply made it impossible for him to admit that he'd been beaten. When undercover Special Agent Droujinsky had given him the code name "Checkmate" Lipka had either failed to recognize that he was beaten, or he continued the game with the hope that he could control the outcome. This would explain his efforts to minimize his activities to investigators, despite the damaging information he provided to Droujinsky—including the flimsy alibi he'd concocted about working on behalf of Milt Robey.

All this begs the question: Were any of these reasons adequate for Lipka to refuse to cooperate with investigators to significantly reduce his jail time? Or is there something else Lipka knew, something that he was so fearful of disclosing that he would never admit it, no matter what the stakes? We'll never know.

EPILOGUE

Many of the retired FBI Special Agents who returned to the Philadelphia Division for the conference regarding their 1960s investigation of Peter and Ingeborg Fischer have since passed away. Their courage and continued devotion to duty made a lasting impression on the prosecutors and the investigation team who met with them. Those who are still alive are mostly in their late eighties. Norris Harzenstein, the FBI supervisor who ran the Fischer investigation, died about one month after meeting Whiteside's team for the Lipka investigation. Despite his poor health he had found the strength to make it to the meeting, and provided valuable insight in the ongoing investigation. His smile when he told AUSA Cohan that his men were "Harzenstein trained" will be long remembered by everyone who saw it. Bob Wade, Bob Broderick, Jerry Phelps, Nick Hand, Russell Liskey, Bill Birnbaum, Carl Lunkenheimer, Tom McWade, Ray Bott and Frank Gaffney—other retired FBI agents and support personnel who'd given information— have all passed away as well.

Ned Hecht, the postman who befriended Peter and Ingeborg Fischer at the behest of the FBI and eventually sold their furniture, had maintained an entire file on his correspondence with the Fischers. Hecht suffered from cancer during the Lipka investigation; he would lose his courageous battle with the disease shortly after Robert Lipka was sentenced.

Most of the FBI Special Agents who were on active duty during the Lipka investigation and worked all or parts of the case have been retired and are working in second careers, including SAs Brennan, Rochford,

Whiteside, Auld, Droujinsky, Reutter, Horan, Pruitt, Kimmel, DeBuvitz, Kibbie, and Feehery. Many of the support personnel who assisted in the investigation, both in Philadelphia and at FBI Headquarters, are still serving in analytical positions and in the Special Support Group, conducting surveillances of high-priority counterintelligence and terrorism targets around the nation.

The employees who comprised the investigative team of the National Security Agency are for the most part still employed at that agency. They continue to serve the nation in keeping it secure from the threats and hostile intents of other nations around the world.

Judge Charles Weiner, who was appointed to the Federal court by President Lyndon Johnson while Robert Lipka had been spying for the KGB, passed away at the age of eighty-three on November 9, 2005.

AUSA Barbara Cohan left the United States Attorney's office several years ago and entered into private law practice. She also owns a successful restaurant in Philadelphia, PA with her husband, a noted chef.

Departmental Attorney Michael C. Liebman left the Espionage Unit at the Department of Justice and is now serving as an Assistant United States Attorney in the District of Columbia in Washington, DC. John Dion is presently the Chief of the Counterespionage Section at the Department of Justice in Washington, DC.

Pat, Robert Lipka's ex-wife, continued to work as a registered nurse in Maryland until she contracted a brain tumor. Sadly, Pat died on August 25, 2000, at the young age of fifty-two. Her daughter, Kelly, continues to reside with her husband and children in Maryland.

Vasili Mitrokhin was not needed to testify in court as a result of Lipka's guilty plea. While living in the United Kingdom he wrote several books about the KGB, which have been published in the United States and abroad. Mitrokhin co-authored *The Sword and Shield: The Mitrokhin Archive and the Secret History of the KGB* with Christopher Andrew; it's a popular account of KGB activities targeted against the West, and included a brief account of Lipka's espionage activities.

The follow-up book, also co-authored by Christopher Andrew, is titled *The World Was Going Our Way: The KGB and the Battle for the Third World*. But Mitrokhin was angry at MI-6 for not giving him as much credit as he thought he deserved in writing the books, so he subsequently published two more books under his name alone, *The KGB in Europe and the West* and *KGB Lexicon: The Soviet Intelligence Officer Handbook*.

Mitrokhin and SAs Rochford and Whiteside would meet again on the West Coast in February 2000 to discuss the ramifications of another espionage case that Mitrokhin had brought to the attention of the FBI. Mitrokhin was seventy-seven years old at the time, and still energetic. He was emotionally drained, however, because his beloved wife, Nina, had contracted the same neuromuscular disorder their son suffered from, and she passed away in 1999. One evening, sipping iced Stolichnaya vodka and eating Russian black bread, Mitrokhin broke down in tears talking about his wife and son. It was evident that he had suffered much over Nina's untimely death and the uncertain future for his ailing son.

SAs Rochford and Whiteside would not see Mitrokhin again once his plane left California at the end of that week. During the next several years his health began to fail. On January 23, 2004, Mitrokhin died of pneumonia in a London hospital. He was eighty-one years old. He and his wife Nina are survived by their son.

On December 8, 2006, Lipka was released from custody by the Federal Bureau of Prisons, having served 130 months of a maximum of twelve years, or 144 months. AUSA Cohan had recommended that Lipka be transferred from the Fairton Federal Correctional Institute near Philadelphia to the "supermax" prison facility in Florence, CO based on his attempt to publicly disclose Vasili Mitrokhin's identity. Lipka served one year of his sentence there, and the rest back in the Fairton prison in New Jersey. Surprisingly, no one at NSA was made aware of his pending release by the Bureau of Prisons. Under the old sentencing guidelines, the maximum amount of time Lipka would have had to spend in prison was 144 months, or two-thirds of his actual sentence. He was fortunate to be released without completing the last fourteen months of his sentence.

Now sixty-eight years old, he is currently residing in the area of Meadville, PA, living with a female associate and fellow horse player. The Presque Isle Downs Racetrack and Casino opened nearby in 2007.

Deborah Lipka divorced Robert Lipka sometime during his prison term. She sold the house in Millersville, PA and moved away with her two sons.

***

AUTHOR'S NOTE

Stanislav Levchenko, a former KGB defector, called intelligence operations the world's second oldest profession. He may be correct; in the Bible in the Book of Numbers, Chapter 13, Moses has led the Israelites to the land of Canaan, and tasks some of his men, called "spies" to gather the same information intelligence services gather today: How many of the potential enemy inhabits the area? How fortified is their complex? Where are the food and water supplies, and how likely is it that they could withstand a siege? What type of weapons do they possess?

But to Levchenko in his book, *On the Wrong Side*, there's only one crucial difference between intelligence operations and the world's oldest profession: "One seduces the body while the other seduces the soul." What is it that motivates individuals to betray their countries? Despite recruitment efforts by professionals in intelligence operations, individuals often make independent decisions to approach intelligence agencies and volunteer information against their own country.

This book is based on the true story of the American spy Robert Lipka, who walked into the Soviet Embassy and volunteered information to the KGB. All of the people named in the book are real, with the exception of two, Judy Lee and Harry Spencer, who are pseudonyms for security purposes. All dialogue between Lipka and his ex-wife, and dialogue between Lipka and Dimitry Droujinsky is accurate, though edited for length. All actual recording transcripts are available for public review in archived Federal court documents.

The reasons people volunteer classified information to the enemy vary, but are usually related to three behavioral drives: Least common is an ideological motivation, wherein a person believes it important to assist a nation he feels close to by reason of birth, past history or current situation. Another popular reason has always been revenge. Someone who loses a job or has been humiliated, transferred, demoted or otherwise belittled or punished may become so angry that espionage becomes an instrument of retribution. However, the most common reason that a person commits espionage is simple greed. Spying can be lucrative, and many people will do anything for money.

Both Lipka and Vasili Mitrokhin volunteered classified information (Lipka against the U.S. and Mitrokhin against Russia). While the first is motivated by greed, in the end so is the second, although revenge was his first motivation. The Soviet Union (now Russia) and the United States view spies in similar ways, both praising their respective hero and despising their respective traitor. But this story, while a victory of sorts, is essentially a tragedy. Whenever a trust is betrayed—trust that can cost possible lives and fortunes— little joy can be gained, no matter how well justice is served.

This book was completed in 2009. Or so I thought. It was forwarded to the pre- publication review units at both NSA and the FBI for approval prior to being published. That review took nine months and requested changes were made. Once an approved manuscript was obtained, I sought out an editor to improve the manuscript where possible. I want to thank Rachel Zanders who began the editing process for her early work, and then for recommending another editor when she was unable to continue her editing. Jenny Gavacs of Chicago, IL became the primary editor for my manuscript. We worked together for many months, finally agreeing on the book you have just completed. Jenny did a wonderful job turning a bland manuscript into one filled with energy and excitement. Any success this book has is directly related to her exceptional editing. I also want to thank Ed Comstock for his review of my initial manuscript and for his comments and assistance in getting a final draft prepared.

Special thanks go out to my attorney Mark Zaid who has stood by me in my dealings with the pre-publication review units during the second round of reviews. Following Jenny's editing of the original manuscript, I was again required to run the manuscript through the pre-publication review process at NSA and the FBI. This time it took ten months before the manuscript was approved once more for publication. Mark is one of the finest and best known attorneys in the Washington, DC area and his assistance was invaluable to me.

Others played an important role in my efforts to publish this book. Thanks to Bill Leidy, Olga Goncharenko and her mother Ilona, I was able to have Russian translation services as needed for a portion of the book. Their efforts were a great help to me and I am grateful for their assistance. Special thanks to David Kilgore for suggesting the title for my book.

My colleagues at NSA, Bob Hallman and Jim Ohlson, continued to encourage me to write the book and assisted me in trying to locate a publisher. I am grateful for their assistance and continued friendship.

My family and friends continually encouraged me to press on despite all the difficult issues associated with writing a book. Thanks to all of them for their patience and encouragement.

When asked by my editor Jenny why I was writing this book, I told her I had several reasons. In no particular order of importance, one reason was that I found the case to be fascinating in all of its component parts and thought it would make for a great read. Another reason was to create somewhat of a historical primer for those investigators who follow me when working "false flag" approaches. I tried to include both the successes and mistakes that occurred in the investigation. While every case in the future will be somewhat different, and every "false flag" approach utilized will be tailored for the individual circumstance, I thought this case would be beneficial to read about so as to improve on the technique and to be made wary of pitfalls. I had no such benefit when working this case. Lastly, I wrote this book to recognize all of the people who played a role in its success. I initially included every FBI employee who gave me written permission to include their name in the book, as well as all NSA employees.

Unfortunately, many of the names were taken out by my editor for literary reasons. She seemed to think that too many names made the book too confusing for the reader. So, to all of you who do not appear in the story, know you were there in the original manuscript. And to all of you, this book is dedicated. And I thank all of you for your help in sending Robert Lipka to prison for the crime of espionage.

Any mistakes are mine alone, and were not intended. I tried to keep the story as accurate as possible. I have tried to reach out to Lipka's former KGB handler without success. I had hoped we could get together and discuss our mutual interest in this case, now that we are both retired. I am still hopeful for such a meeting in the future. Lastly, I would like to thank my agent and publisher for seeing that this book finally gets onto the bookshelves.

As I look back on my thirty year career with the FBI, I realize how fortunate I've been to work with the finest group of people in law enforcement. The job was filled with many challenges and thrills, and all the while serving the American public. It is for all of you, my fellow Americans, that I give you this story.

JWW

SELECTED BIBLIOGRAPHY

Andrew, Christopher, and Oleg Gordievsky. *KGB: The Inside Story.* New York: Harper Collins, 1990.

Andrew, Christopher, and Vasili Mitrokhin. *KGB: The Sword and the Shield.* New York: Basic Books, 1999.

Andrew, Christopher, and Vasili Mitrokhin. *The Mitrokhin Archive: The KGB in Europe and the West.* London: Allen Lane The Penguin Press, 1999.

Barron, John. *Operation SOLO: The FBI's Man in the Kremlin.* Washington, DC: Regnery, 1995.

Bagley, Tennent H. *Spy Wars: Moles, Mysteries and Deadly Games.* New Haven: Yale University Press, 2007.

Cherkashin, Victor, and Gregory Feifer. *Spy Handler: Memoir of a KGB Officer.* New York: Basic Books, 2005.

Earley, Pete. *Comrade J.*
New York: The Penguin Group, 2007

Grimes, Sandra, and Jeanne Vertefuille. *Circle of Treason: A CIA Account of Traitor Aldrich Ames and the Men He Betrayed.* Naval Institute Press, 2012

Kahn, David. *The Code Breakers: The Story of Secret Writing.* New York, The Macmillan Company, 1967.

Kalugin, Oleg and Fen Montaigne. *The First Directorate: My 32 Years in Intelligence and EspionageAgainst the West.* New York, St. Martin's Press, 1994

Kessler, Ronald. *The Bureau: The Secret History of the FBI.* New York: St. Martin's Press, 2002.

Kessler, Ronald. *The FBI: Inside the World's Most Powerful Law Enforcement Agency.* New York: Pocket Books, 1993.

Polmar, Norman, and Thomas B. Allen. *The Encyclopedia of Espionage.* New York: Gramercy Books, 1997.

Wise, David. *Cassidy's Run: The Secret Spy War Over Nerve Gas.* New York: Random House, 2000

Wise, David. *SPY: The Inside Story of How the FBI's Robert Hanssen Betrayed America*. New York: Random House, 2002.

Wise, David. *The Spy Who Got Away*. New York: Random House, 1988.

CPSIA information can be obtained at www.ICGtesting.com
Printed in the USA
LVOW01s1828050615

441366LV00031B/1281/P